Next Time, She'll Be Dead

Next Time, She'll Be Dead

*Battering &
How to
Stop It*

ANN JONES

Beacon Press
Boston

Beacon Press
25 Beacon Street
Boston, Massachusetts 02108-2892

Beacon Press books
are published under the auspices of
the Unitarian Universalist Association of
Congregations.

Excerpt from "She Swallowed It" by L. Patterson
and A. Young, Ruthless Attack Muzick (ASCAP),
© 1992, used by permission, all rights reserved;
excerpt from "Mind of a Lunatic" by Brad Jordan,
Willie Dennis, and Keith Rogers, Geto Boys, used
by permission of Rap-A-Lot Records, Inc.

99 98 97 96 95 94   8 7 6 5

Text design by Diane Levy

Library of Congress Cataloging-in-Publication Data

Jones, Ann, 1937–
    Next time, she'll be dead : battering and how
to stop it / Ann Jones.
        p.   cm.
    Includes bibliographical references and index.
    ISBN 0-8070-6770-9 (cloth)
    ISBN 0-8070-6771-7 (paper)
    1. Abused women. 2. Abused wives. I. Title.
HV6626.J66   1994
362.82'92—dc20   93-24630
                                        CIP

Contents

Acknowledgments

This book springs from a lifelong endeavor to understand the violence that marked my own childhood. It is the product of years of interviews and conversations with women who have been battered and with others who work on their behalf. The names of those to whom I owe thanks would fill many pages, so I can acknowledge here only some special debts. I'm grateful to the Millay Colony for the Arts for once again providing precious workspace and peace, and to Mount Holyoke College for a travel grant that enabled me to conduct several interviews. Many students at Mount Holyoke College—young women who represent the future—helped me out in one way or another as I wrote this book: Giulietta Swenson, Jennifer Rodrigue, Susan Gehrke, Kristin Meausky, Kathleen Lyons, Iris Fischer, Margaret Rooks, and Jennifer Fisher. The librarians of Mount Holyoke College and Joan Grenier and Lily Sibley of the Odyssey Bookshop found everything I asked for. Mary Haviland assisted me with legal research. Anne Ganley, Erika Munk, Laurie Woods, and Elizabeth Schneider read one or another chapter of this book with critical eyes. And Susan Schechter, with whom I collaborated on a previous book, proved once again a wise and thoughtful colleague; she read the whole manuscript more than once and encouraged me beyond measure.

I cannot adequately thank my many other friends and colleagues in the battered women's movement for debts incurred over the years, but I would like to acknowledge particularly the work and help of Ellen Pence, Holly Maguigan, Jean Grossholtz, Angela Browne, David Adams, Marie Fortune, Beth Richie, Valli Kanuha, Suzanne Pharr, Sara Buel, Sue Osthoff, Donna Ferrato, Anne Menard, Esta Soler, Joan Zorza, Betty Levinson, Michael Paymar, Barbara Hart, Lenore Walker, and Evelina Giobbe. I want also to thank my friends who, although they are not affiliated with the battered women's movement, help me through countless acts of kindness to imagine a world without violence: Joan Silber, Patricia Lewis Sackrey, Ann Ellen Lesser, Valerie Martin, Janie Geiser, Phyllis Grosskurth, Marilyn French, Lois Gould, Liz Knights, Marilyn White, Nell Schofield, Fran Moore, and Dan Domench. I am grateful to Charlotte Sheedy and Octavia Wiseman for friendship as well as literary agency, and to Lauren Bryant, Marya Van't Hul, and Wendy Strothman at Beacon Press for infinite patience and expert guidance.

My greatest debt, of course, is to all the survivors of assault and battery who told me their stories over the years in hopes that my retelling might help other women to escape or to change the conditions of our lives. This book is for them.

Introduction

Violence changes those it touches. A generation of veterans home from Vietnam taught us that. But I'm thinking now of other veterans of violence closer to home—violence *in* the home. We label this violence "domestic," as if it were somehow tamer than the real thing, but newspapers and newscasts list casualties. They report that such violence rages wild among us, as uncontrolled as an epidemic. People who go through it, as victims or as witnesses, learn (among many things) to fear violence, to avoid violence at all costs, or to be violent. Many veterans of family violence suffer recurrent, paralyzing flashbacks, just like war veterans, afflicted with the same psychiatric disorder: post-traumatic stress. Many skid into alcoholism, drug addiction, assault, suicide—as if to finish the destructive process begun by someone else. Others find that memory mends itself, blotting out the worst of violence, so they can get on with life, troubled only now and then by some imperfectly forgotten wound. But once you're struck by violence, its prospect covers things, like shade. Survivors may develop a determination to stop violence, and they may work toward that goal. But even then they may never quite cheer up.

I speak from experience. My father was a drunk, a wife beater, and a child abuser. That's never the whole story, of course, so he was also other things: a modestly successful businessman, a civic leader, a war hero, an athlete, a prize-winning angler, a church-goer, a tenor, a patriot, a Republican, a baseball fan, a formidable player of gin rummy. And more important, a delightful and funny man. Of all my family, all now long gone, it's my father I miss.

When I was about five, my father went to a rehabilitation center *again*; this time he sobered up, joined Alcoholics Anonymous, and—as far as I know—stopped hitting my mother. Perhaps because I was so young during the worst of his attacks on her, I don't remember much about them at firsthand; but I recall the family stories—like the one about the time my father loaded his revolver, threatening to shoot my mother, and she walked up an enclosed stairway straight into the gun and took it away from him. My mother knew how to stand up for herself. Which may explain why he hit me instead.

The beatings I got from him I remember much better, but even they dim in memory, thanks to the mind's readiness to minimize and deny what's too painful to retain. So I can't recall when he started hitting me (I don't remember a time when he *didn't*) or how often he beat me up; I can't call to mind my father's face when he attacked me, but half a century later, I can remember exactly the look of the floorboards under my bed, the one place, when I was small enough to scrunch into the far corner and cling to the bed leg, where he couldn't quite get at me.

What I remember most of all is my father's weepy, groping attempts at "making up" after he'd pounded me with his belt buckle or fists. He'd creep into my room in the middle of the night and sit on my bed. If he said anything, I've forgotten it. He would take me in his arms and press his face, always wet with tears, against mine, and give me big slobbering kisses. He was feeling sorry, not for me but for himself. I'd sit bolt upright in his embrace, terrified by it—for nobody ever hugged or kissed in our family in the normal course of things—terrified by his wet tears and spittle on my face and the hand worming between my legs.

I blamed my mother. If only she wouldn't talk back to him or nag and complain so much about the same old things all the time. (Why *couldn't* he leave his hat on the dining table?) If only she'd be nicer, more loving and understanding, and not set him off. (Of course this is what my father said, too.) It's true that *I* couldn't control his outbursts of violence by *my* conduct, but I was just a kid; and even when it was me he went after, I could see he was really mad at her. Now I believe that she did the best she could to stop him. I'm sure she thought she was doing the right thing for my sister and me by staying married to our father, even though she no longer cared for him. Divorce carried a terrible stigma, and how would she have supported us? She had no money of her own, and although she held a master's degree and had supported herself before marriage as a schoolteacher, the teaching profession in our town was closed to married and divorced women. Besides, she was in very poor health and always "nervous"—the result, she said, of what my father put her through. So she stayed with him, but she slept in a bedroom of her own, and she answered him back and "nagged" him—and he took it out on me.

I became what family systems psychologists call "the family scapegoat," and for at least a dozen years—until I was seventeen—I was the one everybody yelled at and the only one my father hit. He taught me to fear him, to love him, to manipulate him, and to copy him. And he taught me to hate my mother.

He hit me for the last time when I was seventeen and came home from college for a visit. (The argument—I still remember—was about my midterm grade in math: a B, and not good enough for him.) I told him that if he hit me one more time I'd never come home again, and I meant it. I had tried all along to resist: I'd learned to run out of the house or scream at the top of my lungs because he was embarrassed to continue if he thought the neighbors noticed. Once I totally ignored him for several months. I got a key for my bedroom door and kept it locked always. But only this last real threat stopped him. After that he was never violent again, but he remained—as he had been all along—two people: publicly charming and delightful, privately sullen, angry, and morose.

Almost every summer night of my childhood, when our minor league baseball team played at home, I went with him to the ballpark where he sat in the grandstand behind third base, high-spirited among his pals, joking, laughing, full of life and good cheer. When the first black players were assigned to our lily-white town, it was my father with his famous sense of humor who silenced racist opposition with a barrage of ridicule. Pointed hoods for pointed heads, he said. I was old enough then to be proud of my brave father for standing up for the rights of others. What he never could get straight was our rights at home. Or how to be brave and cheerful *there*.

When in his eightieth year he lay in the hospital dying, my father drifted in and out of consciousness, laughing. From his incoherent mumbling, we gathered that he had slipped back into his youth, to a time when he was all promise, a practical joker famous for his wild adventures, his generous heart, his wondrous good looks. What went wrong with his life? War intervened, and alcohol, and the Depression. Perhaps his Nordic temperament bent him toward sullenness and rage; perhaps his mother, whom he said he never saw smile; perhaps his dictatorial father who never gave her cause. I know only this: from my earliest memory he was a sad and violent man. It shouldn't have been up to my mother to stop him. And it shouldn't have been up to me.

I mention these things by way of stating my credentials: I'm a veteran of violence too. And to let you know why I came to believe—and why I will try to persuade you—that women and children have *an absolute right* to live free from bodily harm. And further, to let you know why I believe that safeguarding women's rights is the key to safeguarding children. Extend to women—all women—our fundamental right to freedom from bodily harm, and afford women—all women—equal opportunity to emotional and economic self-sufficiency, and most women will protect their children. Make a woman's identity and livelihood and safety contingent upon the favor of some man, and she may be forced to betray her child, as my mother betrayed me. Or she may be compelled to take that man's life to save her own. Or she may die herself, by inches as my mother did, or all at once, by his hand or her own. So it's women I want to talk about—and women's rights.

I believe that women and children—like men—have an *absolute* right to be free from bodily harm, a right that ought to be self-evident but that is seldom acknowledged at all, much less acted upon by our social institutions in any reliable and effective way. Increasingly, women are insisting upon that right, reporting sexual harassment, rape, and battering, and demanding that men who violate that right suffer some consequences. But faced with a report of battering we are still inclined to look to the woman (and to her psyche) for explanation. We are still inclined to regard battering as a marital "problem" rather than a crime. We are still inclined to mediate rather than to punish the offender. We are still inclined to prescribe counseling (for the woman as often as for the assaultive man) rather than criminal prosecution. We are still inclined, in short, to regard whatever "right" the abused woman has in these circumstances as merely formal, contingent, conditional, and in competition with many rights traditionally enjoyed by the man as *pater familias* and upheld by social institutions, religious leaders, public officials, and politicians under the rubric of family values. The way a woman is treated by public opinion, by public institutions—police, social services, medical and mental health facilities—and by the law depends largely upon what we believe her rights (or lack of them) to be. I maintain that to make real progress against battering we must get it through our heads that women have an absolute right to be free from bodily harm—all women, at all times, no matter what their relationship to the assailant: wife, cohabitor, girlfriend, date, acquaintance, total stranger—and we must act on that belief. Shouldn't all people have that right? Even women? Even at home?

Does it seem late in the day to be writing about abused women? Hasn't the subject filled our newspapers and magazines and talk shows? Haven't we seen enough battered women, enough psychologists, enough lawyers, on "Donahue" and "Oprah" and

"Sally"? Haven't we watched these terrible stories dramatized often enough on the TV Movie of the Week? Wouldn't you think that by this time we must know everything we need to know? Why then does the problem persist?

A great many people now agree that men who beat up their wives or girlfriends do a bad thing. Many understand that children who witness such violence against their mothers can only be harmed by the experience. Many sympathize with battered women, and hardly anyone any more—apart from religious fundamentalists—seems to think that women should put up with abuse. What's more, we've seen the crisis hotline telephone numbers march across our TV screens. We've heard about shelters. We may even contribute to our local shelter directly or by giving to the community chest. Attitudes have changed. Services are available.

Given such widespread agreement on this social problem—which all available statistics tell us is immense—do you ever wonder why you keep seeing the same headlines? Like these: "Woman Slain, Police Seek Boyfriend," "Man Charged in Ex-Wife's Death," "Postman Shoots Estranged Wife, Four Others," "Man Slays Wife and Self," "Abused Wife Hired Husband's Killer," and "Slain Wife Had Protection Order." In an average year, murder stories like these appear in newspapers across the country at the rate of a dozen every day. But if we're doing all that can be done to stop assaults on women, how does it come down to homicide day after day? A few years ago the FBI reported that in the United States a man beat a woman every eighteen seconds. By 1989 the figure was fifteen seconds. Now it's *twelve*.[1] Some people take those figures at face value to mean that male violence is on the rise; while others argue that what's increasing is merely the *reporting* of violence. But no matter how you interpret the numbers, it's clear that male violence is not going *down*. As crime statistics go, homicide figures are most likely to be accurate, for the simple reason that homicides produce corpses—hard to hide and easy to count. And homicide figures indicate so clearly that male violence against women is on the rise that some sociologists have coined a new term for the crime: femicide.[2] In Massachusetts, in 1989, one woman was slain by her husband or boyfriend every twenty-two days. In 1990 such a murder occurred every sixteen days. As I write in 1992 it is happening every nine days.[3] How can this be? Why, when things seem to have changed so much for the better, do they seem so much the same? Why, when we actually keep score, do they seem *worse*?

That's what I want to talk about. I want to begin at the beginning to explain where some of the sticking places are, and why— despite all our good will—we slide backwards. Our habitual ways of thinking about what is euphemistically called "domestic violence" have led us astray, I think, and, worse, into complacent assumptions that we've done all that can be done, when in fact we've done very little. So I want to go over the ground again, not so much to describe male violence against wives and girlfriends (although I will do that) but to describe how we think and talk about it—all of us: you and I, the reporter, the cop, the family court judge, the academic "expert," the shrink. I want to describe the way we think in hopes that it might make us think again. To vary an old jibe: If we're so smart, why aren't we safe?

This is not to say that nothing has been done about battering. An immense amount of work has gone into changing our attitudes and our public policies, and—it's important to note—most of that work has been done not by public officials and institutions but by women, and mostly in the last twenty years. As Susan Schechter explains in her definitive history *Women and Male Violence: The Visions and Struggles of the Battered Women's Movement*, the rise of the women's movement in the 1960s and the antirape movement in the early 1970s provided encouragement and a forum for women to speak about violence in our lives.[4] Until then, no one guessed the nature and extent of violence within the home—not even the theorists of the "second wave" of feminism. Betty Friedan's enormously influential *The Feminine Mystique*, published in 1963, is a compendium of middle-class housewifely woes, but assault and battery are not among them; and the first anthologies of the women's movement, *Sisterhood Is Powerful* and

Voices of Women's Liberation, both published in 1970, allude to battery only in a few passing references.[5] Academic "experts" were no better informed; for thirty years, from 1939 to 1969, the index of the scholarly *Journal of Marriage and the Family* contained no reference to violence.[6] The few psychiatrists who published articles on a handful of cases of wife beating in the 1960s saw no social problem but merely the perverse psyches of provocative individual women: frigid, masochistic, and emasculating.

Once feminists encouraged battered women to "speak out" and tell their stories, as women in the antirape movement had done, the circumstances of the battered woman and of the rape survivor proved remarkably alike. Both were doubted and disbelieved, both were charged with making false accusations, both were blamed for provoking violence, both were said secretly to enjoy it, both were blamed for not preventing it themselves, both were shamed into silence—both were victimized by unrestrained male power. And as more and more abused women spoke out, the numbers began to add up: millions of women of all races and social classes isolated *with* the men who abused them in individual homes all across the country—with no place to go. Describing these circumstances as early activists found them, Susan Schechter writes: "As late as 1976, New York City, with a population estimated at more than 8 million people, had 1000 beds for homeless men and 45 for homeless women. In Minneapolis-St. Paul, there were only a few beds available before the first battered women's shelter opened in 1974. A 1973 Los Angeles survey revealed 4000 beds for men and 30 for women and children. . . . In various states, social service or religious organizations provided minimal programs or temporary housing for displaced persons, 'multi-problem' families, or the wives of alcoholics, but there was no category, 'abused women.' Since 1975, the ongoing struggle of the battered women's movement has been to name the hidden and private violence in women's lives, declare it public, and provide safe havens and support."[7]

That was the beginning of one of the most astonishing social reform movements in the history of this or any other country. The movement started with women helping women, and it's still growing. Since 1974, women working in local communities established more than a thousand shelters and at least as many emergency hotlines to provide refuge, information, and advocacy for battered women. Women pressured many states to enact more comprehensive domestic abuse prevention laws, some of them remarkably creative—like the law first passed in Florida in 1978 that levies a surcharge on marriage licenses for the benefit of shelters.[8] Groups of battered women brought class action suits against police departments and court officials to compel them to enforce laws against assault and battery: to arrest and prosecute batterers. They lobbied Congress to hold hearings on "domestic violence," pass legislation, and allocate funds to combat it. They pressured the attorney general and the National Association of Chiefs of Police to change recommended law enforcement policy from mediation to arrest. In many states and municipalities they won by law or public policy a practice of mandatory arrest and prosecution. They established support and educational groups for battered women and provided advocates to help women through the intricacies of social service applications and court procedures. They set up re-education programs for batterers, sometimes as "jail diversion," a mandatory alternative to jail. They devised education and training programs for police, prosecutors, judges, and other public officials. They introduced "domestic violence" awareness programs in public schools to help prevent violence and to help kids already suffering from it. Working with hospitals and child protective services treating physically and sexually abused children, they established advocacy programs for mothers who are unable, without help, to protect their children because they too are being abused. (Some studies have found that at least 50 percent of the mothers of abused children are battered women.)[9] They led campaigns to remove incompetent and sex-discriminatory public officials and judges whose refusal to enforce laws against assault left batterers free, in case after case, to hold women against their will and to murder. They developed legal strategies for defending battered women who, while defending themselves, injure or kill their batterers. They set up support groups inside prisons for thousands upon thousands of battered women (the majority of women in America's prisons) who committed crimes—typically shoplifting, forgery, drug sales, prostitution—under coercion, to avoid another beating. They produced a shelf of studies on the history, sociology, psychology, politics, law, and personal experience of battering; countless reports on local projects that work and don't work; conferences, films, videos, plays, songs, rituals, and innumerable self-help handbooks. They organized nationwide to coordinate programs, develop policy, and evaluate accomplishments. They demanded, coaxed, wheedled, flattered, persuaded, cajoled, threatened, lobbied, badgered, and shamed "the system" to give way. In short, they effected enormous changes which are only just now beginning to be felt.[10]

There have been many movements for reform in this country, but never in American history has there been such an organization of crime victims, denied redress, establishing a *de facto* system of protection for themselves and other victims. Women also help some women and children not only to leave but to disappear— out of sight of batterers who threaten further to abuse and kill them. There is now in this country a busy underground railroad— though it's impossible to say where or how it started, where it goes, or how many women and children it carries away. This underground railroad has only one parallel in American history: the women and children who use it, like slaves of old, are escaping from bondage. If that comparison seems to make light of slavery, it's only because wife beating has been so long hidden away, leaving us in ignorance of what life is like for battered women today. In fact, the worst-case scenarios in both institutions, slavery and marriage, are grimly similar, right down to and including rape, torture, mutilation, and murder. The fundamental difference is that most battered women can and do leave, although, like slaves who fled, many battered women are pursued by men who would capture or kill them. Hence the modern underground railroad.

Thanks to the battered women's movement, we now know that any social, economic, or political development that counteracts

sexism and promotes sex equality helps in the long run to elimi-
nate violence by reducing the *power* men hold, individually and
institutionally, over women. And there is now plenty of evidence
that in the short run the most effective way to protect women and
children, save lives, and cut down violence is to treat assault as
the crime it is: to arrest batterers and send them to jail. (Counselors who work with batterers say that re-education or therapy
will not necessarily induce a batterer to change his behavior unless
he also suffers *real* consequences that underscore strong social and
legal sanctions against violence.)[11] We now know that all the institutions to which battered women and children are likely to turn
for help—hospitals, mental health facilities, social welfare services, child protective services, police, civil and criminal courts,
schools, churches—must join a *concerted* effort to prevent violence
before it occurs and to stop it when it does. All these community
institutions must be alert to identify battered women and children
and to take their part. All these community institutions must deliver the same message: namely that they stand ready to defend
the right of all women to be free from bodily harm. The battered
women's movement has taught us these lessons; and it has demonstrated through an astonishing array of imaginative programs
that communities *can* safeguard women and children from domestic assault, and at far less cost to the taxpayer than mopping
up the widespread social and economic fallout of assault and child
abuse.

Nevertheless, as some people say, making a feeble joke to triv-
ialize the matter: the beat goes on. When the problem of men
battering women seems insurmountable today, we should remind
ourselves of the time—not very long ago—when it was not a *problem* at all. Battering *always* went on, and women always complained of it; but for as long as social problems and "private affairs" have been defined exclusively by dominant white men,
battering has been hidden in the latter category. There is no problem without a person who suffers from it, who complains of it,
and whose voice is *heard*. In France, Christine de Pizan complained in 1405 of the "harsh beatings" and "many injuries"

that women suffered "without cause and without reason." In England Mary Wollstonecraft complained of male "tyranny" in the eighteenth century; Frances Power Cobbe and John Stuart Mill decried "wife-torture" and "atrocity" in the nineteenth.[12] In the United States, spokeswomen for the Women's Movement complained of male "brutality" from the moment they organized in 1848, and Susan B. Anthony personally helped battered women to escape. But credit for "discovering" wife abuse goes to contemporary feminists, although they often find that what they have to say about the subject meets the same derision the batterer heaps upon his wife or girlfriend. (Certainly women would not have had to build the elaborate network of shelters and services, or establish the underground railroad, or carry out any of the projects I've mentioned if existing institutions had been willing to do the job.) Social policy makers (much like batterers) tend to recognize a problem only when it's their own. So battering or "domestic violence" came to be noticed as a "social problem" only as men of influence noticed its effect upon them, and particularly on their pocketbooks.

Advocates pointed out to businessmen the economic costs of battery: federal officials estimate that "domestic violence" costs U.S. firms four billion dollars a year in lower productivity, staff turnover, absenteeism, and excessive use of medical benefits.[13] One New York City study of fifty battered women revealed that half of them missed at least three work days a month because of abuse, while 64 percent were late for work, and more than three-fourths of them used company time and company phones to call friends, counselors, physicians, and lawyers they didn't dare call from home.[14] As surgeon general, C. Everett Koop labeled the "epidemic" of battering a leading national health problem and pointed out the costs to hospital emergency services, public health, and mental health facilities. A few worried legislators and penal officials, who can't build prisons fast enough to contain America's violent men, suddenly noticed that many violent prisoners had once been kids in violent homes. Could their home-grown violence be, as battered women's advocates suggested, another immense public cost of "private" violence?

City administrators woke up when women brought class action suits against police and family courts. Some police departments, which first complained about time wasted on "domestic" calls, reconsidered when battered women or their survivors sued them for their failure to protect victims of "private" violence. Alarmed insurance companies reexamined liability insurance rates for municipalities which did not protect abused women and children by arresting batterers. Some state legislatures, faced with the prospect of municipal treasuries drained by "failure to protect" lawsuits, enacted statewide mandatory arrest and prosecution laws. And once battered women knew that a call to the police would bring *help*, the number of calls rocketed off the top of the charts, creating more difficulties for cops and budget makers and taxpayers. Connecticut advocates identified fourteen thousand battered women in the year before a new state law mandated that police arrest batterers and give battered women printed information about their rights and available services; then the number of battered women identified by advocates and the criminal justice system jumped to more than thirty thousand.[15] Another example: in the first year after the San Francisco Police Department adopted a new policy of making arrests in domestic assault cases, arrests increased 60 percent, doubling the time police spent writing up cases; within three years, reports of serious "domestic disputes" (felonious aggravated assault) jumped 123 percent.[16] There was no getting around it: in the course of a decade, "domestic violence" had become a *real* social problem.

The battered women's movement arose among women from immediate need, not abstract theory. It was taken up by concerned policy makers largely for reasons of politics and economics, not justice. So we have a situation in which social action *precedes* the premise from which it should follow: namely, that all women have an absolute right to be free from bodily harm. It is no longer enough to offer some victimized women safety and sympathy, any more than it would have been enough to offer Rosa Parks that seat at the front of the bus without granting the principle of social equality behind it. Grant the principle and all the rest falls into place. For women in the United States, that principle has not yet been recognized.

So it happens that while we profess to believe it wrong for men to beat women, we tend to make allowances in individual cases for men who do, finding in these cases particular circumstances which suggest that the woman is really to blame. Popular discourse derived largely from Freudian psychology and macho tradition fills our minds with prefabricated phrases, exonerating the abuser and blaming the victim. We understand that he was under "stress" of one sort or another, while she was emasculating, cold, provocative, self-destructive, hysterical, masochistic, and free to leave. Although many people now agree *in principle* that it's wrong to hit women, many of us also seem to believe that under certain circumstances it's almost bound to happen. And those circumstances are so elastic that in effect almost every abused woman gets blamed. In most cases, the very fact that she was *there* is enough to bring her under suspicion. And whether we blame battered women or pity them for their plight, we tend to think of them as a kind of pariah group, rather like prostitutes, who apparently choose to live "abnormal" and dangerous lives because of some peculiar kinks of background and personality. (After all, we think, she *could* leave.)

Knowing public attitudes, abused women often keep silent out of shame and a fear of being blamed, thereby appearing to acquiesce to violence. But if the abused woman appears complicitous, so do we; making excuses for the abuser in this case, blaming the victim in that case, we *approve* violence. Is it any wonder then that battering continues?

Our thinking about battered women is hindered by some pernicious habits of mind. First, there is the popular conviction that if abused women seek help from the law, they get it, when in fact the law itself *contributes* to the abuse they undergo. Second, our general ignorance of the real nature and seriousness of battering. Third, the commingling in the popular imagination of sex, anger, aggression, and violence. And finally, and perhaps most important, the persistent tendency to blame victims for "their" problems. I will discuss these impediments to clear thinking and action in the first five chapters of this book. Then I will illustrate how these habits of mind coalesce to the detriment of all women by discussing public reaction to a single notorious instance: the victimization of Hedda Nussbaum.

The Nussbaum story, like battering in general, has been repeatedly discussed—so much so that we may feel we know much more than we care to know about it. What more can there possibly be to say? Yet I've chosen this case precisely because so many have said and written so much about it. As an extreme case of woman abuse and child murder it throws into high relief the kinds of problems millions of women and children face to a lesser degree every day. And more important, because it elicited so much public commentary, it serves as a kind of Rorschach test to evaluate the temper of the times, just as public attitudes toward sexual harassment were revealed by the Senate hearings on the appointment of Clarence Thomas to the Supreme Court. The story of Hedda Nussbaum and the public reaction to it make plain the ill-informed or *dis*informed habits of mind that prevent us from acting effectively, despite a wealth of good will, to stop violence against women.

Finally I'll offer some suggestions for thinking differently and acting more effectively to safeguard the persons and the rights of women and children. It strikes me that we've settled into a habit of neglect, just as the government during the Reagan-Bush years settled into a habit of neglecting the health and general welfare of the vast majority of our citizens. Programs to aid battered women and abused children have been cut back or canceled altogether, like so many other social programs. When so many Americans are denied the fundamental necessities of life—jobs, housing, education, basic health care—it isn't surprising that abused women and children should be overlooked as well. Even feminists sometimes seem to have forgotten about violence against women; while Marilyn French fearlessly documents worldwide violence against women in *The War Against Women*, the two bestselling feminist books of 1991–1992—Susan Faludi's *Backlash* and Gloria Steinem's *Revolution from Within*—scarcely mention it, perhaps because the threat of violence to women is now so pervasive as to be part of the very air we breathe.[17] Yet just as poverty and homelessness need *not* always be with us, neither must we abide male violence against women.

In the last fifteen years I've interviewed hundreds of women who have survived male violence, women of every description all across this country. There are millions of them—in every walk of life, in every neighborhood, every workplace, every church and synagogue. You know some of them, though the chances are that you don't know you do. It's not a piece of history a woman is likely to bring up in conversation, knowing the listener is apt to think a little less of her, suspecting she complied with, perhaps even contrived, the violence she survived.

Individually and collectively the stories I've heard from survivors have revealed to me a history of male violence against women that defies imagination. They made me think again about the violence that violence has done to women's conception of commonplace terms like "love" and "family" and "home." And they left an abiding impression of women, even in the most wretched and terrible situations, hanging on, fighting back, getting even, getting out, laughing last, going on; women rich in intelligence, common sense, humor, ingenuity, love, and power; women whose histories are heartbreaking, often appalling, and inspiring at once. Women whose lives were touched and forever *changed*—as mine was—by violence.

More than a century ago in England in one of the first essays written in English about domestic assault, Frances Power Cobbe told "horror stories" of wife abuse, appealing to the essential fairness of good and true Englishmen to right these wrongs. In this book I tell some horror stories too, in the same spirit though perhaps with less optimism. Many women deliver themselves from violence, and their stories are at once an inspiration to other women in adversity and an indictment of the society that fails to help them. But many other women simply do not survive. The wrongs of which Frances Power Cobbe wrote have not been righted. Shall we try again?

1

Against the Law

As Americans, we believe that we possess certain fundamental inalienable rights, and we assume that the right to be free from bodily harm is among them. We share a conviction, so deeply felt as scarcely to need articulation, that people have a right to bodily integrity, to freedom from physical intrusion. The right to be secure in our persons is mentioned in the Bill of Rights, just as freedom of speech, freedom of assembly, and freedom of religion are, but it may be even more important.[1] In his classic analysis of the rights of individuals, Blackstone gave the highest priority to "security from the corporal insults of menaces, assaults, beating and wounding," and next in importance after "personal security" he ranked personal liberty and personal property.[2] What do our other freedoms amount to after all if we are not safe in our persons? As one judicial decision noted: "No right is held more sacred, or is more carefully guarded . . . than the right of every individual to the possession and control of his own person, free from all restraint or interference of others."[3] We assume that it is the task of government, then, to keep the peace among us, to keep us all safe from the state itself, from enemies abroad, and *from one another* so that we may go about our business, exercising our freedoms, pursuing our happiness.

Our right to freedom from bodily harm underlies our laws against physical assault, providing their moral foundation. Without laws to forbid assault and battery and rape and homicide, and without a government to enforce those laws and punish offenders, we'd have to defend ourselves. We can imagine how terrible such lawlessness would be. Our Hollywood Westerns have taught us the value of a decent lawman to fight our showdowns for us. Threatened by an attacker, we don't want to fight it out for ourselves, and we don't think we have to. We call the cops. We good citizens cede to authorities—to police and prosecutors and judges—our right to defend ourselves, and they in turn are supposed to act on our behalf to protect our right to be free from bodily harm and to punish those who try to violate that right. That's the deal we make with the state—a basic clause in the social contract. And at the most rudimentary level, this is what a government of law is all about. Civilization rests upon the shoulders of an upright sheriff.

It doesn't rest easy, for despite the idealism of our assumptions, the right to be free from bodily harm has never been absolute. Like all our other rights, it was for a long time the privilege of only some of the "people"—mainly those well-to-do white men who drafted the laws and administered their enforcement. English men enjoyed privileges that were enshrined in the common law as their legal *rights*, and among them was the right to rule the family.[4] Building on the foundation of English common law, American legislation and jurisprudence imported those male "rights" wholesale. And just as English women had complained for centuries about the undue power men held over women and children, American women also began to campaign for equal rights, especially for equal rights *within the family*.

Historically, the law distinguished between public matters and private family matters, leaving the family under the governance of the husband and father. English common law made a Husband and a Wife legally *one* entity, and that one was the Husband. When she married, a woman ceased to exist before the law; she was "covered" by her Husband. If Wife ran up debts, pummeled a neighbor, or stole a cow, Husband had to answer for it at the bar of justice. Obviously then, the law had to arm Husband with a stick to keep Wife in line. Fair's fair. Today, of course, every woman is legally accountable for her own acts; so there is no longer any basis for the legal justification of wife beating. But for centuries the law concerned itself with the larger problem of keeping order among *men*; it delegated to each individual man the task of keeping his own household in line. The law gave him the right— even the obligation—to "chastise" *his* women and *his* children and *his* servants. American law in the early nineteenth century permitted a man to chastise his wife "without subjecting himself to vexatious prosecutions for assault and battery, resulting in the discredit and shame of all parties concerned."[5] The law drew a curtain of privacy about each man's household to shield it from legal scrutiny.

But behind that curtain, men committed acts against women and children which would have been considered crimes if committed against other men. Stories of household atrocities, such as we see in our newspapers today, have always circulated; and, gradually, under pressure from humanitarians and women's rights activists, some lawmakers came to face facts. They recognized that laws against assault and battery which protected men from bodily harm at the hands of others should apply to women and children as well—even when the assailant was the husband. Yet efforts to expand the legal category of "people" protected from assault inevitably collided with the accumulated precedents of privacy law. The two sometimes collided within a single judicial decision, producing hopeless ambiguity. Consider, for example, an 1874 decision of the Supreme Court of North Carolina. The court nullified the husband's right to chastise his wife *"under any circumstances,"* then added: "If no permanent injury has been inflicted, nor malice, cruelty, nor dangerous violence shown by the husband, it is better to draw the curtain, shut out the public gaze, and leave the parties to forgive and forget."[6]

The first English law against "Aggravated Assaults Upon Women and Children" was passed by Parliament in 1853. (Parliament seems to have been caught in a particularly charitable mood, for this law followed upon a great wave of legislation to protect domestic animals.) The act provided fines and prison terms of up to six months for men convicted of beating their wives or children under age fourteen. The United States, however, was slow to follow this example. Protesting the commonplace physical and sexual abuse of wives, American feminists and temperance leaders in the late nineteenth century railed against the "brutality" of violent and drunken husbands. And eventually they convinced policy makers, in that Darwinian age, that such privileged male behavior was an evolutionary throwback to the order of "brutes," unworthy of Nature's crowning achievement: Man— which is to say, men. By 1880, many states had made laws to restrict the "right" of men to "chastise" their wives and children, but few provided any punishment for men who exceeded the limits.[7] And because the laws were not enforced, the lives of women were little changed.[8]

The North Carolina decision that nullified the husband's right to chastise and then in effect nullified that nullification exemplifies the progress of American law. Not until this century did a court rule that while Husband was still obliged to "teach the wife her duty and subjection," he could no longer claim "the privilege, ancient though it be, to beat her with a stick, to pull her hair, choke her, spit in her face or kick her about the floor, or to inflict upon her other like indignities."[9]

Laws against assault, of course, were on the books in every state, but being intended to regulate the conduct of one man to another, they were almost never applied when a man assaulted his wife. Thus, many men continued to claim their ancient privilege, and law enforcement officers, uncertain what the law required of them, and—as one man to another—understandably reluctant to interfere in a fellow's "family" affairs, hesitated to look behind the traditional curtain of privacy. That very distinction between *public* and *private* matters, with the law regulating only weighty public affairs, effectively diminished women's concerns to inconsequential private complaints beneath the dignity and majesty of the Law. Thus, for the better part of a century, only the most atrocious crimes came to the attention of the courts, while run-of-the-mill batterers like my father carried on undeterred in the sanctified privacy of home.

In the 1970s, when women began fleeing to shelters, many of them told the same story. They'd called the cops. The cops had insulted them, laughed at them, blamed them, put them down, or ignored them altogether. Some women had gone to court only to be told they had no business there. Prosecutors and judges sent them home to "make up" with their husbands. Battered women's advocates and legal scholars set to work to make the law better, stronger, fairer, and inclusive of women and to persuade the criminal justice system to come to the defense of women's rights. At last a thoroughgoing paper reform took place, with many states adopting domestic abuse prevention acts to strengthen the hand of the authorities and sharpen their focus on assault in the home. Women worked with police, prosecutors, and judges—or tried to—to help them see the issues from the woman's point of view and to understand the seriousness of male violence against female partners. But battered women, still fleeing in growing numbers to shelters, reported little change.

Feminist attorneys, working on behalf of groups of battered women, brought class action law suits against police departments and court officers to compel them to do their job—to enforce laws against assault, make arrests, and help battered women press charges in court. In most cases, battered women won or settled to their advantage out of court. Important victories in Oakland, California, and New York City in 1976 prompted policy and procedural changes in those cities, sparked other lawsuits across the country, and convinced police in some jurisdictions, under pressure from local battered women's advocates, to change their policies without litigation. In addition, the victories inspired the battered women's movement, of which they were a part, to new levels of confidence and work.[10] But the movement had to fight the battle city by city, leaving many localities untouched or unchanged, and even in cities where the movement won, it had to monitor the police continuously to ensure even partial compliance with the law. The victories were monumental, yet battered women described the change as "small."[11]

Then some badly injured individual women and the families of some women murdered by husbands or boyfriends brought suits against police for failing to protect them as they would protect other crime victims, a violation of their civil rights. One woman, Tracey Thurman, won a suit against the police of Torrington, Connecticut, who had stood by and watched while her estranged husband stabbed and slashed and kicked her nearly to death.[12] Awarding her substantial damages, a federal district court ruled that "a man is not allowed to physically abuse or endanger a woman merely because he is her husband. Concomitantly, a police officer may not knowingly refrain from interference in such violence, and, may not automatically decline to make an arrest simply because the assaulter and the victim are married to each other."[13] This sensible decision was handed down only in 1984, and only after Tracey Thurman and thousands upon thousands like her had been beaten and beaten and beaten.

The more women pressed for law reform and law enforcement, the more they realized what an impenetrable body the law is, and how intransigent the system that administers and enforces it. Again and again during the last two decades women assaulted by men turned to the legal system for help. Again and again the system let them down. In one six-year period alone—1967 to 1973—battering men killed 17,500 women and children in the United States. To grasp the enormity of that figure consider that only a little more than twice as many men—39,000 to be exact— were killed during the same period in combat in Vietnam.[14] Thankfully the war in Vietnam ended, but the count of women injured and killed by men on the home front continues. In 1991 more than 21,000 domestic assaults, rapes, and murders were reported to the police every week.[15]

The law has never been able to address battering effectively because of its own peculiar structure. Written by men for men, the law is designed to protect men from the power of the state and to adjudicate conflicts between men, to preserve order in a society of men. We may believe the law to be rational, objective, impartial, and fair, but many legal scholars find legal procedure, legal language, legal logic, and even the binary "either/or" mode of legal thought masculine to the core. To critics, the law seems simplistic, regimented, confrontational, adversarial, and overly technical—in a word, *macho*. A trial is a showdown: somebody wins, somebody lies bloodied in the dust. This result is called "justice." But how can this sort of macho justice be applied to the complex issues raised when a man assaults a person who is also his intimate partner or wife, and when the welfare of children also hangs in the balance? The fact is that there's something fundamentally wrong with the law. Dickens's Mr. Bumble pronounced the famous indictment: "The law is an ass." Worse. The ass seems to be *masculine*. Worse still, when women's rights are at issue, the ass ambles backwards.

The problem is not simply that the law is biased in favor of the male gender (though it is), but that the law itself, in the way it goes about things, is "gendered." Thus, the practice of law changes only very slowly as women enter the field, for female law students are subjected to the same rigorous training in the system of "male" language, logic, and procedures as their male counterparts; and subsequent success in the profession usually depends upon sticking to the rules.[16] Certainly, among women in the law, feminist legal scholars engaged in critical analysis of the law are a minority. The fact that so many women in the law behave much like men in the law is then taken as evidence that the law is indeed objective, impartial, ungendered, true, and universally applicable. But, unfortunately, it is not.

In any conflict, the law casts the parties as adversaries, but conflict between parties who share a household and perhaps children is never that simple. A battered woman may want her husband arrested to deter him from beating her again, but if feeding the children depends upon his wages, she may not want him jailed or even prosecuted. In that case, the prosecutor is likely to say that she's wasting the court's time; and the judge may admonish *her* instead of her assaultive husband. She has to play it the court's way, or not at all. Yet the court is singularly unable to remedy her complaints because by the very nature of its thinking, geared to simple good guy versus bad guy situations, it cannot comprehend them. Is this man, who is at once her husband and her assailant, her adversary or not? The battered woman may have to answer yes *and* no—an answer which disqualifies her complaint. On the other hand, if a battered woman wants her assailant locked up *forever*, as many do, the court is certain to remind her that the man is her husband. In either case, the prosecutor or the judge may conclude that there's something wrong with *her*: she's indecisive, uncooperative, manipulative, masochistic, stupid, angry, a "bitch" *using* the law to "get back at" her husband or boyfriend. In fact, it may be that adversarial law is simply inadequate to gratify her best interests, or even to understand them.

Harvard psychologist Carol Gilligan, studying moral conflict and choice, concluded that women make ethical distinctions that are different from those of men. Earlier studies of people in ethical dilemmas concluded that the ability to reason from abstract principles (as the law purports to do) is the highest level of moral development; but Gilligan noted that those studies were based almost entirely upon male subjects. The few women studied were found "deficient" in abstract reasoning and branded morally "inferior." Gilligan agreed that women—given their different social conditioning and experience of life—seemed to reason differently; but she posited a second moral "voice," neither better nor worse than the male interest in abstract principles, but "different"— more concerned with real human relationships and connectedness. Beside the male ethic of "justice" she placed the female ethic of "care."[17]

Gilligan's work is controversial among psychologists who don't like to admit they've based a "science" of human behavior almost exclusively on the behavior of white males, and among some feminists who see differences between the sexes (particularly differences that may be regarded as essential) as potential obstacles to equality. But her observation that women often make different ethical distinctions from men goes straight to the core of what's wrong with the law. Faced with a classical ethical problem—should a poor man whose wife is dying steal the drugs she needs?—men take the poor man's side or the law's; they argue one side or the other. Women say things like: "Maybe if he explained the situation to the druggist, they could work something out." Interestingly, philosopher John Stuart Mill also observed these differing habits of the female mind in the nineteenth century, differences produced, he said, "merely by circumstance," or perhaps simply attributed to women by men. Mill thought women were "extremely unlikely to put faith in any speculation which loses sight of individuals, and deals with things as if they existed for the benefit of some imaginary entity, some mere creation of the mind, not resolvable into the feelings of human beings." Further, he said, "Women are comparatively unlikely to fall into the common error of men, that of sticking to their rules in a case whose specialities either take it out of the class to which the rules are applicable, or require a special adaptation of them."[18]

The law, on the other hand, sticks to the rules of its own devising. Faced with a typical battering case, the law remains judiciously "neutral," weighing the "adversaries" in the scales of "justice" as though they were equally matched, quarreling man to man, instead of what they are: a criminal and a crime victim (who also are, or have been, involved in an intimate relationship). But by not taking the part of the victim, the law takes the part of the assailant; just when it professes to be most "objective," it is most clearly biased. And rarely does a judge bother with the "special adaptations" that common sense calls for when criminal and victim are parents. One Massachusetts court worker reported in 1992 that in four hundred cases in which she helped women get restraining orders, only three judges ordered temporary financial support and worked out child visitation arrangements.[19]

Almost as if they recognize the limitations of the law's masculine moral enterprise, judges often tell the battered woman to do what women are supposed to be able to do so well—to go home and work things out. Or, they order victim and assailant into mediation or joint counseling for "conflict resolution," as if they were business rivals or merely neurotic. No wonder feminist legal scholars see the law as cruelly irrelevant to the concerns of women, or worse, oppressive.

Today, when women complain of this treatment, when they sue police departments and court and municipal officials for violating their constitutional rights to due process and equal protection of the law, they are told (as we shall see in chapter 2) that our Constitution is merely a charter of "negative liberties," forbidding the state to deprive its citizens of life, liberty, or property, but in no way obliging it to protect them against "private violence."[20] This is a charter and a jurisprudence for rugged individualists—independent, self-sufficient, powerful, and brooking no interference. (Here is the masculine perspective once again.) But from the standpoint of women and children—the common objects of "private violence"—this perspective is inappropriate, and cruelly so. As legal scholars have pointed out, this " 'hands off' view of the law effectively abets the batterer . . . and turns a deaf ear to the battered woman," who often has no other options.[21] In the context of that charter of "negative liberties," the legal concept of privacy (which usually means *male* privacy) "operates as a mask for inequality, protecting male violence against women."[22] Thus, the law is "not separate from the violence" against women, but part of it, for the failures of the law and those charged with enforcing it to intervene in "domestic violence" are "public, not private, actions."[23] Catherine MacKinnon, a legal scholar who has argued women's case against the law persuasively and at length in her work on feminist jurisprudence, sums up a multiplicity of problems in a single sentence: "The law sees and treats women the way men see and treat women."[24]

The law has *always* seen women this way—and developed legal theories accordingly. Current legal thought and procedures follow "naturally" from this venerable tradition of legal and extralegal sexism. Today in the eyes of the law, any assault is both a criminal offense and a personal tort, or wrong; any assault may be the basis for a criminal prosecution or a civil action, or both. If you attack me in the street, the state can put you on trial and send you to jail for assault and battery, and I can sue you for damages. But in a great many jurisdictions, even today, a domestic assault is not regarded as a *real* assault—that is, not really criminal. When police refuse to arrest, prosecutors to prosecute, and judges to sentence a man because the victim he assaulted is (or was) his wife or girlfriend, the state redefines this criminal assault against a woman as a special category of violence immune from criminal law. The state magically transforms a crime into a noncrime.[25] When a battered woman takes her case to criminal court, it may be dismissed as a trivial complaint, or worse, a "vexatious prosecution"—that is, an unfounded and malicious action intended merely to harass the "victim" of the complaint, which is to say the poor man accused of assault.

More often the complaints of battered women are shunted into municipal or family courts to be heard by civil judges—which makes the offense complained of *by definition* a civil matter and not a crime. Indeed, in many jurisdictions this strategy was deliberately adopted during the feminist wave of paper reform to augment existing assault laws (which weren't enforced against batterers) by creating "a constructive middle way, short of either criminally prosecuting or ignoring the violation of the law."[26] At the time, many battered women's advocates preferred to use family courts because so many battered women wanted a means to protect themselves short of prosecuting their assaultive husbands; and in some jurisdictions where judges take domestic assault seriously, civil courts can serve women's interests well. But, unfortunately, the family court proceeding, by its very nature, suggests that what has happened is not as bad as all that. In some jurisdictions, where all battering cases go to family court, men alleged to have committed felonious assault, or even attempted murder, may evade criminal prosecution altogether.

The practice of bringing assault cases in civil courts may also place women at greater risk because civil court judges do not receive and review as a matter of course the criminal records of men who come before them. In case after case, civil judges set free battering men who are subject to outstanding criminal warrants. To cite just one example, Massachusetts municipal court Judge Lawrence Shubow granted 21-year-old Kristin Lardner the restraining order she sought on May 12, 1992, against ex-boyfriend Michael Cartier, then turned Cartier loose. Before the month was out, Cartier gunned down Kristin Lardner in the street, then killed himself. A civil court judge, Shubow didn't know when he set Cartier free that the man had a criminal record described by *Boston Globe* reporters as a "lengthy and bizarre history of violent crimes, especially against women." Nor did he know that Cartier was on probation, subject to a stayed six-month jail term for attempting to slash a previous girlfriend with a scissors. After Cartier murdered Kristin Lardner, Judge Shubow said he was sorry that he had not reviewed Cartier's criminal record; but Samuel Zoll, chief justice of the Massachusetts district courts, explaining standard legal procedure to the press, said: "You can't mix civil and criminal records." It was an idea, Zoll said, that probably couldn't even be considered.[27]

Judges may be moved to consider it, however, as more and more batterers demonstrate how dangerous they are by committing assaults within the courthouse. On January 19, 1993, judges in Dallas staged a spontaneous walkout, protesting the lack of court security, after Van Hai Huynh shot and killed his wife Ly Thi Dang, wounded a bystander, and killed himself in a courthouse corridor just before a hearing on the woman's application for a restraining order.[28] Reporters unofficially tallied more than twelve such "courthouse slayings" in the previous twelve months, including one incident just six months earlier in neighboring Fort Worth in which a man who lost custody of his children shot and killed two lawyers and wounded two judges and a prosecutor. In another case in Grand Forks, North Dakota, in May 1992, a former city councilman shot and wounded a judge who called him to account for unpaid child support.[29] All of these assaults and killings occurred in civil or family courts. All of them were committed by men. And if one can judge from the facts presented in the press, all of them were assaults aimed at women who were trying to get free, women who were seeking orders of protection, divorce, child custody, or child support. In some cases, like those in Fort Worth and Grand Forks, the violent man also targeted court personnel who must have seemed to him to be aiding his wife. Discussing these cases, reporters wrote of gender-neutral "emotional outbursts," "emotionally charged" circumstances, and explosive "passion"; and judges talked of metal detectors, not undeterred male violence. But in most if not all of these cases, the man's violence was consistent with his previous "private" behavior, could have been predicted by his wife, and probably was.

Nevertheless, judges often abdicate altogether their responsibility for dealing with assaultive men and hand cases of "domestic" assault over to court-appointed mediators for resolution. For a battered woman, however, mediation is just as inappropriate as an adversarial contest or a civil proceeding. Like the family court hearing, mediation suggests that the matter at hand—actually a criminal assault—is not very important. And like civil court proceedings, it may place a woman at greater risk. Mediation may be effective in disputes between parties who both have bargaining *power*—like General Motors and the United Auto Workers, for example; but when one side has muscle and the other merely fear, mediation is bound not only to fail but to *make matters worse for the weaker party*. In battering cases, mediation in effect minimizes both the woman's injury and the man's responsibility. (We don't ask men charged with assault against strangers to negotiate a settlement with the victim.) A "successful" mediation—that is, one that reaches a conclusion "acceptable" to both parties—is necessarily a victory for the assaultive husband, for it lets him off the hook. For the battered woman, mediation may mean double defeat: she gets no relief, and she is led to question the legitimacy of her own complaint.

Until quite recently, with the development of divorce law and child custody law that considers "the best interest of the child," the law did not even acknowledge that family members might have competing interests. Traditionally, the law assumed that the interests of the *pater familias* and the interests of the family were the same (or would be made the same by that stick in Husband's hand). These days, those competing interests often clash in court, for many men use child custody suits as one more weapon to punish and control a woman who is trying to get free.[30] And even now, the law commonly takes the rights of the husband and father to be clearly established rights—that is, to take precedence over the rights of wife and children. For example, the law is reluctant to evict an assaultive husband from the family home because a man has a right to enjoy "his" home as "his" castle, even when it is the scene of his crimes. (Hence the great need for shelters to house the women and children who must flee "his" home. Since the criminal is not jailed, the victims must lock themselves in sanctuary; the shelter is prison in reverse, a jail for crime victims.)

The law is even more reluctant to deny a man's right to "his" children. Although some experts estimate that 70 percent of batterers also abuse children in the household, men who seek custody have a better than even chance of getting it, whether or not they have a history of violence.[31] In one study, 59 percent of fathers who won custody had "physically abused" their wives, and 36 percent had kidnapped the children.[32] Another study found that in many cases where fathers received custody with the supposed agreement of the mother, the father had forced her to agree by threatening her safety, reputation, or financial security.[33] Clearly, men can continue to control and abuse "their" women by gaining control of the children, but judges often reason that "domestic violence" has nothing to do with a father's fitness as a parent. In 1978, in one of the earliest of many so-called landmark cases in the history of battered women's litigation, a New York jury awarded two million dollars in damages to Dina Sorichetti and her mother Josephine; yet legislators and judges seem to have learned little from the example.

In 1975, Josephine Sorichetti brought a divorce action after her battering husband Frank, who had previously been arrested six times for drunkenness and assault, attacked her with a knife. He threatened to kill her and the children if she went ahead with the divorce, and she applied for an order of protection. The judge who granted Josephine Sorichetti's order of protection gave Frank Sorichetti the right to take six-year-old Dina for the weekends. Even when Frank tried to assault Josephine outside the courtroom, the judge refused to rescind the father's parental rights.

Josephine turned her daughter over to her husband as ordered and immediately reported to police that Frank had again threatened to kill both mother and daughter. Those threats violated Josephine's order of protection, but the police refused to arrest him or to retrieve the child; even when Frank Sorichetti failed to return the child on time, police did nothing. Later that day, Frank Sorichetti's sister found Dina in his apartment. He had attacked the little girl with a fork, a knife, a screwdriver, and a saw. He had slashed her from head to toe, inflicted many internal injuries, and attempted to saw off her leg. Dina Sorichetti survived, but she was severely and permanently disabled.[34]

More recently, courts have held in the cases of Joseph Pikul in New York and James Lutgen in Illinois that a man cannot be considered an unfit parent merely because he has murdered the mother of his children. Lutgen, who served less than three years in prison for voluntary manslaughter after strangling his wife Carol (who had just obtained an order of protection) in front of their two young daughters, was adjudged "a fit and proper person to have care and control of his minor children."[35]

Similarly, when a man abuses a child, judges are reluctant to believe it. If a woman repeats her allegation of child sexual abuse, or if she seeks more evidence to confirm her child's allegations, the judge may find her "paranoid," "delusional," or "obsessed" with sexual abuse and consequently an unfit parent. Worse, the judge may see her as a vindictive woman seeking revenge on a hated husband by "brainwashing" the kids to cry sexual abuse, a woman whose spiteful manipulations he may consider far more damaging to children than "mere" sexual abuse. This view that vengeful women use false charges of child sexual abuse as a weapon in divorce and custody proceedings is advanced with increasing frequency and fervor by fathers' lawyers and expert witnesses and by spokesmen for the Fathers' Rights movement. If believed, it

"proves" not only the father's innocence, but also the mother's viciousness. (An example is Woody Allen's much publicized allegation that Mia Farrow is an unfit mother.) Such charges are newly
legitimized by pop psychiatrists such as Richard A. Gardner, a
man who single-handedly invented a new "psychiatric disorder"
common in women: "Parental Alienation Syndrome." Its pathological symptoms in women include making sarcastic remarks
about the children's father and complaining about his failure to
make child support payments.[36]

If an abused woman, or the mother of an abused child, takes
matters into her own hands and runs away to save herself and/or
the child from physical and/or sexual abuse, she can be charged
with kidnapping and deprived of all parental rights in favor of the
"nonoffending" father. This means that one of the easiest ways for
a man to get sole custody of his children may be to abuse and
terrify their mother until she has no choice but to run, either taking the children with her ("kidnapping") or leaving them behind
("abandonment"). In short, so devoted is the law to the father's
best interests, and so given to seeing things his way, that the more
abusive and violent a man is, the more likely he is to get sole custody of his children.[37]

The ordeal of Dr. Elizabeth Morgan of Washington, D.C., il-
lustrates the lengths to which courts may go to enforce paternal
rights. It seems an extreme case because it has been highly publicized, but its details are duplicated in courtrooms again and
again.[38] When District of Columbia Superior Court Judge Herbert Dixon Jr. ordered Morgan in 1987 to send her daughter Hilary, then five, to the child's father for a two-week visit, Morgan
sent her instead into hiding. During a long custody fight, Morgan
had alleged that the father, her former husband Dr. Eric Foretich,
sexually abused Hilary during visitations. One of Foretich's previous wives alleged that he had sexually abused her daughter too,
and a medical specialist found similar injuries in both girls. Judge
Dixon, being "unwilling to find as more probable or not that the
alleged abuse occurred or did not occur," presumed the father innocent and upheld his right to "his" child, even though the child

in question had not yet been born when Morgan left her husband.[39] Morgan went to jail for contempt, losing her medical practice in consequence and running up debts in excess of $1.5 million. She served twenty-five months in a Washington jail—the longest jail term for civil contempt in United States history—and was released in September 1989 only in response to extraordinary public pressure. It took a special act of Congress, limiting imprisonment for civil contempt in the District of Columbia to one year, to set her free.[40]

Then, in February 1990, the child was found, living in Christchurch, New Zealand, with her maternal grandparents; and the case was taken up on the other side of the world. In what sounded like a victory for Elizabeth Morgan, New Zealand Family Court Judge P. D. Mahoney awarded her sole custody of her daughter and barred Foretich from visiting the child "in the immediate future." But Judge Mahoney also seized the child's passport and decreed that she could not change her address or her school without the court's permission. Morgan could have her daughter, but only if she abandoned the medical practice she had resumed in Washington, her second husband (a federal court judge), and her country. (The rulings of the District of Columbia court still apply, should Morgan and her daughter ever return to the United States.) Foretich, who said he didn't want to give up his dental practice to move halfway around the world, did not bother to contest the custody decision. "I'm an American," he said.[41]

Having made this remarkable decision, Judge Mahoney let TV reporters know what he thought of Elizabeth Morgan. Like Judge Dixon in Washington, Judge Mahoney found her an unreasonable woman because she would not give in and allow Foretich to play "a meaningful part" in the child's life. Having stripped the woman of everything else she cared about in the world, Judge Mahoney told the press that Elizabeth Morgan was "preoccupied" with her daughter.[42]

Many judges make pronouncements like this to the press or from the bench in cases of battery, child abuse, and child custody. They speechify about such extralegal matters as a wife's "duty" and her "place" in the home, her "preoccupation," and the essential frivolity or vindictiveness of her complaints against her husband. When they make such speeches to the press, they certainly influence public opinion. When they make them from the bench, they elevate to legal standing their own traditional biases. Often they talk in legalese, but sometimes they use words that sound like plain English—words that turn out to mean something quite different from what a woman complainant might have supposed. The judge who says that he won't break up a family, for example, means that he won't remove or punish an assaultive man; for very often in law the word "family" means merely "father." In this context, then, women's complaints of battery and sexual abuse—of *crimes* men commit upon them and upon children—are anything but frivolous. In fact, they call into question concepts dear to our hearts and to legal tradition. Concepts like *fatherhood*, *authority*, and *justice* itself.

Instead of safeguarding woman's right to be free from bodily harm, the law itself does her harm.[43] It preserves male privilege by asserting "his" prior rights, by turning a deaf ear to her complaints, by providing "remedies" that are at best inappropriate, by declining to treat as a crime what is in fact a crime on the books of every state, and by cruelly punishing women who injure or kill men while defending themselves and their children.[44] The law no longer explicitly states (as it used to) that women have no right to be free from bodily harm, but in the peculiar ways it contrives to avoid punishing women's assailants, and in the devious ways it *reasons* about "domestic" harms, it enforces that ancient policy. In case after case, the law itself is deeply implicated in battering the battered woman, with disastrous results.

Pamela Nigro Dunn was only twenty-two when she went to Somerville (Massachusetts) District Court four times early in 1986 to seek restraining orders against her assaultive husband whom she had left. Although he granted the restraining orders, Judge Paul P. Heffernan berated Pamela Dunn for wasting the court's time with trivial complaints. He belittled a police officer who had escorted her to collect her belongings from the marital apartment. To her husband Paul Dunn, Judge Heffernan remarked: "If you want to gnaw on her and she on you, fine, but let's not do it at taxpayers' expense."[45] In March 1986, he told Pamela Dunn that he was "not interested" in her fear that her husband would attack her again. In August Paul Dunn did attack again as Pamela walked home from work, accompanied by her mother. He blinded Pamela's mother with mace, shot Pamela as she tried to run away, pushed her into his car, stabbed her three times, strangled her, and dropped her face down in a puddle at the Lexington town dump where she died by drowning. Paul Dunn was apprehended a few months later in Florida, convicted of first degree murder, and sentenced to life in prison.[46]

After someone turned over tapes of Judge Heffernan's courtroom harangues to the *Boston Globe*, reporters learned that battered women had filed complaints against nearly two dozen Massachusetts judges who, it was demonstrated, had refused to enforce the Commonwealth's model 1978 Abuse Prevention Act, a law designed specifically to protect them. A task force appointed by then-Governor Michael Dukakis subsequently found among Massachusetts judges "a widespread pattern of noncompliance" by which women often were "denied completely the protections the law provides or subjected to verbal and psychological abuse from the very people they've turned to for help."[47] The 1978 law, designed *for* women in recognition of woman's right to be free from bodily harm, simply didn't square with *the* law as many Massachusetts judges understood it, muddled with their personal and woefully biased beliefs. District Court Judge Paul H. King of Dorchester, denying a battered woman's plea to have her husband barred from her home, said flatly: "I don't believe in breaking up families."[48]

Studies of gender bias in state courts turn up similar cases. In Georgia, for example, a 1991 study cited a judge who "mocked," "humiliated," and "ridiculed" a female victim of repeated assaults and "led the courtroom in laughter as the woman left." The woman's assailant—her estranged husband—subsequently murdered her.[49] Clearly, the law and the legal system are deeply implicated in the abuse of women and children.

The story of Pamela Guenther, documented by the public television news program "Frontline," is another example of how the law and public officials charged with enforcing the law become accomplices to the lawbreaker. Pamela Guenther, of Westminster, Colorado, married her husband David when she was fifteen and for the better part of the next fifteen years tried to get away from him. According to her friends who appeared in the televised documentary, she was fun-loving and full of life, while her husband David was "kind of strange": an immature, temperamental, and surly man who quarreled with all the neighbors and couldn't hold a job. At first, when Pamela thought about leaving him, her best friend advised: "If you love him, it's worth fighting for—you don't want to just throw it away." Then David threatened to kill Pamela if she tried to leave, and it seemed *safer* to stay. She went to work in a doughnut shop—she supported David and their two children—but he kept her from her friends. He was "terribly jealous," they said. So Pamela and David "lived very quiet lives" at home.[50]

David Guenther tried to run the neighborhood too. He called the police so often to complain about his neighbors that he became something of a joke among them. On April 20, 1986, after a drinking party, some of them went to Guenther's house to get back at him by harassing him. David Guenther suddenly burst from his house with a 357 Magnum. He killed one woman and seriously wounded her husband and another man. He argued in court that he had been defending his wife and property, and that he was well within his rights under the terms of Colorado's controversial "make my day" law which gives homeowners immunity from prosecution for shooting intruders. A judge agreed and dismissed charges against him. Pamela Guenther already knew that her husband was a dangerous man; now the police had reason to know it too.

Not long afterward, Pamela discovered that David had beaten their son; and she took the children into hiding at a women's shelter. Counselors there described her as terrified but outwardly calm and businesslike; they said she had grown used to terror and had learned to carry on in spite of it. When David found Pamela at her job, he assaulted and tried to kidnap her. Police charged him only with an incidental matter—driving away from the scene of a motor vehicle accident—and let him go. Pamela had to quit the job and get another where she wouldn't be alone. David wrote her letters threatening to kill her. He phoned her former boss, who had become her boyfriend, threatening to come after both of them "with a gun." Pamela got a restraining order that evicted David from the family home and restored it to her and the children. The policeman who accompanied her during the move found David "cooperative."

Two days later David forced his way in and held Pamela at gunpoint, ordering her to have sex with him (though he proved impotent) and ranting about murder. Police surrounded the house, but David Guenther held them off for five hours, using Pamela as a hostage until she finally persuaded him to surrender. The police took him away and charged him with "burglary." The court set bail at $10,000. Within eight hours he had paid the 10 percent— $1,000—required to go free.

The investigating police officer, a man, said he had "no reason not to believe" David Guenther when he said he was sorry (he had only wanted to "talk" to his wife) and that it wouldn't happen again. On the other hand, the officer distrusted Pamela Guenther. She was "too calm," he said, for someone "who had been through what she *said*," while David Guenther seemed genuinely "upset." As if to prove his "impartiality," the policeman said he hadn't let David Guenther's previous shootings color his thinking about this "incident" at all; and as for Pamela Guenther's restraining order— well, that was a civil matter.

The next day David bought another gun, using Pamela's credit card; and a week later, on March 1, 1987, in the parking lot of a restaurant where she and her children and her boyfriend had eaten dinner, he shot and killed her. Her boyfriend, shot four times, survived.

Interviewed in the "Frontline" documentary, Denver psychologist Michael Lindsey, who counsels abusive men, commented on the way the criminal justice system had handled David Guenther all along: "He got essentially no consequences. He's never been given any consequences . . . for anything that he's done. So it just sort of systematically lets him get further and further out on the edge, believing that he's going to be able to do anything he wants." Pamela Guenther's family and friends and advocates thought David Guenther should have been locked up long before, but District Attorney James Smith commented after the murder: "I didn't feel the system let Pamela Guenther down. I'm not sure any domestic violence policy would have prevented her death." Then, however, he reconsidered the incident when David held Pamela hostage only a week before her murder. Belatedly, he added to the burglary charge additional charges of "failure to leave premises" and "false imprisonment," bringing the bond to one million dollars. Had he done that at the time of the offense, Pamela Guenther might still be alive. Instead, when David Guenther at last was convicted of first degree murder and sentenced automatically to life in prison, D.A. Smith pompously told "Frontline" reporters: "We learned from the Guenther case that *at some point in time* most criminals are held accountable for their actions."

These days we hear stories like Pamela Guenther's all the time, for women die every day at the hands of battering men. Their ordeals make absorbing magazine features and TV movies. The reports always "shock" and "sadden" press and public alike. Often some official board investigates, some official report is issued, some official wrist is slapped. Someone gets transferred or reassigned or takes early retirement. Some policy is remanded to committee for further study. And some bereaved relative of the dead woman explains to reporters that the murder victim *did* call the police, she *did* get an order of protection, she *did* leave home, and yes, she *did* say over and over that he was trying to kill her. We feel outraged because we can see so clearly that somebody could have saved that woman's life. But somebody messed up. And always in the same way. Somebody—often *everybody* in the criminal justice system—discounted her complaint, trusted the man who terrorized her, and wrote off criminal assault *as if it had not occurred*. Somebody underestimated the dangerousness of the terrorist. Because he was dangerous only to *her*, the law acted as if he wasn't dangerous at all.

But how are law enforcement officials to know? How can they assess, as the jargon of criminology puts it, a man's "potential lethality"? How are they to tell the difference between a man who is "really serious" and one who is "only a batterer"? The question is doubly disingenuous in the case of David Guenther, who already had shot three people, killed one, and kept the town's police force at bay for five hours while he held his wife hostage; but it would not arise at all if the law and everyone charged with enforcing the law treated *all* assault cases as serious and potentially lethal offenses. It wouldn't arise at all if the law could *hear* women. It wouldn't arise at all if the law assumed, as it should, that all women have the right to be free from bodily harm.

In 1979 in Nebraska Lynn Ditter charged her husband with sexual assault and battery in what was to have been the state's first trial for marital rape. In January 1979 she asked the court to revoke his bond and lock him up; he was following her and threatening her, she said.[51] But the court was guided by a report from a Nebraska Mental Health Clinic psychiatrist who said that defendant David Ditter "presents every evidence of good emotional and physical self-control" and should not "be considered assaultive or dangerous to be at large at this time." The court continued his bond, leaving David Ditter at large. He shot and killed his wife, just as she had said he would.[52]

On April 2, 1979, Jeanette Tedesco of Fairbanks, Alaska, reported to police that her boyfriend Charlie Walton had kidnapped, assaulted, and raped her, but police failed to investigate and Assistant District Attorney James Doogan declined to prosecute unless Tedesco passed psychiatric and lie detector tests. Before she could finish the exams, Walton killed her.[53]

A decade later, in the space of ten days in December 1988, three women in Suffolk County, New York—each with an order of protection—died at the hands of their estranged or former husbands. Joseph Grohoski chased his twenty-four-year-old wife Lydia to the basement of her home, kicked down a locked door, shot her in the face with a 12-gauge shotgun, and then shot himself.[54] Two days later William Croff rammed the car of his estranged wife Elizabeth, aged thirty, and fired a rifle at her, then chased her down in his vehicle when she fled on foot carrying her two-year-old daughter. He shot her in the head, wounded the child, then shot himself.[55] A week later the body of thirty-four-year-old April LaSalata was found on her doorstep; her ex-husband Anthony had shot her twice in the head as she returned from work.[56] Police found him several days later in a car parked in a rest stop on the Long Island Expressway; he had shot himself.[57]

Elizabeth Croff's mother, with whom she lived, told reporters: "She wanted him arrested, but the police wouldn't do anything."[58] The courts also refused to take seriously the threats against these three women. Three days before her death, Elizabeth Croff, trying to get a warrant for her husband's arrest, told the court that he had assaulted her, in violation of her order of protection. When she was killed, the warrant hadn't been typed yet. (She didn't know, and the judge hadn't told her, that she didn't need the warrant; in New York state, police can, and should, arrest on the strength of a protected victim's verbal complaint.) Lydia Grohoski was waiting for her husband to stand trial for reckless endangerment, assault, and menacing—charges brought against him when he assaulted her three weeks earlier—but Joseph Grohoski was free on $10,000 bail. Eleven months earlier, in February 1988, Anthony LaSalata had broken into April LaSalata's home armed with a sawed-off rifle and a knife and stabbed her several times in the chest. Charged with attempted murder, he was released in August 1988 on $25,000 bail. Prosecutors and April LaSalata herself appealed to Suffolk Criminal Court Judge Rudolph Mazzei to increase the bail and jail Anthony LaSalata, but the judge refused. April LaSalata was also denied a permit for a gun with which she might have protected herself.[59]

Every year, according to FBI statistics, roughly three thousand men murder their current and former wives and girlfriends in circumstances like these.[60] A simple calculation, then, tells us that during the decade that elapsed between the murders of Lynn Ditter and Jeanette Tedesco in the seventies and the murders of Lydia Grohoski, Elizabeth Croff, and April LaSalata in the eighties some thirty thousand American women were murdered by men who once claimed to love them.

Reporting on some of these murders in *Redbook* magazine, writer Sheila Weller commented with remarkable restraint: "The alarming incidence of these cases raises disturbing questions about the adequacy of the system designed to protect us, and the attitude of those who administer it."[61] But the delusion that batterers are not dangerous to be at large is so widespread that in any particular case the machinery of that system designed to protect us almost certainly will be jammed—whether by a judge, a prosecutor, a cop, a psychiatrist, a prison official, a parole officer, a social worker, or even a telephone operator. In June 1988, twenty-five-year-old Carol Kudelycz called the New York City emergency number to report that her ex-boyfriend William Elliott was trying to break into her house. The operator didn't think it important to tell the police dispatcher what Carol Kudelycz had told him: that Elliott had assaulted her before, and just three months earlier had attempted to kill her by dousing her with gasoline and trying to set her on fire. The operator reported only a "violent man banging on door," the dispatcher gave it low priority, and thirty-seven minutes later, when police reached the scene, Carol Kudelycz was dead of a gunshot to the chest.[62]

The system that is supposed to protect us is so haphazard, and the judgment of many of those who administer it so skewed by sympathy for men, that even when the system appears to be working, it may break down altogether. Consider the story of Lisa Marie Bianco who—like so many other women—predicted her own murder.

When she married Alan Matheney, a plumbing contractor, in 1978 he was "a perfect gentleman," but in 1985 Bianco fled with her two children from her home in Mishawaka, Indiana, to a

South Bend women's shelter. She was badly beaten, deeply ashamed, and scared; and by the end of the year she was divorced. In retaliation, Matheney kidnapped the children. On Bianco's complaint, he was arrested in North Carolina and brought back to Indiana. There he was released on bond. He broke into Bianco's house, beat her, tried to strangle her, and told her he was going to rape her. In a videotaped statement Bianco told the prosecutor: "I told him I didn't want to die. . . . I decided I'd rather be submissive and go along with his wishes because I didn't want to be bothered anymore. . . . I had to save myself any way I could. . . . I have to [prosecute]. If I don't do something, it's just going to happen again."[63]

A probation consultant recommended *against* jail time for Matheney, advising the court that the defendant and his ex-wife "very possibly could have been having a wonderful social affair with sex involved." So the rape charge was dropped. But Matheney was sentenced to five years for the remaining charges of kidnapping and assault.

From prison one hundred and fifty miles away, Matheney telephoned Bianco, threatening to kill her. Bianco, who was working as a counselor at the Elkhart (Indiana) Women's Shelter, told a co-worker: "I know he's going to find me. But if I start running now, I know I'll never stop, so I might as well stay here and help out." To another friend she said: "If I'm killed it'll have to be a closed casket, because if he ever gets a hold of me, it's not going to be a pretty sight." Bianco, who had looked to law enforcement and the courts for protection, continued to do everything by the book. She reported Matheney's threats to the prosecutor and the prison; and the prosecutor secured a promise from prison officials to notify both his office and Lisa Bianco if Matheney should ever be let out. For their part, prison officials were pleased with Matheney and the "clear conduct record" he established behind bars. "Subject relates well and seems to have adjusted . . . very well," an official wrote in December 1988. "Subject" appeared to have "no mental impairments that would hinder his ability to function in society."

On March 4, 1989, Matheney was released on furlough into the custody of his mother and ordered to remain in the vicinity of the prison. Instead he drove one hundred and fifty miles to Misha-waka, dropped off his mother, stole a shotgun from a friend's house, and smashed in Lisa Bianco's door. Bianco's ten-year-old daughter ran to a neighbor's to call the police while Bianco, fresh from the bathtub and wearing only her underpants, fled screaming toward the street. Matheney caught her in the yard and clubbed her twenty times with the shotgun, breaking the gun into three pieces and smashing Lisa Bianco's head to bits.

The story went out on the wire services and turned up in the *New York Times*, a paper that covers only the most "significant" killings.[64] But what made the story news was not the failure of the state to protect a battered woman but the failure of the state's prison furlough system. Press and public had been well schooled only a few months earlier, during the 1988 presidential campaign, by slick Republican commercials blasting Massachusetts Governor Michael Dukakis for furloughing murderer Willie Horton. With a finger to the political wind, Indiana Governor Evan Bayh suspended his state's prison-release program; and the state corrections department, admitting to "poor judgment," fired two officials who had approved Alan Matheney's furlough. Everyone concerned expressed amazement, outrage, and shock. But Lisa Bianco—one more woman who turned to the criminal justice system for protection from bodily harm—had seen it coming.

Women usually do. And in states that publicized new "get tough" policies on violent men, endangered women turned increasingly to the courts for protection, encouraged to believe, as Lisa Bianco was, that their best hope for safety lay in the law. In Massachusetts 31,000 restraining orders were issued to battered women in 1990, and 37,000 in 1991, yet the death toll of women possessing restraining orders continued to mount during those years.[65] May 12, 1991: Peter Nguyen of Lowell stabbed his wife Nancy Nguyen to death, set the house on fire, and killed himself. Their seven-year-old daughter Joanna died in the fire. Nancy Nguyen had a restraining order. November 18, 1991: Joaquim Alameida of New Bedford allegedly shot his ex-girlfriend *and* his estranged wife and one of her friends. The estranged wife, Beth Lovering, had a restraining order. January 27, 1992: Louis Johnson, Jr., of Medford allegedly shot and killed his girlfriend Pamela Watkins and her ten-year-old daughter Kimberly. He also wounded his fourteen-year-old daughter Nekeya Gomez. Pamela Watkins had a restraining order; and the police had Johnson in custody on the evening of the shootings, but they let him go. February 6, 1992: Ernest Anthony of Waltham kidnapped his ex-girlfriend Donna Manion and killed her mother, Gertrude Manion. A week later Donna Manion escaped and Anthony killed himself. Donna Manion had obtained several restraining orders. March 7, 1992: Joseph Owens strangled his ex-girlfriend Sandra Anzalone of Chelsea and hanged himself in front of their three-year-old son. Anzalone had a temporary restraining order.[66]

April 5, 1992: Juan Torres of Lawrence shot and killed his common-law wife Delfina DeLeon, two teenage friends, and himself. Before her death Delfina DeLeon had filed a long series of complaints. She had left Torres, but he broke into her house at least twice and raped her. In March, in violation of a restraining order, he broke in, tied her up with telephone cord, put a gun to her head, and said, "This is the second time. The third time you will die." But when Torres went to court on March 25 on a warrant charging him with violating a court order to stay away from DeLeon, no one appeared to give information against him. Neither DeLeon nor her legal advocate nor the arresting police officer, who believed that Torres presented an "immediate danger," had been notified of the hearing. The prosecutor recommended no bail, and Judge J. Dennis Healey released Torres on his own recognizance. Questioned about the hearing ten days later, after Torres killed Delfina DeLeon, two bystanders, and himself, Judge Healey couldn't recall the case; but he told reporters: "Our capacity to forecast, to predict dangerousness is imperfect and inexact. You just make the calls, and some of them unfortunately have tragic consequences." District Attorney Kevin Burke agreed. "There's just no predicting a tragedy like this," he said.[67]

But of course there *is*. Every one of these women knew. And every one of them told police and judges what to expect. Massachusetts Governor William Weld called the situation "a total outrage." He said, "The current [legal] system is absolutely cockeyed in not taking into account the dangerousness of an individual to the community."[68] He proposed reforms that would permit judges to consider a defendant's dangerousness when assigning bail, and not merely the likelihood of his showing up for trial. But legislators demurred. You can't hold a man for crimes he *might* commit, they said. Not on the strength of a woman's vexatious prosecutions.

Then, in May 1992 Michael Cartier gunned down Kristin Lardner in broad daylight on a crowded public street. He had been sentenced to a year in prison after assaulting his previous girlfriend, but a judge had released him after six months and sent him instead to a course of six weekly therapy sessions for abusive men. While he was attending "Alternatives to Violence," Cartier terrorized and beat Lardner. When he completed the program, he killed her.

Such stories, which hit the news often these days, send a message both to battering men and to women. As columnist Margery Eagan noted, batterers get the message that "they can get away with it . . . and indefinitely, in a disorganized court system all in disarray, where the certainty is not of punishment swift and sure but of punishment maybe never, or in the distant future, and only minimal if at all."[69] Women get the message that the law will not make them safe. The system does not protect them from assault at home, and it does not protect them when they leave.

When David Guenther killed Pamela Guenther, battered women at the shelter that had taken her in were reportedly "very, very scared." One advocate said: "We had women go back to their batterers because they would rather stay alive and live with being beaten periodically, and verbally abused periodically, than to end up dead."[70] The battered woman has to look out for herself. And she knows, better than anyone else, the extent of her danger. One advocate in Suffolk County, New York, said that after the murders of Lydia Grohoski, Elizabeth Croff, and April LaSalata in 1988, battered women in her shelter felt like it was open season on women.[71] They were right. In the two previous years twelve women with orders of protection had been murdered in Suffolk County alone, while others, like Audrey Thomas, stabbed twenty-three times, came close to death.[72] ("Many times I saw him, and I called the police," she said, "but they never showed up.")[73] In the first seven months of 1992, seventeen women were murdered in Massachusetts, ten of them with orders of protection; the *Boston Phoenix* headlined a story about the murders with the familiar words: "Open Season on Women."[74] Charmaine Grimm, hiding out in a shelter with her little boy and an order of protection, told a reporter, "I see what happened to these women with their orders and I think that I could be any one of them, that I could be next." She suffers from a recurring nightmare in which her ex-boyfriend, a carpenter, pursues her with a chainsaw through a house full of children.[75]

In Colorado, after fifty-one-year-old Jane Campbell was shot to death in 1985 by her second husband, Blonde Cole Hunter, a man with a long history of beating wives and girlfriends, many men made the killing an object lesson. An "avalanche of calls" hit Colorado women's shelters from women "who said their husbands were deliberately leaving newspaper accounts of the murder around the house and warning them to pay careful attention to what had happened to Jane Campbell."[76] And once again it was a lesson reinforced by the heedlessness, impotence, and downright sexist malice of the legal system. Writing in *The Village Voice* in 1985 about the life and death of Jane Campbell, Jan Hoffman asked questions that we might ask today about the death of Delfina DeLeon or Kristin Lardner: "What would it have taken to save [her] life? . . . Police who paid attention to her? A court system that would have expedited the case and made it easier for charges to be pressed without the [woman] suffering the consequences? A restraining order that meant more than the paper it's written on? A judge who would treat domestic assault as a more serious offense than jaywalking?"[77] The correct answer, of course, is *all of the above*, and more: police, court system, community institutions, and public opinion working together to guarantee every woman's right to freedom from bodily harm.

But just when the law should be moving forward to that end, it rolls backwards instead—and mangles women's rights under the wheels.

2

Rights and Wrongs

In October 1989, America watched *A Cry for Help: The Tracey Thurman Story*, the NBC Movie of the Week. It's just the kind of saga American television audiences love: terrible things happen, but in the end, thanks to the efforts of one good man (Tracey Thurman's lawyer Burton Weinstein), justice is done. Tracey Thurman is the Connecticut woman who in 1984 won a landmark lawsuit, reminding law officers across the country that they might be held to account for violating the rights of battered women. But after the *Thurman* decision, other cases came before other courts and gave the law a chance to think again.

It's all well and good to recognize the rights of women and children, but what about the rights of the state? Don't they come first? And the rights of those who act for the state—like the police? Yes indeed, said the courts. By the time Tracey Thurman's story reached the television screen, five years after her victory in court, the law had fashioned new precedents, new principles, new obstacles for battered women seeking their constitutional rights. The TV audience that applauded the dramatized vindication of Tracey Thurman's rights wasn't told that eight months before the telecast, in a decision known as *DeShaney v. Winnebago County Dep't of Social Servs.*, the Supreme Court of the United States had snatched the legal rug from under Thurman's victory.[1] Any battered woman inspired by Tracey Thurman's story to seek redress for the violation of her own constitutional rights would find herself standing on slippery ground.

In 1982 Tracey Thurman left her battering husband Charles "Buck" Thurman after a brief, violent marriage. With her she took her only child, Charles Jr. For eight months, she lived apart from Buck, but he refused to divorce her. Instead he harassed her by phone and in person, and he threatened publicly to kill her. He smashed the windshield of her car when she was in it, and the court placed him on probation. When he violated his probation, again threatening to shoot his wife and son, the police refused to arrest him. Tracey Thurman complained, but the police told her to come back in three weeks and referred her in the meantime to the city's Family Relations Office. Three weeks later, Tracey Thurman returned to the police with a court order restraining Buck from assaulting or threatening her, but the police told her they couldn't attend to it until after the holiday weekend; and after the weekend they told her that the only officer who could help her was on vacation. Members of Tracey Thurman's family and her friends also complained to the police time after time—with no better results. As Tracey Thurman later told reporter Dan Rather in a television interview, "I went as far as, if my ex-husband would call me on the telephone and threaten me, I would call the police department immediately and tell them, 'I want this put down on record,' because I figured that if they heard Charles Thurman's name enough times, they're going to finally pick him up."[2] But the police did *not* pick him up.

Tracey Thurman called them again on June 10, 1983, to ask them to arrest Buck. Once again he was standing outside her house, loudly demanding to see her. The officer dispatched stopped by the police station first to use the toilet, and when he pulled up in his cruiser twenty-five minutes later, he parked across the street and sat in the car while Buck chased Tracey across the yard, grabbed her by the hair, slashed her cheek with a knife, stabbed her in the neck, knocked her to the ground, face down, and stabbed her twelve more times. When the officer finally came in to the yard, he persuaded Buck to give him the knife but made no attempt to arrest him. Instead, the officer stood by and watched while Buck attacked Tracey again as she lay on the ground. Buck kicked her in the head and broke her neck. Then he ran upstairs to Tracey's apartment, seized their son, returned with the child and dropped him on Tracey's body. Again he kicked her in the head. Other officers arrived, but it was only later, as they were lifting Tracey into an ambulance and Buck moved to attack her again, that they at last restrained him and took him into custody.[3]

Tracey Thurman survived—permanently disfigured and partially paralyzed. Buck Thurman was convicted of assault and sentenced to twenty years in prison.[4] Then Tracey Thurman sued the City of Torrington and twenty-four individual police officers on behalf of herself and her son. She claimed a violation of her constitutional rights as set forth in the Fourteenth Amendment to the United States Constitution, which says in part: "nor shall any State . . . deny to any person within its jurisdiction the equal protection of the laws."[5] Such violations are actionable under Section 1983 of the U.S. Code, a section emanating from the Civil Rights Act passed by Congress in 1871 to provide a federal constitutional remedy for African-Americans harmed when officials in Jim Crow states refused to protect them from Ku Klux Klan assaults after the Civil War.[6] Initially, the equal protection clause was applied only to cases of race discrimination, but in 1961 the Supreme Court held that section 1983 afforded a more general "federal right in federal courts because, by reason of prejudice, passion, neglect, intolerance or otherwise, state laws might not be enforced and the . . . rights guaranteed by the Fourteenth Amendment might be denied by state agencies."[7]

Since then, members of many other groups discriminated against by local and state laws have sought redress under its terms; and it seems particularly applicable to the complaints of battered women whose situation today so much resembles the situation of African-Americans during Reconstruction. Legal scholar Amy Eppler, writing in the *Yale Law Journal*, points out the similarity: "Just as racial prejudice stopped police from enforcing laws and arresting offenders, so contemporary sexist attitudes underlie the police's failure to respond to battered women's pleas for help."[8] Tracey Thurman turned to the federal courts for her constitutional rights, arguing that the City of Torrington and its police had denied her equal protection of the laws as a victim of domestic assault. By following a policy of not arresting assaultive husbands, she said, the Torrington police failed to provide the same protection to abused wives and children as they afforded the victims of similar assault outside a domestic relationship.

The federal district court agreed. It held, in part:

> City officials and police officers are under an affirmative duty to preserve law and order, and to protect the personal safety of persons in the community. . . . This duty applies equally to women whose personal safety is threatened by individuals with whom they have or have had a domestic relationship as well as to all other persons whose personal safety is threatened, including women not involved in domestic relationships. If officials have notice of the possibility of attacks on women in domestic relationships or other persons, they are under an affirmative duty to take reasonable measures to protect the personal safety of such persons in the community. Failure to perform this duty would constitute a denial of equal protection of the laws.[9]

A federal court jury which heard the cases in 1985 awarded Tracey Thurman $2.3 million in compensatory damages.[10] And almost overnight the State of Connecticut adopted a new comprehensive domestic violence law calling for the arrest of assaultive spouses. In the twelve months after Connecticut's law took effect, the number of arrests for domestic assault increased 93 percent from 12,400 to 23,830.[11]

The Thurman case was not the first dramatic victory for battered women in the courts. Ruling in 1977 in *Bruno v. Codd*, a New York state court judge wrote: "For too long, Anglo-American law treated a man's physical assault of his wife as dif-

ferent from any other assault, and, indeed, as an acceptable practice. . . . in reality, wife beating is still condoned, if not approved, by some of those charged with protecting its victims."[12]
But the feminist attorneys who brought that class action suit were
not seeking damages; instead, they sought injunctive relief to re-
vise the policies and practices of New York City police and court
officials. No money changed hands.[13] Thus, as so often happens
in the United States, the *Thurman* decision with its multimillion
dollar prize appeared to be more important.

Here, it seemed, was a promising source of help for battered
women and their children—though not necessarily in Torrington,
where less than a year later Joanne Tremins sued the same police
department for refusing to arrest her estranged husband, even
when he violated a valid restraining order. Police dismissed Tremins as a "copycat" even after her husband assaulted her so violently
in public that he was convicted and sentenced to two years in
prison.[14] In 1988 Police Chief Mahlon Sabo explained to a reporter why he didn't like to see batterers arrested, especially for
what the reporter characterized as "minor, first time altercations."
Sabo said: "You get handcuffed, taken out of your house in front
of your kids, searched, locked up and the doors close behind you.
Now you've got an arrest record. We labeled these people."[15] Of
course, that disgrace, which can make many a "first-timer" think
twice about repeating assault, is precisely the point of arrest.

Despite the reluctance of Torrington police to learn from experience—Thurman's attorney described their learning curve as
nearly "flat"—battered women's advocates across the country took
heart from Thurman's victory.[16] Not only had she won substantial
damages for herself and her son, but countless other women stood
to gain protection as other, brighter police departments changed
their policy and began arresting batterers. It was extremely difficult to win a case like Tracey Thurman's, for the burden of proof
on the plaintiff was very large. But for battered women denied
police protection, it was certainly worth a try.

In subsequent cases, what the law calls "the pattern of facts"
presented to the court was generally the same. A battered woman

sought protection from state officials: usually the police, sometimes the police and the courts. She received inadequate protection and then was injured or killed by the batterer. For the violation of her constitutional right to bodily integrity, she (or her survivors) brought a claim against the responsible state agents and sought redress from the court. That pattern, so clear in Tracey Thurman's case, is repeated in the case of Jena Balistreri, who was terrorized for years before she sued the police department of Pacifica, California. Because so many of us still assume that the police stand ready to help abused women, it's worth repeating Jena Balistreri's story here. Hearing the same "pattern of facts" over and over again, the truth finally comes home to us: this story of women denied the protection of the law is not the exception, but the rule.

These are Balistreri's allegations as set forth in the opinion of the Ninth Circuit Court of Appeals in *Balistreri v. Pacifica Police Department*:

On February 13, 1982, Balistreri was severely beaten by her husband. The Pacifica police officers who responded to her call for assistance removed the husband from the home, but refused to place him under arrest, and were "rude, insulting and unsympathetic" toward Mrs. Balistreri. One of the officers stated that Mrs. Balistreri deserved the beating. Although Balistreri was injured seriously enough to require treatment for injuries to her nose, mouth, eyes, teeth and abdomen, the officers did not offer Balistreri medical assistance.

Sometime after the incident, an unidentified Pacifica police officer pressured Balistreri into agreeing not to press charges against her husband.

Throughout 1982, Balistreri continually complained to the Pacifica police of instances of vandalism and of receiving hundreds of harassing phone calls. She named her husband, from whom she was now divorced, as the suspected culprit.

In November 1982, Balistreri obtained a restraining order which enjoined her former husband from "harassing, annoying or having contact with her." Subsequent to the service of this order, Balistreri's former husband crashed his car into her garage, and Balistreri immediately called the police, who arrived at the scene but stated that they would not arrest the husband or investigate the incident. During the remainder of 1982, Balistreri reported additional acts of phone harassment and vandalism, but the police "received her complaints with ridicule," denied that any restraining order was on file, ignored her requests for protection and investigation, and on one occasion hung up on her when she called to report an instance of vandalism.

On March 27, 1983, a firebomb was thrown through the window of Balistreri's house, causing fire damage and emotional anguish to Balistreri. The police took 45 minutes to respond to Balistreri's "911" call. Although police asked Balistreri's husband a few questions, they determined he was not responsible for the act; Balistreri complained that the investigation was inadequate, to which the police responded that she should either move elsewhere or hire a private investigator.

Throughout 1983–85, Balistreri was continually subjected to telephone harassment and vandalism. Balistreri contacted Pacific Bell to "trace" the calls. Pacific Bell reported that some of these calls could be traced to the former husband's family, but the police refused to act on this information.

Balistreri, represented by counsel, filed a complaint alleging that these acts violated her constitutional rights and caused her to suffer physical injuries, a bleeding ulcer, and emotional distress. The complaint asserted that the defendant police officers had deprived Balistreri of due process and equal protection of the law. . . . The district court dismissed the complaint.[17]

Balistreri based her suit in part on the equal protection clause of the Fourteenth Amendment, as Tracey Thurman had done. But

in addition Balistreri cited another key provision of the Fourteenth Amendment, the due process clause, which reads: "Nor
shall any State deprive any person of life, liberty or property,
without due process of law." Precisely what "process" might be
"due" in any particular instance, however, has never been fixed.
Rather, the dimensions of due process expand or contract with the
attitudes of the judges who apply it. In any particular case, it can
consist of whatever the judge thinks is fair. Defining due process,
Justice Felix Frankfurter explained how it mirrors the prevailing
attitudes (including the biases and prejudices) of the historical
moment. He wrote: "Representing a profound attitude of fairness
between man and man, and more particularly between the individual and government, 'due process' is compounded of history,
reason, the past course of decisions, and stout confidence in the
strength of the democratic faith which we profess. Due process is
. . . a delicate process of adjustment inescapably involving the
exercise of judgment by those whom the Constitution entrusted
with the unfolding of the process."[18] But are judges who think of
due process in terms of *"fairness between man and man"* likely to
consider the interests of women?

Two out of three judges of the Ninth Circuit Court of Appeals
did. (Both of these judges were women; the third judge, a man,
disagreed.) They ruled that the facts of Jena Balistreri's case might
convince a jury that the police were guilty either of "intentional
harassment" or "deliberate or reckless indifference to her safety."
They noted that the remarks of the police—(one officer allegedly
said he didn't blame Balistreri's husband for hitting her because
of the way she was "carrying on")—and their conduct "strongly
suggest an intention to treat domestic abuse cases less seriously
than other assaults, as well as an animus against abused women."
And citing *Thurman v. City of Torrington*, they noted that "police
failure to respond to complaints lodged by women in domestic
violence cases may violate equal protection."[19] In other words,
Balistreri had a case, and the court of appeals sent the better part
of her charges back to the lower court for further proceedings.

But Balistreri's due process claim raised another troublesome issue. Due process, like the equal protection provision, is designed to protect men from the state (and those who act for the state)—not from each other. In many different circumstances, courts have ruled that "state officials generally have no constitutional duty to protect members of the public at large from crime." But "such duty may arise by virtue of [a] special relationship between those officials and particular members of the public."[20] Jena Balistreri argued that she had a "special relationship" with the state because, for one, the police knew she was being terrorized, and for another she had obtained a restraining order. Two judges ruled that the state's knowing about Balistreri's "plight" wasn't enough to oblige it to *do* anything, but add in her restraining order and Balistreri might indeed have a claim to a "special relationship." The state might, after all, have "a duty to take reasonable measures to protect Balistreri from her estranged husband."[21] But Judge Laughlin E. Waters, dissenting from the majority opinion, took a narrower view. Balistreri's restraining order "heightens the state's awareness" of her "risk of harm," he wrote, but "the mere existence of the order" creates no "special relationship" to the state, imposes no constitutional duty on the state to protect her.[22]

Legal reasoning is tedious, but I go into these details to illustrate how far removed it is from the everyday thinking of those of us who apply to ethical problems our basic moral principles and our common sense. With some remarkable exceptions, such as *Thurman v. City of Torrington*, legal "thought" flies in the face of common sense, and overrides it—a fact that surprises most citizens, for most of us continue to have "reasonable" (common-sense) expectations of the law. We expect the police to try to protect people, for example. We assume that if the police know that a citizen is in danger, they'll take particular care to protect that person. And if the citizen has an order of protection from the court, we expect the police to be particularly watchful and diligent. After all, isn't that their *job*? In the *Balistreri* case, two out of three judges answered, "Maybe." And one said, "Absolutely not."

When Nancy Watson sued the City of Kansas City, Kansas,

her assaultive husband Ed Watson was already dead. After he broke into her home on January 19, 1984, and raped, beat, and stabbed her, she escaped by leaping through a picture window, attracting the attention of a neighbor who came to help her. Ed Watson fled and then killed himself. Ruling on Nancy Watson's suit, the Tenth Circuit Court of Appeals recounted a "long history of domestic violence"; and because Ed Watson was a cop, the pattern of facts in this case was especially grim. It was bad enough that the police declined to arrest or discipline Ed Watson, but Ed's captain allegedly threatened that if Nancy called the police again, he would arrest *her* and see to it that she lost custody of her two children.[23] So Nancy Watson was afraid of the police as well as her husband, and after he very nearly killed her, she thought she had a grievance.

She charged, as Tracey Thurman had, that the city police department and individual police officers violated domestic abuse victims' rights to equal protection of the law by failing to provide the same police protection to victims of domestic assault that they did to victims of nondomestic assault. Citing Kansas City police records, she pointed out that in 1983 in nondomestic assaults 31 percent of the perpetrators were arrested, in domestic assaults only 16 percent. In addition, she said, this policy discriminated against women, who constitute at least 95 percent of the victims of domestic assault. The district court ruled in favor of the police on every score; but the Tenth Circuit Court of Appeals reversed part of that decision. Watson could proceed with her equal protection claim, the higher court said, because she had enough evidence to show that the police policy of nonarrest in domestic assault cases resulted in her being treated "differently." But "such a policy is gender-neutral on its face," the court said, and Nancy Watson had "failed to present *any* evidence . . . that a policy which discriminates against victims of domestic violence adversely affects women."[24]

This ruling, of course, is like requiring African-Americans to prove that Jim Crow laws or "separate but equal" schools adversely affect blacks, propositions that would be denied only by the bigots who enjoy the benefits of racist policies. Lawyers fabricate technical distinctions between differently based standards of discrimination and different levels of judicial scrutiny appropriate to each standard, but the upshot of these legal intricacies—restrictions clapped on *all* women's equal protection claims by the Reagan federal courts—is a giant step backward from the *Thurman* decision. Tracey Thurman alleged only that police discriminated against victims of domestic assault; the *court* drew the self-evident conclusion that because almost all victims of domestic assault are female, Thurman's claim was *by implication* one of sex discrimination. But the sex discrimination that judges in Connecticut could so readily infer in 1984 had become invisible in Kansas four years later. And even if Nancy Watson *could* prove that police policy "adversely affects women," the court said, she would have to prove in addition that the police adopted the policy *purposefully* to discriminate against women.[25]

When Nancy Watson's equal protection claim went back to the district court for reconsideration, the judges reminded her that "this is not a gender discrimination case."[26] Then they granted all but one of the individual police officers immunity from liability—on the grounds of ignorance. The officers could not have known that responding differently to domestic and nondomestic assault might be a constitutional violation, the court said, because that principle had been established only weeks before the present case in *Balistreri v. Pacifica Police Department*. The principle was "established" all right, but not—as the court required—*"clearly* established."[27]

Alesia Hynson was shot and killed by her former boyfriend, Jamil Gandy, the father of one of her two children, on October 15, 1984, a few days after her third order of protection expired and a few days before her new order was officially signed. Her mother and the children sued various municipal agencies and individual police officers of the City of Chester (Pennsylvania), the first step in a complicated legal process. The district court dismissed the family's due process claims against individual police officers, but it permitted their due process claims against the city and their equal protection claims against the police and the city to stand. The individual police officers appealed that decision, seeking to have all claims against them dismissed; and by the time their appeal was heard in 1988, the courts had seen the hand-writing on the wall. The Third Circuit Court of Appeals noted that the Hynson case "reflects a growing trend of plaintiffs relying upon the due process and equal protection clauses . . . to force police departments to provide women with the protection from domestic violence that police agencies are allegedly reluctant to give."[28] And the court knew that its decision would have wide social effects. "It is obvious," the court said, "that lawsuits re-questing injunctions and monetary awards for damages resulting from such policies will cause municipal and metropolitan police agencies to reconsider their policies toward domestic violence."[29]

Accordingly, the appeals court set out to clarify and articulate "a standard for the district courts . . . to follow" in such cases "arising from domestic violence situations."[30] The court went on and on about *Balistreri* and *Watson*—but whether by carelessness or design, it failed to understand the legal theories at issue in this line of cases. For example, the court referred to *Thurman* as "one of the first cases dealing with the issue of a due process violation," although the central issue of *Thurman* was not due process, but equal protection.[31] Such mistaken analysis leads to mistaken law, as the *Hynson* court demonstrated when it snatched up the finely discriminated threads of the *Watson* court and tied them in a knot, the better to flog women. The *Watson* court had distinguished be-tween gender-based discrimination and class-based discrimina-tion; and while it threw out Nancy Watson's claim that police policy discriminated against her as a woman, it allowed her to carry on with her claim that police policy discriminated against her as a member of the class, "victims of domestic assault." The burden of proof for the two claims was different; and while Nancy Watson brought plenty of evidence (from police arrest statistics and training manuals) to claim class-based discrimination, she was not able to shoulder the heavy burden of proof the court re-quired for a claim of sex-based discrimination. Now, setting out righteously to enunciate a clear standard for all cases of this sort, the *Hynson* court mixed up the two kinds of discrimination and then applied the double burden of proof to *both*.[32]

Tracey Thurman had won her case simply by showing that the police treated *her* differently than they would have done had Charles Thurman not been her husband, but the *Hynson* court followed the *Watson* court in adding to the woman's burden of proof. Henceforth, even to make a simple claim of class-based discrimination, the plaintiff would have to bring a load of evidence not only that the police had a policy or custom of providing less protection to victims of domestic assault than to victims of nondomestic assault, but also that "discrimination against women" was a "motivating factor" in this policy, and that the plaintiff was injured as a direct result.[33]

As if that were not enough to discourage a woman from trying to claim her constitutional rights, the appeals court also took up another separate issue raised by attorneys for the police in the *Watson* case: police immunity. Historically, the law has always granted a certain qualified immunity from lawsuits to government officials exercising professional discretion in their work. The Supreme Court has ruled that the public interest is best served if public officials are free to do their jobs without fear of getting sued for an honest mistake, as long as those officials respect the clearly established rights of the citizens. The tricky legal phrase here is "clearly established." If the right of battered women to equal protection is not clearly established, officers violating that right can be found "immune." And as long as officers are immune and free to ignore the battered woman's right to equal protection, her right to equal protection can't be considered clearly established.

In the case of Alesia Hynson, the appeals court concluded that police could lose that immunity "*only* if a reasonable police officer would know that the policy [of treating domestic assault differently from nondomestic assault] has a discriminatory impact on women, that bias against women was a motivating factor behind the adoption of the policy, and that there is no important public interest served by the adoption of the policy."[34] (Another tricky legal phrase: the state is always free to discriminate for some *important or compelling public interest*. The law has only to elevate the important private interest of so many judges in maintaining intact families to the status of *public* interest to make police non-arrest policy perfectly legal, and even patriotic; but so far the law has chosen another course.) The *Hynson* court arrived at this standard for determining police accountability, it said, by carefully balancing "the plaintiff's right to pursue his or her claim" against "the individual public official's right to perform his duties without a constant fear of harassing litigation."[35] Once the law protected Husband from "vexatious prosecution" brought by his battered Wife; by the standard of the *Hynson* court, it also protects the cop who backs him up.

Having established these standards, the Third Circuit sent the Hynson case back to the district court with instructions that it make a new decision consistent with the higher court's opinion.[36] Like the shreds of *Balistreri* and *Watson*, *Hynson* would go on grinding through the courts, plucked and skinned and eviscerated by the legal machinery that packages new bodies of law. After the common-sensical decision in *Thurman*, each case brought under the Fourteenth Amendment seemed to be subjected to more and more legal "reasoning." And the more the courts reasoned, the more law they found. The woman's burden of proof grew heavier. The shield of immunity about the police and public officials thickened. Nevertheless, in some cases, after a federal district court threw out a battered woman's claim, an appeals court threw some small part of it back. There seemed to be no single easy way for the law to get around the Fourteenth Amendment rights of battered women. Not until the Supreme Court found one in the case of little Joshua DeShaney.

In March 1984, in Neenah, Wisconsin, Randy DeShaney beat his four-year-old son Joshua into a coma. It wasn't the first time. Emergency brain surgery revealed old hemorrhages, the result of repeated beatings over a long period of time. With half his brain turned to mush, Joshua DeShaney was placed in an institution where he will spend the rest of his life. Randy DeShaney was tried and convicted of child abuse; and Melody DeShaney, Joshua's mother, brought suit on Joshua's behalf against the Winnebago County Department of Social Services and some of its employees.[37] Her complaint charged that they "had deprived Joshua of his liberty without due process of law, in violation of his rights under the Fourteenth Amendment, by failing to intervene to protect him against a risk of violence at his father's hands of which they knew or should have known."[38] The district court and the Seventh Circuit Court of Appeals ruled against Joshua DeShaney, but because they were "inconsistent" in their approach to the issues, the United States Supreme Court took on the case to define conclusively "when, if ever, the failure of a state or local governmental entity or its agents to provide an individual with adequate protective services constitutes a violation of the individual's due process rights."[39]

The facts of the matter, the Supreme Court said, "are undeniably tragic." In 1980 when Randy DeShaney's first wife Melody divorced him, he obtained custody of the infant Joshua and took him to live in Winnebago County. In January 1982, DeShaney's second wife divorced him and complained to police that DeShaney hit the child and was "a prime case for child abuse." Little Joshua DeShaney, at age two, became a "case" in the files of the Winnebago County Department of Social Services. A year later, when Joshua was admitted to the hospital with multiple bruises and abrasions, he was placed in temporary custody of the state until a "Child Protection Team" determined there was "insufficient evidence of child abuse." The juvenile court returned Joshua to Randy DeShaney, who agreed to take certain measures for the child's welfare—an agreement he subsequently disregarded. During the next fourteen months, a social worker visited the home "nearly twenty" times, dutifully writing down in her case file a description of all Joshua's suspicious injuries. (In all that time, she never notified the child's mother.) Twice, the hospital emergency room reported treating Joshua again for injuries that looked like child abuse. Twice, when the caseworker visited Randy

DeShaney's home, she was told that Joshua was too ill to see her. Still the Department of Social Services left Joshua in the care of Randy DeShaney—until the day he beat the child nearly to death.[40] When the caseworker learned that Joshua had been admitted to the emergency room in a coma, she commented, "I just knew the phone would ring some day and Joshua would be dead."[41]

The miserable life of Joshua DeShaney is another story to shock and sadden us all. In retrospect one can see clearly that *someone* in the public agencies charged with protecting this child should have, and could have, saved him. But that's not the way the Supreme Court saw it. Chief Justice Rehnquist, writing about due process in the majority opinion, took Justice Frankfurter's "profound attitude of fairness between man and man" and whittled it down to the narrowest possible point. The purpose of the due process clause, he said, "was to protect the people from the State, not to ensure that the State protected them from each other." Thus, "State's failure to protect an individual against private violence does not constitute a violation of the Due Process clause"—even when that individual claims a "special relationship" with the state, as Joshua DeShaney did, being the subject of a Winnebago County child abuse case file.[42] "Judges and lawyers," Rehnquist wrote, are "like other humans" in being moved by their "natural sympathy" to try to find a way to compensate "Joshua and his mother . . . for the grievous harm inflicted upon them." But instead of "yielding" to that merely human "impulse," Rehnquist took the high road of legal logic, noting that the harm done Joshua DeShaney "was inflicted not by the State of Wisconsin but by Joshua's father." But what about the responsibility of Social Services with its Child Protection Teams and its stenographic caseworkers? "The most that can be said of the state functionaries in this case," Rehnquist wrote, in a staggering understatement of the facts, "is that they stood by and did nothing when suspicious circumstances dictated a more active role for them."[43]

Dissenting, Justice Brennan maintained that "the Constitution itself 'dictated a more active role'" for state authorities. He argued that when the state invites, or even directs, citizens to depend upon its agencies for help or protection, it has already intervened in their lives. It cannot then "shrug its shoulders and turn away from the harm that it has promised to try to prevent." "My disagreement with the Court," Justice Brennan wrote, "arises from its failure to see that *inaction can be every bit as abusive of power as action*, that oppression can result when a State undertakes a vital duty and then ignores it." Justice Brennan said he thought that the Constitution is not "indifferent to such indifference," but his was the minority opinion.[44] The law had found a way around the Fourteenth Amendment due process claims of Joshua DeShaney—and of battered women as well.

Joshua DeShaney's claim was based only on due process, not equal protection, but as the Fifth Circuit Court of Appeals pondered another case, it quickly saw that *DeShaney v. Winnebago* could be used to block the claims of battered women brought under *either* provision of the Fourteenth Amendment. The *DeShaney* decision was handed down on February 22, 1989, just before the Fifth Circuit Court of Appeals was scheduled to hear oral arguments in a case brought by Gayla McKee. As one dissenting judge in the McKee case would note, the *DeShaney* decision actually had nothing whatsoever to do with Gayla McKee's claim, which was based on equal protection, not due process, but the majority of the court grabbed hold of *DeShaney*, twisted it about, and stretched it to fit.[45] By manhandling the law, the *McKee* court all but obliterated *Thurman*—and did its best to foreclose the Fourteenth Amendment to battered women.

According to her complaint, Gayla McKee called the cops one night in April 1986, to report that her boyfriend Harry Streetman, with whom she shared an apartment, had assaulted her and threatened to kill her. She said that Streetman had also disabled her car, so she couldn't drive away; and once she got out of the apartment to call the police, he wouldn't let her back in to get her belongings. McKee said she asked the two policemen who responded to her call to arrest Streetman, but they refused. She asked them to take her to the station to file a complaint. They refused. (One cop—she couldn't remember which one—told her she was "inappropriately dressed.") She asked them to take her to her parents' home. They refused. Instead, one of them drove her to another apartment, fifty yards away, and left. From there she telephoned her parents, but while she waited for them to pick her up, her boyfriend tracked her down and attacked her with a knife, slashing her right leg.[46]

Gayla McKee sued the policemen and the city of Rockwall, Texas, where she lived, charging "that she had been injured as a result of the officers' refusal to make an arrest, and that this non-arrest was the result of a Rockwall policy that discriminated on the basis of gender."[47] In support of her claim she brought statistics showing different rates of arrest for domestic and non-domestic assault and an affidavit from her mother describing an interview she and her husband had with the Rockwall police chief just after Gayla was assaulted. The McKees had asked the Chief why Gayla's boyfriend hadn't been arrested when she first called the police; according to Mrs. McKee's affidavit, "The Chief responded that his officers did not like to make arrests in domestic assault cases since the women involved either wouldn't file charges or would drop them prior to trial."[48]

The officers and the city asked the district court to dismiss Gayla McKee's complaint on grounds that the police were "insulated from liability by the doctrine of qualified immunity"; but the court found substance in her charges and refused to throw them out. Seeking to reverse that decision, the cops and the city found help from sympathetic judges of the Fifth Circuit Court of Appeals. Although that court said it had no jurisdiction over the city's appeal, it reversed the lower court's decision in regard to the officers and dismissed all charges against them. In a split decision, the majority ruled that Gayla McKee had "presented no evidence at all that the City pursues a discriminatory policy."[49]

In a lengthy dissent, Judge Irving L. Goldberg argued that while McKee's evidence was not extensive, it was enough for a jury to draw "a reasonable inference that the police treated her based upon illegitimate stereotypes and archaic notions of women," or,

in other words, that they had discriminated against her in violation of her right to equal protection.[50] Her complaint should have
been evaluated by a trial jury, Judge Goldberg said, and not by
his dismissive colleagues on the bench. Nevertheless, the majority
found fault with McKee's statistics (saying they contained "a glar-
ing mathematical error"), and wrote off the Chief's remark on
grounds that: "A dislike is not a policy."[51] McKee had nothing to
offer as evidence of discrimination, they said, except the single
incident she described. And her account of that incident they then
proceeded to discredit.

For the majority, the whole case—and the whole issue of discrimination—came to rest on a question of whether or not the
officers involved in the incident had *probable cause* to make an arrest. The majority held that "the officers had no authority to make
any arrests absent probable cause to do so."[52] Ignoring the possibility of police bias, the court reasoned in a tidy circle: if the police saw no cause to arrest, they could not make an arrest, and their
failure to do so could not be found discriminatory. Harry Streetman's second assault on Gayla McKee, however, had exposed the
cops' decision not to arrest him as so clearly wrong that the court
tried to fudge the issue. "Probable cause," the majority said,
"turns not so much upon whether Streetman committed a crime
as upon whether or not the officers had sufficient evidence that
Streetman had committed a crime."[53] And that evidence, the officers claimed in their affidavits, they did not have.

The officers said that when they reached the scene, they saw on
Gayla McKee no physical evidence of a beating, "no welt, bruise,
abrasion, cut, skin discoloration, unneat appearance, or any other
indication" of assault.[54] (As dissenting Judge Goldberg pointed
out, such "physical marks on a victim's body" are not required
under Texas law which recognizes that many assaults—such as a
blow to the belly or a threat at knifepoint—may leave no trace;
but the majority justices who made such an issue of probable cause
seemed strangely unfamiliar with the provisions of the Texas statute.) Besides, the policemen said, by the time they arrived,
McKee was safely *outside* her apartment. (Apparently, it didn't oc-

cur to them that a woman is entitled to be safely *inside* her own home.) And most important, the officers reported "that McKee looked angry rather than hurt, and that Streetman was calm."[55]

The only other evidence presented to the officers at the scene was Gayla McKee's word, and, as Judge Goldberg observed, they did not believe her.[56] McKee reported that the officers told her she was exaggerating. They suggested she talk things over with Streetman. They told her that "after she had calmed down she probably would not want to file a complaint." And McKee said that when Streetman threatened in the presence of the police to "burn her belongings" if she went to the station, the officers "did not respond in any way."[57] (This threat alone, as the court noted, was grounds for arrest, but the cops claimed they didn't hear it.)[58] Instead, according to both McKee and the officers, the two cops stood by while she got her purse and some other things from the apartment, and one of them drove her up the street while his partner remained with Streetman. Then they left.[59]

In short the officers did what police officers often do when called to the scene of a "domestic disturbance." And they seem to have *thought* in the same way, making clear once again that when sex-biased officers look for probable cause, no matter how it is defined by statute, they probably won't find it. Nothing these officers saw or heard that April night dissuaded them from exercising their professional discretion *for* Harry Streetman and *against* Gayla McKee—against arrest. Even after Harry Streetman tracked Gayla McKee down and slashed her with a knife, an incident that one might think would cause the officers to reconsider their position, they continued to blame McKee. When they moved in district court to have her claims against them dismissed, they charged that Gayla McKee "was the proximate cause of her own harm."[60]

This is precisely the sort of discriminatory practice, based on prejudice, that the Fourteenth Amendment was designed to redress. Battered women have complained all along that officer "discretion" is a convenient excuse for discrimination. All too often in domestic assaults, police do *not* exercise discretion to evaluate the particular incident, but rather they routinely refuse to arrest men who assault "their own" women, then chalk up that automatic reaction to "discretion."[61] Even the *Watson* court recognized that "officers' assessments as to whether probable cause exists are colored by whether the disturbance is domestic or nondomestic."[62] In short, police "discretion" is not simply an excuse for discrimination. As it is habitually exercised all across the country, it *is* discrimination.

But not any more—thanks to the *McKee* court. The majority's preoccupation with probable cause, as it turned out, was merely a red herring. In the end, the court ruled that even if Gayla McKee could prove that the police had good cause to arrest Harry Streetman, she still couldn't win. Dragging in the *DeShaney* decision as if the Supreme Court had spoken directly about Gayla McKee's problem with the cops, the *McKee* court reasoned this way: "*DeShaney* goes on to say that even if the officers *could have* arrested Streetman, they were not under any constitutional obligation to do so. The *DeShaney* rule leaves officers and law enforcement agencies with some discretionary authority. . . . McKee cannot . . . prevail merely by showing that the officers knew facts that would have justified an arrest of Streetman. This is the lesson of *DeShaney*: *that law enforcement officers have authority to act does not imply that they have any constitutional duty to act.*" Gayla McKee could make her claim, the court ruled, only by showing that "non-arrest was the result of discrimination against a . . . class," but the court had already discredited all her evidence that this was so.[63] (You can see how "discretion" works among men in a male system: the police believe the man, the court believes the police.) "Absent any evidence of a discriminatory policy," the court concluded, "the only reasonable construction of the officers' action in this case is that they decided that McKee's complaint did not warrant any further response than what they gave."[64] Of course, that's what the officers decided. And that judgment is precisely what Gayla McKee complains of as a violation of her constitutional rights. But according to the *McKee* court, that "judgment is not actionable." *DeShaney*, the court said, makes this "clear."[65]

Overnight *DeShaney* became the rule in every due process claim brought by battered women, and it figured in some equal protection claims as well.[66] And retroactively. Jena Balistreri was moving forward with her due process claim (by herself, because her lawyer had refused to continue after the court initially dismissed the case) when the Ninth Circuit Court of Appeals reversed its earlier decision. It had ruled that Balistreri's order of protection might create a "special relationship" with the state, requiring the state to protect her.[67] Now it quoted *DeShaney*: "The affirmative duty to protect arises not from the state's knowledge of the individual's predicament or from its expression of intent to help him, but from the limitation which it has imposed on his freedom to act on his own behalf."[68] In other words, if the state held Jena Balistreri in *custody*—in jail, or an asylum—it would be obliged to protect her; but short of that, she was on her own. "DeShaney is . . . controlling in Balistreri's case," the court ruled—and threw out her due process claim once and for all.[69]

The district court of the Eastern District of Pennsylvania reconsidered the due process claim of Alesia Hynson's survivors and came to a similar conclusion. Judge Marvin Katz wrote: "In *DeShaney*, the [Supreme] Court limited the responsibility of the state to protect individuals from private violence to those situations in which an individual is in the custody of the state." Judge Katz then contemplated "two basic facts": one, that Alesia Hynson was "not in custody . . . at the time of her death"; and two, that her murder was "an act of private violence." Putting one and two together, he concluded: "no duty existed to protect Ms. Hynson from the violent acts of Mr. Gandy."[70] Out went the due process claim.

To save this claim from what the court called "the fate dictated by *DeShaney*," the Hynson survivors tried a different approach, arguing that Alesia Hynson had an "entitlement" or "property interest" in police protection. Certain individuals may gain a property interest when some source outside the Constitution itself— such as state law—gives them special benefits which they come to depend upon and feel "entitled" to. The state may not then suddenly deprive individuals of their property interests without following procedures respectful of their due process rights.[71] (The classic example is welfare payments which, once given, may not be *arbitrarily* withdrawn.) The Hynson family claimed that Pennsylvania's Protection from Abuse Act, passed in 1984, and Alesia Hynson's temporary restraining order "provided the basis for her understanding that she would have police protection" and thus created an entitlement.[72] It was true, the judge said, that the Protection from Abuse Act modified police procedure and authorized police to arrest without a warrant when they had probable cause to believe an assault had occurred. But, said the judge, "The decisions concerning mode of investigation and whether to arrest a suspect are left to the discretion of the police." And "given this broad discretion . . . there can be no property interest," he said, putting an end to the Hynson due process claim. No matter what protection a woman might think herself entitled to by virtue of state laws and court orders, the protection she actually got—or failed to get—was entirely up to the cops to decide. What little ground *DeShaney* left her was already covered by police *discretion*— the very thing that raised her complaints, or contributed to her death, in the first place.

The courts seemed dead set against the claims of battered women. And they were amassing a thickening stack of unfavorable case law, much of it—like parts of *McKee* and *Hynson*—decided in error or transparent bias. By the time a case brought by the children of Sherrie Stewart against the Board of Police Commissioners of Kansas City (Missouri) reached the district court in 1990, the court had a laundry list of precedents: not *DeShaney* only, but the reversal of *Balistreri*, and the eminently useful *McKee*.

Sherrie Stewart was assulted by her estranged husband Eddie Luster on Christmas Eve 1986. Her niece called the cops and told the first officer to arrive that her uncle was killing her aunt. The officer waited in his car for backup, and by the time police entered the house, Eddie Luster had stabbed Sherrie Stewart "several times." She died on Christmas day. Her children charged that because the police were not properly trained, they had handled this situation in a way that discriminated against Sherrie Stewart because of her race (she was African-American) and "perhaps because of her sex," and thus they had deprived her of due process and equal protection.[73] Since the *McKee* court had mistakenly applied the *DeShaney* decision on due process to a case of equal protection, however, this district court could use the *McKee* decision to dismiss both charges. "In both due process and equal protection analyses," the court said, "the lesson of *DeShaney* is that if 'law enforcement officers have authority to act [it] does not imply that they have any constitutional duty to act.' "[74] Out went the claims of Sherrie Stewart's children. The court dragged in another precedent as well, almost as if it wanted to avoid the appearance of discriminating against victims of domestic assault; citing *Burgos v. Camareno*, the court said that "under *DeShaney* individuals have no constitutional right to receive police protection from *burglaries*" either.[75]

Since *DeShaney*, at least a dozen battered women or their survivors have entered claims in federal courts, initiating the long, arduous process of litigation—the tedious, time-consuming round of pretrial motions and appeals and motions to reconsider. Feminist legal scholars have urged them on, suggesting strategies for the post-*DeShaney* courts. A woman might still prove that the state had a duty to protect her, scholars reasoned, if she could show that the state held her in some broadly construed kind of "custody," or that the state, by its actions, had placed her in *increased* danger.[76]

After an ex-boyfriend shot and killed Kathleen Dudosh, her family brought suit against the police of Allentown, Pennsylvania, charging that the police had not only failed to protect her, but placed her in greater danger. First, the police failed to take decisive action against Richard Miller, the ex-boyfriend (and the subject of an order of protection) who harassed and threatened Kathleen Dudosh for almost a year. (The police said, "It has been our policy not to get involved in matters of this nature.")[77] More important, after Miller broke into her apartment in her absence on March 28, 1985, two police officers escorted Kathleen Dudosh to the door and, having reason to believe that Miller was still inside, allowed her to enter the apartment first. Miller shot and killed her and, as the police retreated, killed himself. Throwing out a due process claim in 1987, the district court ruled that Kathleen Dudosh "willingly and of her own volition" walked to her death. Asked to reconsider, the court ruled again in 1989 that although the officers "escorted the decedent to confront her assailant," despite an outstanding order of protection and his past violent conduct, they didn't *take* her there.[78]

The Seventh Circuit Court of Appeals made a similar ruling in a due process claim brought in Wisconsin by the children of Julie Losinski. On September 13, 1989, by prearrangement with the family court, she had gone with her mother, brother-in-law, and a deputy sheriff to her husband's trailer to collect some belongings for herself and her children. Donald Losinski, the subject of a divorce action and a restraining order, followed Julie from room to room, arguing and harassing her, while the deputy—who was *required* by Wisconsin law to make an arrest if domestic abuse was occurring or likely to occur—stood in the hall. Donald shot Julie twice, and she died three days later.[79] Her family argued that Julie Losinski had been in a kind of state "custody" at the time of the shooting because without the deputy she wouldn't have gone to the trailer or anywhere near her dangerous husband. The deputy undertook to protect her, they said, and then failed to do his job. But the Seventh Circuit Court ruled that what the *DeShaney* decision meant by custody was *involuntary* custody; and "although the state walked with Julie as she approached the 'lion's den,' it did not force her to proceed."[80]

Mary Lee Brown, who sued the City of Elba (Alabama) in 1990 for depriving her daughter Janet Lockett of life without due process, also claimed that the police had placed the woman in increased danger. Janet Lockett was living with her parents, having left her violent common-law husband Randy Walton, when on September 4, 1989, Walton got a police officer to drive him to her house, grabbed the officer's gun, and shot and killed Janet

Lockett and himself. Once again, the court quoted *DeShaney*, ruling that the state was not obliged to guarantee an individual's safety "but rather simply to 'place him in no worse position than that in which he would have been had it not acted at all.' "[81] It seems obvious that Janet Lockett would have been in a better position if a cop had not delivered her killer to her door and provided him a lethal weapon (by allowing him to ride next to the armed officer in the front seat of the patrol car); but the court didn't see it that way.[82]

Legal scholars referred to the concept of "creation of danger" as a new and crucial "post-*DeShaney* test." The murders of Kathleen Dudosh, Julie Losinski, and Janet Lockett couldn't pass it. To date, no battered woman's due process claim has—although in the case of Janet Lockett, the district court did allow that if the police officer himself had shot the woman "the legal issue presented would be quite different."[83]

A second line of argument holds that when the state issues an order of protection, it "unambiguously interposes the state in the private life of a battered woman" and agrees to protect her.[84] Thus, when the state fails to protect a woman who holds an order of protection, she should have a legitimate due process claim, *DeShaney* notwithstanding. Not so, said the *Balistreri* court when it reversed itself after the *DeShaney* decision and threw out Jena Balistreri's due process claim.[85] Kathleen Dudosh had an order of protection, and so did Julie Losinski, but these orders didn't figure in the courts' decisions. Nor did the state laws under which those orders of protection were granted. The fact that local police failed to enforce domestic abuse prevention acts, which many states had passed, was held to be "irrelevant" to the due process claims of women deprived of their rights as a result.[86]

Alesia Hynson's family had argued that her temporary restraining order and the state's Protection from Abuse Act created a property interest or entitlement, providing the basis for a procedural due process claim. The *Hynson* court said no; but two other federal cases seeking a way around *DeShaney* advanced the same argument. Terry Coffman sued the Wilson (Pennsylvania) Police

Department after her estranged husband Wayne Barber shot and permanently injured her in 1988. Barber had harassed and threatened her for months, committing what the court described as "unpleasant acts," and although he had earlier been cited for contempt of a restraining order, the police failed to arrest him.[87] Terry Coffman claimed that this failure deprived her of her entitlement to police protection under the Protection from Abuse Act and therefore violated her rights to due process. The court agreed with Judge Katz's ruling in the *Hynson* case that "the Pennsylvania Protection from Abuse Act creates no enforceable [property] interest in police protection."[88] But, it said, an order of protection *does*.[89] Under certain circumstances, and with many limitations, Terry Coffman might have "the right to reasonable police response"; but the court "stressed" that this seemingly favorable ruling was not "a litigant's bonanza."[90] "The only entitlement here," the court said, "is an entitlement to place before the [police] dispatcher information which if true would require him to conclude that there was an emergency and therefore send [a police car]."[91] But the police might *reasonably fail* to send a police car if "other calls had greater importance," the court said, warning that "there is . . . a great deal of discretion in police work."[92] The *Coffman* decision was a victory of sorts, but it sounded suspiciously like business as usual.

So did the decision of an Ohio district court in the case of Karen Siddle. She brought due process and equal protection claims against the Cambridge (Ohio) police, alleging that they had failed over a period of several months to protect her from the harassment of her estranged husband, despite the fact that she held a protective order. On one hand, the district court ruled that the protective order did create a property interest for Karen Siddle. "When a protective order exists," the court said, " . . . there is a governmental duty to protect the individual." On the other hand, the court said that the extent of that duty is merely "a reasonable protection given the sources of the governmental agency responsible."[93] Karen Siddle had found the cops "rude" and "intimidating" and apparently not very helpful, but the court ruled that the police department had "fulfilled its duty to the individual in this case."[94] Whether a woman was "reasonably protected" seemed to be up to the police, not the woman, to decide. The court threw out Karen Siddle's equal protection claim, too. It could see that the police had in fact treated her "differently" as a victim of domestic assault, but where was the harm in that? The police were perfectly justified in providing such unequal protection, the court said in 1991, because "the criminal area may not be the best place to resolve *marital problems* of this sort."[95]

Obviously the law could and should protect women and redress violations of their constitutional rights. But just as law enforcement has not held batterers to account, the courts choose not to hold the police to account for their failure to protect women, their violation of women's constitutional rights. And who is to hold the courts to account when they enunciate from the bench the fundamental biases of an ancient patriarchy? Not the current Supreme Court, which instead quotes itself, citing *DeShaney* in its controversial *Webster* decision restricting women's abortion rights, and thereby placing *DeShaney* firmly in the lengthening line of cases which advance the view that states have no duty to secure individual rights.[96]

Meanwhile, in an FBI publication that goes out to law enforcement personnel across the country, one of the Bureau's legal experts summed up recent judicial rulings bearing upon police liability in domestic assault cases: "The government has no constitutional duty to protect citizens against private domestic violence," he wrote, echoing *DeShaney*. "Police have considerable discretion in deciding whether and when to make an arrest," he continued. "Proof that the failure of police to protect a victim of domestic violence resulted from a police department policy or practice of treating domestic assaults differently from non-domestic assaults and that women were disproportionately disadvantaged" is *not enough* for plaintiffs to establish an equal protection violation; and "procedural due process claims against police for their failure to protect victims of domestic violence are likely to fail."[97]

Even seemingly promising federal legislation designed to combat violence against women has been whittled down to conform to the strictures of the court. Title III of the Violence Against Women Act, a bill that has been working its way through the Senate Judiciary Committee since June 1990, would provide a civil rights remedy for violent gender-based discrimination. But only up to a point. It will not permit claims "that a governmental entity has violated a citizen's due process rights by failing to protect him or her." The Supreme Court ruled that out, in *DeShaney v. Winnebago*.[98]

Nevertheless, the legal struggle to secure women's right to be free from bodily harm has only just begun. Although *DeShaney* blocked some avenues to relief, feminist legal scholars and law students are mapping alternative routes. They may build stronger equal protection cases and try to move them out of the long shadow of *DeShaney*. They may sue municipalities for their "failure to train" police and prosecutors and other public officials. They may continue to bring claims in state courts, at least in states where the bench is not overcrowded with judges utterly unsympathetic to women's claims. They may press for injunctive relief rather than money damages, in the hope that municipalities will negotiate settlements if they are required merely to change procedures and not to hand over cash. They may press for revision of state laws so that the language of statutes governing orders of protection and mandating arrest clearly establishes duties and creates entitlements of which women cannot be deprived without due process. And although prosecutors and judges enjoy even greater discretion than police, feminist attorneys may also sue them for failing to perform duties and thus effectively denying women their rights under the Constitution and state laws as well. With feminist activists, they may press for new statutes that spell out those duties. They may work to remove negligent and misogynist officials from public office. They will continue to articulate the definition of battery as a violation of civil and human rights. And they will find new legal terrain to explore. For example, seeing the plight of thousands of battered women bound to their assailants by force and fear, one legal scholar suggests bringing federal suits under the Thirteenth Amendment and section 1584 of the U.S. Code, the statute that prohibits involuntary servitude.[99]

None of this litigation will be fast or easy. To hold a municipality liable for failing to train its police to arrest batterers, for example, a woman must prove, among many other things, that the municipality failed to train its officers *because* of "deliberate indifference" to the rights of the public.[100] Yet we may well see a wave of "failure to train" cases following upon the wave of due process and equal protection cases. Laurie Woods, Director of the National Center on Women and Family Law and lead counsel in *Bruno v. Codd*, the 1976 class action suit against New York City police and court officials, takes the long view of feminist litigation on behalf of battered women. "We were successful in holding police and public officials accountable long before *Thurman*," she says, "and we will be successful long after *DeShaney*."[101] Law professor Elizabeth Schneider is also optimistic. Currently, she says, "There is an explosion of battered women's work in the law schools —an amazing, creative burst of thinking, writing, clinical projects, and pro bono litigation."[102]

Still, it's hard to imagine that this creative burst will not be contained by the weight of equally amazing and portentous decisions to be handed down in future by the same bunch that brought us *DeShaney*, now augmented by Clarence Thomas. One has to ask: should it be *this* hard to win the right merely to make a claim in court to a constitutional right so fundamental that most white men don't ever have to think about it? Somehow the social contract doesn't seem to apply to women. But if the police are not to be required to protect women from bodily harm, if orders of protection and state domestic abuse prevention laws and federal legislation are to be merely pieces of paper, if the courts at every level are simply to deny what we thought to be our constitutional rights, then what are women to do? Feminist attorneys will continue their work; but in the meantime, in this mean time, for many battered women only self-help remedies remain—remedies such as flight, hiding, and homicide, the traditional remedies of the noncitizen, the outsider, the alien, the slave. They are the remedies of women who, even at this late date, are not "covered" as much by the law as by the men in their lives.

What's needed then is to change laws to make them inclusive of women and other marginalized Americans. But even more important is to change profoundly the way the law is interpreted, applied, and enforced. And that would seem to hinge upon a transformation of consciousness. It's not impossible. Writing in the *Boston Globe*, Hiller B. Zobel, a justice of the Massachusetts Superior Court, described a great change in the public's attitude as he observed it in cases of "date rape" coming before Massachusetts courts. "Behavior that in 1959 might have passed as standard aggression," he writes, "can today produce a prosecution for indecent assault and battery, with the possibility of five years in state prison or an indictment for rape. R-a-p-e: as in 20 years maximum sentence." Judge Zobel points out that for centuries, although rape was defined as "unconsented-to, forcible penetration," the act was considered rape only if it occurred between strangers; even then, he says, "the law, almost entirely male-crafted, regarded the defendant with a tenderness conspicuously absent when the accusation concerned . . . armed robbery." The woman alleging rape was commonly suspected of making a false accusation and routinely subjected to "brutal cross-examination" focused on her "chastity." Today, Judge Zobel observes among jurors a widespread belief "that a woman would not make the accusation unless it were true" and a "plain increase in willingness to condemn and punish the man who does not understand the new social rules"—namely, that "in plain English, no means no." In short, he writes, "we have . . . arrived at a new interrelation between the law and social behavior" even though *the law has not changed*."[103]

Judge Zobel probably overestimates the transformation in American attitudes toward rape.[104] But he has a point. Just as our consciousness of rape was raised in the last decade, our consciousness of assault and battery must be raised in this one. And that heightened consciousness must somehow come to inform the courts; for most of the cases I've described have not gone to trial to be judged by a jury of ordinary citizens as Tracey Thurman's case was, but have been tossed out, like yesterday's news, by judges whose biases and errors and callousness and simple ignorance are enshrined in their decisions. The sensible, straightforward, and compassionate justice of the *Thurman* court goes down under the crabbed hand of *DeShaney*. The constitutional rights of all American women—to freedom from bodily harm, equal protection, due process—and the very lives of thousands lie at the disposal of cops and prosecutors and judges who still think the subject before us is "marital problems."

3

What Is "Domestic Violence"?

"Domestic violence" is one of those gray phrases, beloved of bureaucracy, designed to give people a way of talking about a topic without seeing what's really going on.[1] Like "repatriation" or "ethnic cleansing," it's a euphemistic abstraction that keeps us at a dispassionate distance, far removed from the repugnant spectacle of human beings in pain. We used to speak of "wife beating"—words that brought to mind a picture of terrifying action, a big, heavy-handed man with a malicious eye, and a slight woman, dazed and bent, raising her arms against the blows, and crying out, "No!" Or we called it "wife torture," the words of Frances Power Cobbe that conjure the scenes *between* beatings: the sullen husband, withdrawn and sulking, or angry and intimidating, dumping dinner on the floor, throwing the cat against the wall, screaming, twisting a child's arm, needling, nagging, manipulating, criticizing the bitch, the slut, the cunt who never does anything right, who's ugly and stupid, who should keep her mouth shut, who should spread her legs now, who should be dead, who will be if she's not careful. Dickens drew such scenes, and Hardy and D. H. Lawrence, Dostoevsky and Zola, Doris Lessing, Toni Morrison, Margaret Atwood, Alice Munro, Alice Walker, Joyce Carol Oates. But we prefer to speak of "domestic violence."

I suspect that some academic researcher coined the term, dismayed by the fact that all those beaten wives are *women*, and reaching for some pretentious and gender-neutral "objective" term. During the Carter administration, when women's issues enjoyed a heady moment of legitimacy in the nation's capital, professionals in mental health and justice, equipped with professional vocabularies, took up the problems of "spouse abuse," "conjugal violence," and "marital aggression"—and a great renaming took place, a renaming that veiled once again the sexism a grass-roots women's movement had worked to uncover.[2] Even feminist advocates for women, who called their cause "the battered women's movement," eventually succumbed; they adopted "domestic violence" in their fund raising proposals, so as not to offend men controlling the purse strings by suggesting that men were in any way to blame for this "social problem." So well does the phrase "domestic violence" obscure the real events behind it that when a Domestic Violence Act (to provide money for battered women's services) was first proposed to Congress in 1978, many thought it was a bill to combat political terrorism within the United States.

It's difficult to face up to the sexism behind the "social problem," for the public mind, like the individual, is apt to minimize, deny, repress, and forget the bad news.[3] Women in particular may have trouble facing the facts of sexist violence against women. Psychiatry professor Judith Lewis Herman observes: "Most women do not in fact recognize the degree of male hostility toward them, preferring to view the relations of the sexes as more benign than they are in fact. Similarly, women like to believe that they have greater freedom and higher status than they do in reality."[4] Nevertheless, it's absolutely necessary to keep that sexism in sight if we hope to make sense of battery, for the immensity and viciousness of male violence aimed specifically at women are otherwise incomprehensible.

Any battered woman, who has surely been called a lot of bad names, can tell you that words have the power of blows; but the words we commonly use to discuss battering aren't up to the task. Male violence disappears in euphemism. The old term "wife beating" named only one piece of male violence and only one relationship—marriage—between assailant and victim; and it focused attention on the victim, not the perpetrator. But at least it suggested what goes on. Current terms like "domestic violence" and its academic progeny "partner abuse," "familial dysfunction," and "spousal dissonance" obscure its nature altogether.

On the other hand, the term "battered woman"—adopted by the battered women's movement from nineteenth century feminist campaigns against "wife beating"—suggests a graphic picture, but one that may also mislead: the picture of a woman more or less constantly subjected to serious physical assault, a helpless victim. It alludes to only one form of male violence against women in the home, and it seemingly excludes so many others that most "battered women," sizing up their own circumstances, don't see themselves as "battered." Again, in emphasizing physical damage, the term "battered" masks the real nature and purpose of the "batterer's" behavior.

The terms "battered woman," "domestic violence victim," and "abused woman," which emphasize a woman's situation as the victimized object of another's actions, also obscure her subjectivity and actions. They suggest that "battered" woman is *all* she is, that "victim" is her identity. Yet women who have lived through such violence, who know the immense daily expenditure of strength and attention and self-discipline it takes to survive, rarely identify themselves as "victims." They think of themselves as strong women who can somehow "cope." Many who escape speak of themselves as "formerly battered women" or "survivors" or "veterans" of violence, but these terms suggest a status achieved after the fact; they do not describe the active woman in the day by day process of coping with, combating, and escaping her "partner's" violence.

The term "partner," by the way, is a politically correct addition to the academic lexicon, neutral not only in terms of gender but also sexual preference. It subsumes battering in lesbian and gay relationships under the discussion of heterosexual violence as if it were the same thing, when in fact the cultural context in which the violence occurs raises very different problems for victims in straight and gay "partnerships." On one hand, history and culture clearly support old-fashioned wife-beating, giving it a legitimacy that sets it apart from "partner abuse" within the marginalized homosexual community. On the other hand, the cultural repression of homosexuals trivializes violence within the homosexual community and writes off its victims, presenting immensely complicated problems to those who need help and must seek it from public authorities. In short, the word "partner" gives a nod to homosexuals while ignoring their real concerns. The usefulness of the term lies in its gender neutrality, for it conveniently hides one undeniable fact: that despite the real problem of violence committed by women against women, the assailant in almost all heterosexual *and* homosexual violence is a man.

The label "battered woman" is dangerously deceptive in other ways as well. The word "battered" names what someone else *did to her*, but since the battering agent is omitted from the phrase, the word "battered" somehow attaches to the woman as if it were an attribute, or part of her own nature—as in *deceitful* woman or *ambitious* woman. The implication built in to the form of the phrase is that *battered* is what she somehow chose to be. Somewhere in the back of our minds, just behind that American folk hero the "self-made man" lurks his dutiful counterpart, the seemingly "self-battered" woman.

The term "battered woman," which puts the focus on her, also encourages us to overlook her children; but there can be no doubt that male violence inflicts terrible damage upon them. Uncounted millions of children live in households dominated by violent men. Millions of children see and hear their mothers beaten repeatedly, a traumatic experience that many experts regard as in itself a form of child abuse. Some studies suggest that children who witness battering may suffer long-term consequences; both as children and as adults they may be particularly anxious, depressed, or aggressive.[5] And one major review of psychological studies of batterers found only one point of common history: many batterers witnessed the battery of their mothers when they were boys.[6] Millions of children become targets of violence as well, for the man who batters a woman is likely to abuse the kids, too. Two studies found that between 53 and 70 percent of men who battered a wife or girlfriend also abused a child; and in households with four or more children, 92 percent of the batterers abused the children.[7] Two other studies of children who received hospital treatment for abuse found that between 45 and 59 percent of their mothers were battered women.[8] Such children, too, are likely to become depressed, anxious, or aggressive; and the physical and emotional damage that will freight their adult lives is beyond calculation and repair.

The term "battered woman" also sets apart women who are victims of one form of male violence, as though there is something peculiar about *them*, and obscures the universal pattern of male dominance. (This is another reason why battered women themselves resist the label.) Labeling separate categories of male violence—battering, rape, incest, pimping, murder, and so on—makes each "problem" seem smaller than it is, a local condition, or a personal one. — w/ no common cause.

In fact, the categories of male violence interpenetrate and merge. What the batterer does inside the family, the rapist and pimp and murderer do outside the family. What the incestuous father does inside the family, the child molester does outside the family. The batterer subjects his wife or girlfriend to a process of seduction and coercion (known as "romance"), while the pimp uses an *identical* process of recruitment and indoctrination (known in the trade as "seasoning") to "turn out" a prostitute. In fact, the batterer often is a pimp, forcing his wife to have sex with other men or with animals. The batterer often is the molester of his own child or stepchild, or of his girlfriend's child. Batterers rape and rapists batter. Many women suffer male violence sequentially at the hands of various men: the girl beaten or sexually abused by her father, stepfather, or older brother runs away only to be picked up by a pimp, raped and battered, and turned into prostitution from which she may try to escape by marrying a batterer if she is not first murdered on the job. In California in 1981 Victor Burnham was convicted of marital rape after not one but three of his wives testified to rape, battery, torture, and captivity (which the prosecutor likened to the experience of prisoners of war) dating back to 1964.[10] He is different in degree but not in kind from the dozens of serial sexual killers who roam the United States slaughtering one woman (or child) after another. Indeed dominance and violence have become so inextricably bound up with male sexuality that some observers see the serial sexual killer as merely the logical extension of what it means these days to be a man.[11] Thus, even to speak of male violence as a "problem" is euphemistic, suggesting that what women and children experience as a fundamental, universal condition of life is discrete and readily overcome or solved, and that it is a malaise rather than an accumulation of undeterred criminal acts.

In short, when it comes to a discussion of "family violence," we are stuck with a vocabulary too flimsy for the subject, a vocabulary powerful only in this one respect: its insidious subversion of our understanding. Throughout this book, I use *battering*, *battery*, and *assault* to name acts of physical violence, although the profound psychological damage men do to women in addition to, or in lieu of, physical violence—the damage implicit in Cobbe's *"torture"*—leaks out around the hard edges of those legalistic words. And when I quote a court decision, a newspaper article, an academic study, a legislative proposal, or a sermon, we are set adrift again on the warm and featureless seas of *domestic violence*.

We are likely to be betrayed by syntax as well, ambushed all at once by the passive voice, just as women *are beaten*, wives *are abused*, children *are abandoned*. By whom? In the scholarship of sociology and psychology, and even in the columns of the local papers, women are less likely to be assaulted by men than by a deadly mob of abstract nouns. Women are victimized by *abuse*, they are threatened by *aggressive behavior*, they are battered by *the relationship*, they are done in by *the cycle of violence*, they are mutilated by *spousal hostility* and murdered by *domestic incidents*. Women are victimized by amorphous verbs, too. Women *experience* battering. They *suffer* abuse. They *undergo* assault. Rarely in the authoritative literature does a man hit a woman: in the gut, for instance, or the face, with his fist, hard—hard enough to split her lip, loosen her teeth, break her nose, lace her eyeball with a red web of ruptured veins—hard enough to make the blood run down the page.[12] In real life it happens all the time.

Domestic violence, battering, wife beating, woman abuse—call it what you will—is something greater than and different from what the terminology and the standard syntax suggest. We must look at the thing itself—at what is really going on.

The actual physical damage to women is real. "Domestic violence" is the leading cause of injury to women in the United States. According to the National Clearinghouse on Domestic Violence, men batter three or four million women a year.[13] According to the National Centers for Disease Control, more women are treated in emergency rooms for battering injuries than for (nonmarital) rapes, muggings, and traffic accidents *combined*.[14] Untold numbers of women suffer permanent injuries—brain damage, blindness, deafness, speech loss through laryngeal damage, disfigurement and mutilation, damage to or loss of internal organs, paralysis, sterility, and so on. Countless pregnant women miscarry as a result of beatings, and countless birth defects and abnormalities can be attributed to battery of the mother during pregnancy. So many battered women have been infected with HIV by batterers who force them into unprotected sex, in some cases deliberately to prevent their having sex with other men, that the National Centers for Disease Control have identified a direct link between battering and the spread of HIV and AIDS among women.[15] And every day at least four women die violently at the hands of men who profess to love them.[16]

After they escape, battered women may be saddled for years with a load of complicated problems ranging from anxiety, shame, and despair to flashbacks and suicidal ideation. These aftershocks are the symptoms of post-traumatic stress disorder, a [PTSD] psychological syndrome seen also in survivors of rape and incest and in veterans of wartime combat. Judith Lewis Herman notes the "horrifying" implications of this shared symptomology: "There is war between the sexes. Rape victims, battered women, and sexually abused children are its casualties."[17] Herman calls post-traumatic stress disorder the "combat neurosis of the sex war."[18] In her view, however, the diagnosis of post-traumatic stress disorder, as it is now defined, doesn't begin to cover the problems of battered women. The current diagnostic criteria are drawn from survivors of discrete and limited traumatic events, such as combat, disaster, and rape; but the prolonged and repeated trauma of battery, like prolonged sexual abuse of a child, is of a different magnitude and resonance. Herman proposes to add to the clinical lexicon a new name for the aftermath of prolonged trauma: "complex post-traumatic stress disorder."[19]

But battering is something more than the sum of all these afflictions. "Emerge," a Boston counseling program for men who batter, uses this working definition: violence is "any act that causes the victim to do something she does not want to do, prevents her from doing something she wants to do, or causes her to be afraid." And they note that "violence *need not involve physical contact with the victim*, since intimidating acts like punching walls, verbal threats, and psychological abuse can achieve the same results." Psychological abuse, which they define as "behavior that directly undermines . . . self-determination or self-esteem," becomes "particularly powerful" when mixed with physical violence. Behavior you might not think of as "violence," behavior you might think of merely as getting things off your chest—such as "yelling, swearing, sulking, and angry accusations"—*is* violence if it coerces or frightens another person. And the likelihood of its doing just that increases exponentially when it's "'reinforced' by periodic or even occasional [physical] violence."[20]

It's vital to understand that battering is *not* a series of isolated blow-ups. It is a *process of deliberate intimidation intended to coerce the victim to do the will of the victimizer.* The batterer is not just losing his temper, not just suffering from stress, not just manifesting "insecurity" or a spontaneous reaction "provoked" by something the victim did or (as psychologists put it) "a deficit of interpersonal skills" or an "inhibition in anger control mechanisms." These are *excuses* for violence, popular even among therapists who work with batterers; yet we all know aggrieved, insecure, stressed-out people with meager interpersonal skills who lose their temper *without* becoming violent. We assume, then, that the grievances of the violent man must be worse, and that under extreme stress he has spun out of control. He looks it, and that's what he says: "I wasn't myself." "I was drunk." "I went bananas." "I lost it." "I went out of my mind." It's lines like these that provide a public excuse and deceive a battered woman into giving one more chance to the so-called *real*, nonviolent man underneath. But in fact that violence *is* himself, perfectly *in* control and *exercising* control.

Counselor David Adams of Emerge observes that how a man deals with stress, or feelings, or conflict depends upon whom he's dealing *with*, and particularly upon the sex and status of that other person. Batterers can be perfectly agreeable, straightforward, or conciliatory to police officers, bosses, neighbors, co-workers, or friends when they think it's in their best interests. If they don't use those "interpersonal skills" with their wives, it's because they think it's *not* in their best interests; they *choose* not to. As Adams puts it: "The violent husband's selectively abusive behavior indicates an established set of *control skills*."[21] No, the violent man is not out of control. He is a man at work on his own agenda, which is to train "his" woman to be what he wants her to be, and only what he wants her to be, all the time.

Those control skills have been well documented, and they resemble nothing so much as the tactics used by Nazi guards to control prisoners in the death camps, and by Chinese thought-reformers to brainwash American P. O. W.'s in Korea. Psychologist Alfred D. Biderman studied brainwashed American soldiers, and his work, augmented by strikingly similar accounts of political prisoners, hostages, and concentration camp survivors, was codified in a "chart of coercion" published by Amnesty International in 1973. That chart of coercive techniques is often reproduced and handed out in support groups at shelters, and battered women come up with endless examples of the general methods in

*Batterers'
use*

Methods of Coercion

Method	Examples
ISOLATION	
Deprives victim of all social support for the ability to resist.	He moved me away from my friends. He didn't want me to go anywhere unless he was with me. He would eavesdrop.
Develops an intense concern with self.	
Makes victim dependent upon interrogator.	
MONOPOLIZATION OF PERCEPTION	
Fixes attention upon immediate predicament; fosters introspection.	I was always scared he'd blow up. I had to dress up for him. Give him sex whenever he wanted. I had to control the children so they wouldn't bother him. It was like walking on eggshells.
Eliminates stimuli competing with those controlled by captor.	
Frustrates all actions not consistent with compliance.	
INDUCED DEBILITY AND EXHAUSTION	
Weakens mental and physical ability to resist.	He wouldn't let me sleep. He started fights at night. He wouldn't let me see a doctor.
THREATS	
Cultivates anxiety and despair.	He threatened to kill the cat. He said he'd take the kids. He said he'd have me committed. He said he'd burn down the house. He said he'd find me if I left.

Method	Examples
OCCASIONAL INDULGENCES	
Provides positive motivation for compliance.	He took me on vacation. He bought me jewelry. He allowed me sex only when we "made up." Once in awhile he really listened to me and seemed to care.
DEMONSTRATING "OMNIPOTENCE"	
Suggests futility of resistance.	He beat me up. He had me followed. He called me deluded.
DEGRADATION	
Makes cost of resistance appear more damaging to self-esteem than capitulation. Reduces prisoner to "animal level" concerns.	He told me I'm too fat. He'd call me names and touch me inappropriately in public. He put me down intellectually and sexually and said I was ugly.
ENFORCING TRIVIAL DEMANDS	
Develops habit of compliance.	The bacon had to be cooked to a particular doneness. I couldn't leave a cup on the bathroom basin.

Source: Amnesty International, *Report on Torture* (1973), as adapted by the women's shelter of Northampton, Massachusetts.

action. The Amnesty International chart is summarized on the left in the preceding table; comments of members of a shelter support group are on the right.[22]

You may not have thought about battering in this way before. Many people haven't. But it's this unspoken agenda of the batterer that makes it so difficult for a woman to think of what to do, or even to grasp what's going on. (Battered women commonly report great confusion and the fear that they must be going crazy.) Most women, wanting to make the relationship work, will try to figure out rationally how they can change their own behavior to help the batterer stop battering. He says he hit her because the house is a mess or she shouldn't go out in shorts or she ought to stay home? She'll clean the house and dress "modestly" and quit her job—anything to stop the abuse. But because the abuser intends a coercion far more profound than any immediate "reason" for any particular incident, whatever the woman does—short of surrendering utterly to his will—must fail.

It's doubtful any living woman could meet the rigid specifications of the batterer. Emerge counselors observe that even when batterers purport to be "working" on their "relationship," they are intent upon *devaluing* their partner rather than *understanding* her. Typically, they denigrate what women say with comments like "She went on and on about nothing" or "She was in a bitchy mood," but when pressed by counselors, David Adams says, "men cannot recall their wives' actual words or specific complaints."[23] Many counselors observe that what a batterer calls "nagging" is a woman's repetition of what she *knows* he hasn't heard. Counseling batterers in Duluth, Minnesota, Ellen Pence noticed that men rarely call the women they abuse by *name*, presumably because they don't see women as persons in their own right. In one men's group session, she counted ninety-seven references to wives and girlfriends, many of them obscene, before a man mentioned his wife by name. When Pence insisted they use names, many men "could hardly spit it out." Pence points out that many women still lose their last name at marriage; marry a controlling man, she says, and "Your front name goes too."[24] Then the batterer tries to pummel this "nonentity" into the "person" he wants: the perfect wife.

It's important to notice that at least three of the methods of coercion on the Amnesty International chart take effect more or less "naturally" when a woman "falls in love." (The more she follows the prescribed formula of soap operas and romance novels, the farther she falls.) She spends less time with friends and focuses her attention on her new lover. He in turn "provides indulgences." And in the early giddy days of a relationship, she may enjoy trying to meet, even to anticipate, his trivial demands. If she's in love with a man (or woman) who feels the same and who respects her life, she may be on the way to a fine relationship. But if she has fallen for a controlling, potentially violent man, she is in serious trouble, because our traditional notions of romantic love have already given him a head start on coercion.

It's important to notice, too, that the Amnesty International chart mentions *no* physical violence. Thoroughgoing coercion—total destruction of the will—can be accomplished *without physical violence*, although batterers commonly add all sorts of bodily assault and sexual sadism, interspersed with those occasional "indulgences" and periods of professed remorse and reformation. Those seductive periods of male contrition, so convincing that psychologists label them "honeymoon phases" of the "cycle of violence" and women mistake them for love, are not respites from battering, as they appear, but part of the coercive process, pressuring women to forgive and forget, to minimize and deny, to *submit*, and thus to appear complicitous: they *are* battering.[25]

In the extreme, physical violence passes over into torture: sleep deprivation, burns, electric shock, bondage, semi-starvation, choking, near-drowning, exposure, mutilation, rape, forcible rape with objects or animals, and so on. Amnesty International defines torture as "the systematic and deliberate infliction of acute pain in any form by one person on another, or on a third person, in order to accomplish the purpose of the former against the will of the latter." The organization says that "regardless of the context in which it is used, torture is outlawed under the common law of mankind" and "may properly be considered to be a crime against humanity."[26] Yet the terrible stories told by war prisoners and hostages delivered from bondage and torture can be matched by the stories of battered women. <u>The batterer may</u> be less skilled than <u>the professional thought-reformer, but he acts to the same purpose: to control the life of another.</u> And even perfect control may not be enough for him. Judith Lewis Herman explains that the dominating man needs the victim's "affirmation" to justify his crimes. In situations of political captivity and domestic captivity alike, the captor is rarely satisfied with simple compliance. "Thus," Herman writes, "he relentlessly demands from his victim professions of respect, gratitude, or even love. His ultimate goal appears to be the creation of a <u>willing victim</u>."[27]

It is equally vital to understand that <u>women are battered *because they will not give in*</u>. One survivor who now counsels abused women put it this way: "Most of the battered women I meet are really strong women, and that's why they get beat—because they don't take no shit. And that's why I got beat—because I wouldn't act like he wanted me to act, talk like he wanted me to talk, be who he wanted me to be."[28] As I've said, the FBI reports that a woman is beaten in the United States every ten seconds or so, but we can better understand what's going on by thinking of it this way: every ten seconds a woman *resists*.

Her concerns are complex. Like most women, battered or not, she probably places a higher value on human connections and the compromises necessary to preserve them than do most men; and despite her shock and anger, there is no one who has greater compassion for the batterer, at least at first, than the battered woman herself. But she also values herself. Under threat of violence, a woman may give up bits and pieces of herself: her preferences, her opinions, her voice, her friends, her job, her freedom of movement, her sexual autonomy. She may learn to lie, or at least to keep the truth to herself. She may learn to say the sex was good when it wasn't, or that she's sorry when she's not. Unable ever to give the "right" answer, she may retreat into silence. It's often easy to mistake her apparent passivity for submission, masochism, complicity. But she does not give in. Uncle Remus and Br'er Rabbit, experts on outwitting violent oppression, called it "laying low." A battered woman lies low while she tries first to make sense of her situation, then to change it, and finally to get out.

In the long run, battering a woman to control her is almost certain to fail, for battered women *leave*. It is not too much to say that from the first moment a man abuses her, a woman begins, in some sense, to leave—emotionally, spiritually, physically. Shocked at first, she may try to stop the violence by trying to become "a better person," but she ends by trying to be in another place. She may embezzle from the grocery money for months, placating the batterer all the while she squirrels away the price of a ticket to freedom. Abused women describe this process of going underground within themselves, hiding out inside, lying low until they can emerge, like some moth shedding caterpillar skin, becoming themselves. Escapees say: "Now I'm *myself* again."

When it comes to getting out, women are enormously ingenious, resourceful, and brave. They have to be because it's at this point—when "his woman" escapes—that the abuser is most dangerous. Absolutely dependent upon her submission for his own sense of power and control, he can not bear to lose her. In many cases, that false sense of power is the only identity a man has; to lose "his woman" is to lose himself. Thus, he is far more likely to kill her (and perhaps himself as well) as she tries to leave or *after she has left*, than if she stays with him. ("If I can't have you, nobody can," he says.)

Battered women know this, and they leave anyway. One formerly battered woman explained to talk show host Sally Jesse Raphael: "It takes a lot of maneuvering, a lot of mental exercise, to get out." At a speak-out for formerly battered women in Seattle, a woman who had been afraid for her life described her escape into hiding: she booked an early morning flight to a distant city, then asked her husband for permission to go regularly to early mass to pray for God's guidance in "being a better wife." "On Monday I went to mass," she said. "On Tuesday I went to mass. On Wednesday I went to mass. On Thursday I went to the airport." Another woman told me how she ejected a battering husband who refused to leave *her* house. "He's a boxer," she explained, "and he had closed in my garage as a workout room. What I did, while he was at work one day, was cut this giant hole in the garage door with a huge power saw, and I backed a truck up to the hole, and I took all his boxing training things and all his clothes and personal stuff and anything I thought he might want, and I put it on the truck, took it to his mother's house, dumped it in the yard, and said, 'Enough is enough.' Since then I'm on my third restraining order."[29]

In the short run though, battering *works*. It may be mean and cowardly and cruel and criminal and an evolutionary throwback, but for the batterer's immediate gratification, it works fine. Just as many parents use physical force, or the threat of it, to make children "behave," many men know that there's nothing like a good pow in the kisser, or the threat of it, to keep the little lady in line. Individual men beat individual women to make those women do what they want. And the widespread practice of wife beating intimidates all women and reinforces our society's habitual pattern of male dominance. A little muscle gets a guy a little sex, a little peace and quiet, a little attention, another drink, and in the great cosmic scheme of things, it helps keep a man's world a man's world. What could be more efficient?

It's not that abusive men think of themselves as soldiers in the cause of male supremacy; their demands and their disappointments are individual, specific complaints which they can enunciate, and do, often in very loud voices. Historian Linda Gordon studied nearly a century of family violence in Boston and found this to be true. She reports that down through the decades, men who beat their wives were "not ideologues defending the dominance of their sex. . . . They were using violence to increase their control over particular women, defending real, material benefits."[30] Dinner on the table, cold beer on call, sex on demand, quiet kids, clean socks—all those benefits to which a man "naturally" feels entitled. Among the historical wife beaters Gordon studied, "their sense of entitlement was so strong it was experienced as a need."[31] Listen in on a batterers' counseling group to-day, and you'll hear the same "need" still frustrated. "She forgot to buy gin." "She said she had a headache." "She knows I hate macaroni." The grievances are trivial and deeply felt, the pitiful outcry of men who consider themselves victimized by women who simply will not or can not behave as they "ought." And their response is immediate—pow! For wife beaters, violence is not a last resort. It's a weapon of choice.

Batterers *expect* things to go their way. Frustrate those expectations and violence results. It is at this point that batterers part company with nonbatterers, for there is no logical, psychological, or physiological reason that assaultive rage should necessarily follow upon disappointed expectations. Anyone who ever fell in love knows what it is to have frustrated expectations. To most of us, that's life: as much a source of wonder and amusement as anger. To the batterer, frustrated expectations are an immense personal attack, a cosmic betrayal, a calculated injury, a deliberate wound, a fucking insult, or as *he* would put it, wielding the verbal equivalent of a blunt instrument: a fucking *fuck*.

I recall a conversation with the son of a woman who was on trial for shooting her battering husband. After enduring years of abuse for the sake of keeping the family together, she finally shot her husband when he started to abuse the children, including the boy I was talking to. The boy said he loved his mother, but "none of this" would have happened if she had "acted right"—which meant, as her husband had wanted her to. As his own bride, the boy intended to find "a girl who does everything right"; he had recently broken up with his girlfriend because she took a sip from his can of beer, and he considered girls who drink "immoral." I asked him if he ever had any doubts about *his* ability to do "everything right," and it was clear from his bafflement that the question had never crossed his mind. Living up to another's impossible expectations was not *his* job, but *hers*. He was fourteen years old.[32]

The male sense of entitlement, and the use of force to insure it, seem always to have been so strong that early nineteenth century Americans attributed wife beating to the "nature" of men, as characteristic of the sex as whiskers. But what did it mean to be a "man"? Historian Carroll Smith-Rosenberg describes two competing models for the bourgeois male in Jacksonian America: the rebellious, violent, misogynist frontiersman, and the dutiful, sexually repressed family man, a paragon of self-control.[33] Both models presumably were entitled to all the privileges of masculinity, but the self-controlled fellow was supposed to be able to get his way without throwing his physical weight around. As the century advanced, wife beating, and "brutality against the weak" in general, says Linda Gordon, came to be seen not as part of man's nature but as the cowardly act of the "unmanly."[34] Men who subscribed to that definition passed laws to make wife beating illegal; while men who didn't subscribe to it—or who couldn't bring off the symbolic force required to control a woman without punching her out—went on beating their wives.

To this day, similar definitions of manliness compete. Robert Bly, a guru of the men's movement, finds the dutiful, self-controlled family man of the Jacksonian era all around him—the "nice boy who pleases not only his mother but also the young woman he is living with"—although Bly mistakenly thinks him an invention of the last twenty years, a sissified byproduct of feminism.[35] Revitalizing some of the most violent and oppressive figures in the iconography of patriarchy, Bly invites this "soft male" to make a "clean break" with his mother and enter the woods (literally) to be transformed by patriarchal mumbo jumbo into a golden-haired warrior, a Wild Man, a King—an "unnice" man who will be able to brandish his sword, "to shout and say what he wants."[36] The immense sales of Bly's book *Iron John* and the popularity of his weekend retreats suggest that "soft men" are indeed unhappy being "nice"; but battered women, who could use some *ironing* Johns, report that the living rooms and bedrooms of the nation are already filled with hairy men shouting relentlessly about what they want.

Generally, those "soft males" who so disturb Bly believe that it's wrong to hit women—wrong and foolish to resort to violence in any case—and many of them simply *don't* do it. Others do, but deny or try to hide it precisely because they believe it would discredit them if it were known, or perhaps even if they admitted it to themselves. Plenty of other men, like many of the Boston working-class men Linda Gordon studied, don't buy this "feminized," middle-class definition. Or they learn from the instruction manuals of popular culture—from films and rock videos and pornography and beer commercials—more up-to-the-minute manliness scripts, conflating violence and sex. No one claims these days that battering is part of man's essential nature, for there are lots of men—probably more than half the male population—who never have done it and never will. But no one claims that battering is "abnormal" behavior for men either. Rather, it is "an extreme form of normality, an exaggeration of how society expects men to behave."[37] Great numbers of men, in every segment of the population, still swagger through "relationships" with all the finesse of Rambo. And many young men—the MTV fans who are fast making date rape and fraternity gang rape campus traditions—seem to regard the use of violence against women as, if not part of man's nature, certainly man's *right*.

Given the structure of this "man's world," men can scarcely think otherwise. And violence against women is so sturdily buttressed by cultural supports that it can almost be mistaken for the national pastime, as indeed it is by groups of men who gang rape women just for the fun of it, or murder women just for the thrilling rush of power it brings. After more than a decade of talking to wife beaters and beaten wives, Ellen Pence, founder of the Duluth Domestic Abuse Intervention Project, describes the cultural context that supports and encourages battering. Every part of life, she says, is affected by hierarchical structures—the school, the church, the military, the government—so it seems "natural" to us always that someone be "in charge" and others be subordinate. In the family, that someone in charge is the man. (Female-headed households, though they are rapidly coming to outnumber male-headed households, still don't count as *real* families; and couples who try to share authority equally will find that the world's representatives—the banker, for example, or the car salesman—see the man as *really* in charge.) "Every abuser," Pence says, "operates out of the belief that there is a natural order to things, and that by virtue of his sex, he should be at the top of the family system." Secondly, the culture objectifies women in pornography, videos, ads, adult "entertainment," TV shows, beauty contests, and the like, encouraging the abuser to think of women, especially *his* women, as available and intended for his use. Thirdly, the culture compels women to submit through a combination of psychological conditioning that trains them to "understand" and take care of men, economic arrangements that plunge female-headed households into poverty, and legal license that permits men to coerce *their* women by threats and violence.[38]

Summing up the discussion of a group of formerly battered women, Pence says: "We're living in a world in which occasionally, when a man wants to control us, he gets to walk up to us and kick us or hit us or bite us or throw us down or threaten to take away our kids, or threaten to kill us, or threaten to kill our mothers or our fathers or any other man who would ever have us. He gets to call us 'whore,' 'slut,' 'bitch,' 'cunt,' or any name he wants. He gets to tell us how to have sex, when to have sex, where to have sex. He gets to look at whatever grimy little pictures he wants and then come back to us and say, 'This is what I want to do.' Whenever we don't want to do what they want, men get to do all these things. The reality of our lives is that we're being terrorized. And then men get to tell us that they love us. They can't live without us."[39]

That's the way the world of male privilege looks to women who have been battered. And if Pence seems to overstate the case, consider what the world must look like to Kathleen Kaplan of New Hampshire. When she was fourteen her stepfather raped her. She ran away from home, into the arms of Morton (Jack) Kaplan, then forty-seven, who married her at fourteen and during the next ten years, beat her "often," compelled her to have an abortion, and forced her into nude dancing and prostitution. When she asked for a divorce, he threatened to cut the fingers and ears off their baby. She tried to kill herself. According to a *New York Times* report: "The police refused to intervene. When a friend offered to kill Mr. Kaplan, Ms. Kaplan thought it was a joke. But the friend called her later and said he had killed Mr. Kaplan, and she paid him."[40] She pleaded guilty to second-degree murder and was sentenced to thirty years in prison. (The hit man was acquitted.)[41] Her case hit the news again when New Hampshire Governor John Sununu, just before leaving for Washington to become President Bush's chief of staff, granted Kathleen Kaplan a conditional pardon; after fifteen months of working outside the prison, she was to be released, having served little more than eight years in prison. One condition of her pardon was that she relinquish all rights to her son.[42] Raped as a youngster; beaten, terrorized, and sold for a decade; imprisoned for eight years and deprived of her child— Kathleen Kaplan is now expected to be grateful to the man who released her rather than keep her locked up, as the law prescribed, for another twenty-two years. And many good citizens of New Hampshire opposed the early release of this "murderer."

This is not an extreme case. In fact, it's quite routine. Like Kathleen Kaplan, women in danger often seek help from police and prosecutors and judges who, as we have seen, decline to protect them. It is left to women, then, to help themselves as best they can. So it should come as no surprise that some women kill the men who abuse them. The number of women who kill has decreased steadily since battered women's shelters opened in the 1970s, indicating that women do not want to kill their assailants but to escape from them. (During the same period the number of men killing wives and girlfriends has gone steadily up.)[43] Currently, in the United States about five hundred married women and about half as many unmarried women every year commit what some legal scholars have termed "self-help homicide": in self-defense or as a last resort, they kill the men who rape and batter them.[44]

Perhaps the best known is Francine Hughes, of Dansville, Michigan, the subject of Faith McNulty's powerful book *The Burning Bed* and a 1987 television movie starring Farrah Fawcett.[45] In 1977, after years of rape, battery, and terror from which she was unable to escape even after divorce, Francine Hughes doused her sleeping ex-husband's room with kerosene and struck a match. Today she—or Farrah Fawcett playing her part—seems the very image of the battered woman who strikes back. Yet the case of Francine Hughes is extraordinary in several respects—in addition to the fact that she is confused in the popular imagination with a glamorous movie star. For one thing, she killed James "Mickey" Hughes between attacks, as he slept, a circumstance quite understandable if the woman doesn't stand a chance when he's awake, but which nevertheless suggests stealth, premeditation, and cold blood. Most battered women who kill violent husbands or boyfriends, however, do so in the midst of a beating to fend off the attack and save themselves; there is nothing devious or premeditated about it.[46]

Secondly, Francine Hughes's legal defense was that she was temporarily insane, made so by the severity of her ex-husband's abuse; but while the courts are quite prepared to hear that a woman who kills a man is crazy, they are unnerved by the simple plea of most battered women: self-defense. The notion that a woman might kill a man for a sane, sound, and *justifiable* reason is so unsettling that psychologists must be paraded for the defense to explain the battered woman's crime in terms of her peculiar state of mind, her "syndrome," making her crime seem "reasonable" to the jurors—if they take into account the battered woman's oddly hot-wired and "helpless" mind. A woman who can't afford the expense of such sophisticated psychological testimony, to present her as not really crazy but not quite "normal" either, usually goes to prison, becoming the political prisoner of a legal system that can't judge her act of self-defense against domestic assault as justified because it doesn't take domestic assault seriously. As long as the law—and prospective jurors—think domestic assault is no crime, a woman who kills a batterer must be seen as overreacting, without justification.

What's more, the theories that profeminist attorneys and psychological expert witnesses devised to help women charged with homicide now often count against them. Trying to explain to jurors why women who killed battering men hadn't simply left, experts argued that battering leaves many women with a sense of helplessness. The courts, which at first refused to admit the experts' testimony, have now accepted the concept of "battered women's syndrome" with a vengeance. They have whittled the legal understanding of "battered woman" to such a fine point that few living women fit the description. These days, battered women who got angry, or fought back, or called the cops, or took the batterer to court, or bought defensive weapons, or *left*—which is to say, most women who are battered—don't. qualify as "helpless." Put up against the legal definitions of the "battered women's syndrome," they seem to be impostors—not *real* battered women at all, but bad girls and heartless killers.[47] They are punished accordingly.

In that regard, too, they differ from Francine Hughes; for Hughes was acquitted, while most battered women who kill go to prison for very long terms, and often for life. In Missouri, battered women convicted of murder for what they describe as self-defense homicide are commonly sentenced to fifty years *without parole*.[48] At least fourteen of the thirty-three women on death row in the United States in 1991 killed a husband or boyfriend. (We don't know if all of them were battered because in many cases their own defense attorneys didn't bother to inquire.)[49] Sweet-looking young women, the kind of women who wear white gloves to church and know the hymns by heart, and who killed their husbands to save themselves, will live out their lives in a state prison, or be put to death within its walls. So it happens that battered women are battered once again by the law, and hundreds of women every year, who are denied equal protection of the law and who kill the men who assault them, live to repent in prison. Most of them say they feel freer and safer there than they did at home.

Before he left office in 1990, Ohio's Governor Richard F. Celeste reviewed the cases of about one hundred women serving time in the state prison for assault or homicide and granted clemency to about a quarter of them.[50] These women, he said, were "victims of violence, repeated violence," but because Ohio's courts prior to 1990 refused to admit expert testimony about the experience and state of mind of battered women, women who defended themselves against batterers were prevented from defending themselves in court. In a brave, unpopular act, Celeste freed twenty-one women (and scheduled four more to be freed a short time later) in the first mass release of women prisoners in the nation's history. He freed the women not out of charity, but as a matter of law because they had been unfairly tried and wrongly convicted.

Every governor in the country has the power to release such women—battered by men, battered by the law—but no governor had ever thought to do such a thing before, and only one, Governor William Schaefer of Maryland, has done so since. In February 1991, he commuted the sentences of eight women who had been "abused and threatened repeatedly" and who had "reason to fear for their lives" when they struck back at their assailants.[51] Like Ohio, Maryland had prevented them from presenting evidence of abuse at their trials or putting on expert witnesses to testify in their behalf. One of the women released was Juanita Stinson, who "endured 30 years of severe abuse," suffering "miscarriages and other injuries." She was convicted of murder and sentenced to eight years. Another was Patricia Washington, whose husband beat her, inducing a miscarriage, and repeatedly threatened her with a gun. She was convicted of murder and carrying a deadly weapon and sentenced to thirty years. Mytokia Friend, a former police officer, "tried for months to get assistance, fearing for her and her son's lives" and finally killed in self-defense during a beating that had lasted five hours. She was convicted of murder and handgun use and sentenced to fifteen years. Bernadette Barnes's abusive husband shot her in the head while she slept. (The bullet is still lodged in her head.) He was sentenced to *three months* in prison and made "repeated death threats" until she paid a man $5,000 to kill him. She was convicted of murder and conspiracy to commit murder and sentenced to life.[52]

The law had made an example of these women to deter other women from following their course and to impress upon us all the heinousness of killing one's husband, a crime that has always been considered far worse than killing a wife. (Under English common law, killing a wife was an act of homicide, while killing a husband was an act of treason punishable by burning at the stake.[53] That inherent disparity appears in case after case today as lesser charges are brought against men who kill wives and girlfriends and lesser sentences are imposed upon them.) Perhaps because husband killing is still commonly seen as an act without reason or mitigating circumstance, the Federal Bureau of Justice Statistics, which tabulates crime in this country, has never bothered to learn how many of the women who kill men are battered women killing the man who has battered them. Only in the last few years, and only in some cases, has evidence that a woman defendant was assaulted by her "victim" been found relevant to the homicide and admissible at her murder trial. So we simply don't know how many women languishing in our prisons could tell us stories like those of Francine Hughes or Kathleen Kaplan. But certainly such women are not hard to find. In 1990 a survey of imprisoned women in the United States found that "over half were victims of physical abuse, and 36% had been sexually abused."[54]

In January 1989, 3,765 women in the United States were serving time in prison for murder.[55] Most of them killed a man—a husband, a boyfriend, a pimp. You don't have to be a detective, or an FBI statistician, to figure out why. You only have to glimpse the systematic, socially sanctioned brutality masked by that mild phrase: "domestic violence."

4

The Language of Love

Women report rape, battery, broken bones, miscarriages, knife and gunshot wounds. Men talk about "marital problems." Women walk around with bruises, brain damage, paralyzed limbs, shredded genitalia, bullets in their heads. Men mention "domestic disputes." Deborah Evans complained to Detective Felix Grabowski of the Roselle, New Jersey, police that Clifton McKenzie had abducted her, assaulted her, and held her prisoner for three days in her apartment, repeatedly slapping her, raping her, and threatening her life. When Detective Grabowski learned that Deborah Evans had formerly lived with McKenzie "in an intimate fashion," he told her to come back next week and advised the prosecutor that there was nothing to prosecute. The following Monday morning, when Deborah Evans headed for the police station again, she disappeared. She was found in the trunk of a car in the parking lot of a motel where McKenzie had overdosed on drugs. He had beaten her up, locked her in the trunk, and left her to freeze to death. Later Detective Grabowski said that in all his years on the force "he had not filed a single domestic violence complaint or report," although he was required to do so by the New Jersey Domestic Violence Act; and he "made a practice of *not* informing victims, such as Evans, of their rights and options under the Act."[1]

Why is it that the violence women endure and describe seems

to so many men—including so many men with the power to do something about it—to be no more than ordinary "marital problems" or "lovers' quarrels," mere skirmishes in what some jokingly call "the battle between the sexes"? Certainly the answer to that question is complex, but part of it lies in the way we conceptualize violence in intimate relationships. The way we *talk* about "the problem" is part of the problem.

Throughout history, men have had things their way, thanks in large part to their strategic use of coercion and violence. And history, as we know, is written by the victors, not the vanquished. Thus, men who shape events also *define* them. When men and women experience an interchange differently, it's men who specify what happened. When men and women look at an event differently, it's men who apply the label. Men are privileged to call an assault an "argument," or rape "making love." Battered women in particular find their violent and terrifying world tamed—domesticated—transformed by gray flannel nametags into a benign, cheery, and vaguely titillating place. They say it makes them crazy.

In defining common experience, batterers are backed up by the best authorities. The "science" of sexology, for example, has assured us, ever since it was invented at the turn of the century, that men find pleasure in inflicting pain on women during sex, and that women welcome it. In *Ideal Marriage*, a book that went through forty-five printings in the United States between 1930 and 1965 and shaped the sex life of generations of middle-class Americans, the Dutch sexologist Van de Velde wrote: "What both man and woman, driven by obscure primitive urges, wish to feel in the sexual act, is the essential force of *maleness*, which expresses itself in a sort of violent and absolute *possession* of the woman. And so both of them can and do exult in a certain degree of male aggression and dominance—whether actual or apparent—which proclaims this essential force." He quotes with approval the opinion of the eminent British sexologist Havelock Ellis that "a certain pleasure in manifesting his power over a woman by inflicting pain upon her" is a "quite normal constituent of the sexual impulse in man"; and, in any event, the "normal manifestations of woman's sexual pleasure are exceedingly like those of pain"—a "very significant fact."[2] From the decidedly male point of view of Ellis and Van de Velde, it was all the same.

Such ideas persist. In *The New Joy of Sex: The Gourmet Guide to Lovemaking for the Nineties*, an updated version of the perennial bestseller, Alex Comfort reminds readers again and again that "our image of love is uptight about the very real elements of aggression in normal sexuality. . . . To need some degree of violence in sex, rather than the glutinous unphysical kind of love which . . . tradition propagates, is statistically pretty normal." (He does not provide the statistics.) In his version of "normal" sexuality, however, women "who dig an extra sensation of violence and/or helplessness" seem to require artificial restraints—being "held down or tied up"—while for men, intercourse itself can be delightfully violent. "Men can take out quite a lot of the violence component," Comfort says, "in the actual process of penetration and working for orgasm." He mentions in passing that "real, spiteful violence from a partner is a common cause of death or injury in women," but he maintains that the masculine "range of needs" for violence is not in itself "scary." Violence "can be stopped spilling out of sex into cruelty," he writes, and while "normal resentments" build up between people who live together, violent sex "tends to discharge them."[3] He doesn't say how.

Psychologists get into the act, too, touting the beneficial effects of aggression. It stands to reason that if a little violence mixed up with sex is good for us, then unalloyed aggression must be positively therapeutic. A whole school of psychology said it was so. The "ventilationists," as they came to be called, became popular in the early 1970s with the publication of several bestselling books proclaiming what seemed then an iconoclastic and "liberating" notion: anger is good for us. Restrain anger, the books said, and it will build up inside like water behind a dam until it suddenly bursts out; better to drain off the "reservoir" by expressing anger whenever you feel it, preferably often. Better to "blow off

→aggression promotes more aggression

steam," "get it off your chest," "let it all hang out." Such spontaneous venting of anger supposedly produced countless benefits: it was said to relieve depression, cure psychosomatic ills, produce "catharsis," make relationships "real," and incidentally get you what you wanted. All over America, therapists' offices filled with angry patients screaming and attacking pillows with fabric bats. (One is reminded of Robert Bly's new Wild Man running out of the woods to "shout and say what he wants.")[4] In 1970, the Book-of-the-Month Club peddled a bestseller, significantly titled *The Intimate Enemy*, which promised to teach readers how to fight with their marriage partner.[5]

The first curious thing to notice about the ventilationists is their assumption that intimate partners are necessarily resentful and hostile—in a word, enemies. This conception of marriage as an adversarial relationship is reminiscent of the American "justice" system which, as we have seen, also proceeds by hostile confrontation. It reminds one, also, of Simone de Beauvoir's famous dictum that for Man, the essential subject, Woman is the inessential object, the Other.[6] It seems that men conceive of the whole of life in terms of opposition, that they simply can't get along without an object who is not only Other but enemy. Robert Bly says the 1950s model of manhood (of which there are many examples around, including Ronald Reagan) "isn't sure that he is alive . . . unless he has an enemy."[7] And Bly too sees the eternal male and female as "opposites" exemplified in flamenco dance: "defender and attacker . . . , attractor and refuser, woman and man. . . . Each is a pole with its separate magnetic charge, each is a nation defending its borders, each is a warrior enjoying the heat of extravagant passion."[8] Bly eagerly leads his followers away from women altogether; his concern is a man's self, not his wife and kids. But the ventilationists, having defined women and men as enemies, advised them how to conduct the battle of their relationship. They defined the antagonism between them as "love."

Unfortunately, there was no scientific evidence for ventilationist theory. It was popularized chiefly by practicing therapists who apparently drew their ideas from their own infuriated patients, while ignoring or distorting the findings of experimental psychology. The authors of *The Intimate Enemy*, for example, cite the famous experiments of psychologist Harry Harlow, who raised monkeys with mechanical surrogate mothers only to find that when they grew up, although they appeared normal in most respects, they didn't play with other monkeys and they didn't reproduce. To the ventilationists the experiment improbably "showed that an exchange of hostilities is *necessary* between mates before there can be an exchange of love."[9] Harlow himself thought it showed that to learn how to interact with others, a monkey needs a *mother*.

Another bestseller (from 1974), with topics like "Fight for Better Sex," counsels: "Lovers who exclude aggression from their bedroom cheat themselves of a total and exciting experience, and in fact will probably be unable to achieve genuine erotic fulfillment."[10] The authors note that married men impotent with their wives have "no problem" with prostitutes with whom they are "not afraid to be themselves" and to "behave aggressively" and make "authentic demands for sexual satisfaction" without having to worry about being "insensitive or harsh."[11] Without having to worry, in other words, about the feelings or desires or "needs" of another *person*.

It can hardly be coincidence that the bestselling anger mongers all were men. In the first place, the easy equation of anger and aggression is not one a woman is likely to make. Aggression may be a basic human drive, as Freud would have it, but it manifests itself in ways shaped by context, by culture, and, as a growing body of psychological research and theory demonstrates, by gender. A man or a woman in the grip of the aggressive drive might just as well ask for a raise, close a business deal, or practice the trombone as get angry. An angry man or woman might take a walk, count to ten, work out, cry, write a letter to a senator, sulk, join a picket line, have a drink, run around the park, go to a meeting of Alcoholics Anonymous, call a friend, mow the lawn. In other words aggression is not anger, and anger need not be expressed aggressively. And when anger is at its worst, the angry woman is more likely to *smile* than to throw a punch, especially if the person she's angry with is bigger than she is.[12]

We can trace the anger mongers' notions back to Freud's contention that "aggressiveness forms the basis of every relation of affection and love among people," but Freud at least noticed that mothers seemed to love their children (their *male* children, he said) *without* aggression.[13] (As always it was women—what *do* they want?—who eluded his rules.) All these years—until the anger mongers came along with their account of "mutual" conflict in marriage—psychology has studied the *absence* of "normal" (read "male") aggression in women as a *problem*. (Indeed, the closest thing to the anger books by and for women at the time was a popular little self-help book called *How to Be an Assertive (Not Aggressive) Woman in Life, in Love, and on the Job* which coached women to overcome "mousiness" without falling into "unfeminine" aggression.[14] More recently, the 1985 bestseller *The Dance of Anger* instructed women *not* to stupidly blow off steam, but rather to manage their anger, firmly and *quietly*.)[15] The world might be different indeed if psychology had studied as a *problem* the presence of abnormal aggression in men, the absence of normal human *care*.[16] But the male psyche—aggression, hostility, anger, and all—has always been taken as the "human" norm.

The ventilationists elevated anger to a therapeutic tool, and what they seemed particularly to like about anger is its single immediate benefit to a *man* in an intimate relationship: it intimidates his partner. Take this pronouncement: "Anger, directly and constructively expressed in a spirit of good will, energizes its communicator and grabs the ear and involvement of the person it is directed against. While it may be threatening to the other person, if it is motivated by a desire to communicate a genuine feeling and not to overwhelm, it creates a communication reality."[17] One wonders how anger can be expressed in a spirit of good will, since anger by definition is what we feel when all good will has flown.

But who can doubt that a threat creates a "communication reality"? Short of a punch or a gunshot (which often follow) a threat is about as real as communication gets.

One may also wonder about the relative size of the "communicator" and the poor person whose ear is grabbed by the communicator's genuine emotion. But the ventilationists proceed as though an angry woman and an angry man ventilating have an equal impact upon an intimate "enemy." Psychologist Carol Tavris notes the danger for women in that false egalitarianism. In her wise book *Anger: The Misunderstood Emotion*, she quotes a rhetorical question from another ventilationist bestseller, this one by a male psychoanalyst: "'Are you aware that your anger will not kill anyone and that no one's anger will kill you?'" And she answers: "Yes, but only because I am a woman who has never been beaten by her husband or father. I imagine that thousands of battered wives in this country would have a far different response."[18] Tavris points out what experimental psychology and our own observations can tell us: "that the people who are most prone to give vent to their rages get *angrier*, not less angry." She concludes that "the major side-effect of the ventilationist approach has been to raise the general noise level of our lives, not to lessen our problems."[19]

In fact the ventilationists have increased the problems of women by foisting upon women and good-natured men a "general" psychological theory apparently based upon nothing more than the experience of some angry male psychologists and their angry patients. And the theory persists in therapeutic practice, even though it has long been discredited in the literature of both psychological research and popular psychology. Psychotherapist Harriet Goldhor Lerner, for example, reported in *The Dance of Anger* in 1985: "The old anger-in/anger-out theory, which states that letting it all hang out offers protection from the psychological hazards of keeping it all pent up, is simply not true."[20] Nevertheless, one woman I interviewed told me that when she persuaded her abusive, alcoholic husband to seek help in 1990, his "therapy," based on ventilationist theory, made things worse. "His therapist said he needed to get his anger out," she reported, "so he was supposed to shout whenever he felt like it. But every time he started shouting, what he shouted was *abuse*—and the more he shouted the more vicious it got. When he got tired of shouting, he'd have a few more drinks and go to sleep; and I'd sit up all night shaking." He felt relieved, she felt terrified. He felt liberated, she felt oppressed. He felt free of anger, she felt furious. "If I'd ever shouted about how mad it made *me* to have to listen to that," she said, "he'd have broken my jaw. But he and his therapist couldn't have been happier about his great progress. They took what I thought was his 'sickness' and made it much worse, and then they called it 'mental health.' Before therapy he was abusive and apologetic; after therapy he was abusive and self-righteous."[21]

Scorning self-control, restraint, politeness, and common civility, ventilationist psychology gave new license to bullies already too free to grab ears. It brought aggression into the bedroom in service of Eros (incidentally, a male god) so that "sensitivity" became dangerously "inhibiting" to the "hostility" necessary for sexually "liberated" love. And it so grabbed the ears of America that we've heard little else for two decades. The self-serving notions of ventilationist psychology so thoroughly became our popular assumptions, that you may not even notice we've passed into the land of doublespeak—the land where violence is love, and vice versa.

Try this bit of doublespeak from *The Intimate Enemy*: "We recognize that there are times when roughness can be pleasurable and sexually stimulating. . . . We believe that the exchange of spanks, blows, and slaps between consenting adults is more civilized than the camouflaged or silent hostilities of ostensibly well-behaved fight-evaders who are 'above it all' . . . Fists, fangs, and fingernails come into play quite naturally for many (and perhaps most) spouses and lovers."[22] So physical *blows* are both "natural" and "civilized"; and friendly, peaceable, good-natured folks are just devious "fight-evaders," secretly seething. Clearly, for placid men and women, this is a no-win situation.

Some ventilationists even rose to defend batterers. Take, for example, this lament for the plight of the poor wife beater, perse-

cuted by strident victims and by a society which unreasonably
considers him a criminal. (The authors use the euphemism "mate
beating" and throw in an unconvincing female example, but it's
evident that they have wife beating in mind.)

> Everybody is against mate beating. Legal and moral author-
> ity encourage the righteous protests of its victims. "How
> dare you hit me!" they shout. Or, "You must be insane!" Or,
> "Only a coward would beat a woman!" Or, "No real lady
> would attack a man!" And even though a tongue lashing may
> hurt more than physical violence, a physical fight between
> adults constitutes criminal assault and places anyone who
> switches from verbal to physical blows *at a great disadvantage*.
> He may become a *target of shame* and condemnation and may
> even *provide the victim with an excuse to exit* and "win" a di-
> vorce. Unfortunately, society's judgment does not help
> people understand why many perfectly "civilized" partners
> *occasionally blow their cool* and turn to violence. The fact is that
> such violence *may not be irrational*. Like the violence perpe-
> trated by the American colonists against the British crown
> in revolutionary times, it may be a desperate bid to be taken
> seriously when nonviolent measures failed. It may be a *cor-
> nered* mate's last stand, a final attempt to show *deep concern*.[23]

This is doublespeak with patriotic frills: battering and the Boston
tea party, wife beating as revolutionary duty—though you'll recall
that the colonists sought freedom *from* tyranny.

But it gets worse: "Intimate fighters should also understand the
psychoanalytic discovery that people sometimes unconsciously desire to get hurt. . . . There are people who all but specialize in
getting beaten, exploited, robbed, or raped."[24] (Here we arrive at
another popular, and untenable, position: *blaming the victim*, about
which I'll have more to say in the next chapter.) Sex becomes violent, and violence sexy. We're not talking sadomasochism here;
this advice arrived courtesy of the Book-of-the-Month Club, not
in a plain brown wrapper. We're talking ordinary everyday normal
"erotic fulfillment" for Mr. and Mrs. Middle America. But so

snarled become the conceptions of sex and violence that the terms "sadism" and "masochism," which used to distinguish certain extraordinary practices from "normal" sex, become meaningless. And we are only a step away from the so-called "rough sex" murders: women choked to death, smothered with duct tape, strangled, and mutilated because *they* got "carried away" with sex.[25] What could be trendier? And the trend continues. As Alex Comfort puts it in his "gourmet guide to lovemaking for the nineties": "If you haven't learned that sexual violence can be tender and tenderness violent, you haven't begun to play as real lovers."[26]

This thrilling intermingling of sex and violence is familiar to millions of women steeped in the ideology of modern romance, piped in like nerve gas through television, movies, pop music, "women's" magazines, paperback romance novels, and advertising. It's always some variation on the same old story: some beautiful woman (an Elizabethan virgin, a neolithic cavewoman, a stockbroker, an astronaut, etc.) breaks through the ruthless, arrogant crust of the violent, untamed, craggy-faced hero (named something like Damian Savage or Stone Fury) to find the warm, sweet, cuddly, soft-hearted teddy bear within by the sheer "power" of her selfless love for him, and then is swept away, surrendering passively, breathlessly, to the overwhelming force of his bruising but tender passion. This is a fairy tale, of course, but such a pervasive one that it impinges upon real life. For one thing, it inspires many an abused woman to keep "working on" her "relationship" with an arrogant crust, waiting in vain for the non-existent teddy bear to put in an appearance. And it inspires bystanders to overlook violence in anticipation of the joyful ending. When Peter Martins, artistic director of the New York City Ballet, was arrested for assaulting his wife, the ballerina Darci Kistler, a spokesman for the company dismissed the incident as a "personal matter" and said: "People hope that they can live happily ever after."[27]

While women succumb to novels of sexy "smoldering" (suppressed) violence, men enjoy scenarios of violent sex, or plain violence, in which men do *whatever they want* to others, usually women.[28] Men study pornography. They get off on the fabulous fantasy at its heart—the fantasy of dominating and totally controlling another human being. The pornography industry—which sociologist Michael Kimmel describes as "men producing images for men to consume"—is a billion dollar business in the United States, and growing all the time.[29] Its customers are millions of *normal* men. There can be no doubt that it affects the lives of all of us. In his famous studies of American sexual behavior, Alfred Kinsey found that pornography was one of the most common sources of a boy's first information about sexuality, and today, as Michael Kimmel notes, pornography "is one of the major sources of sexual information that young males have about sexuality, and thus a central mechanism by which our sexuality has been constructed."[30]

Campaigning against pornography during the last decade, radical feminists charged that pornography *is* violence against women (real women are coerced and raped in the making of it), that it *causes* violence against women, and that it numbs consumers to the violence around us. A great many of the abused women I have interviewed during the last fifteen years—survivors of battery, rape, incest, attempted murder—described their male partners as pornography consumers, who in many cases coerced them to act out the pictures.[31] (Indeed, it would be hard to find better instruction manuals for batterers than those for sale at any local porn shop.) These painful firsthand accounts, describing a direct causal connection between pornography and violent "sex," are discounted by social scientists as merely anecdotal evidence; but research psychologists now confirm that "experimental evidence is clear with respect to the effects of [aggressive] pornography"—that is, pornography which shows "injury, torture, bleeding, bruised, or hurt women in sexual contexts."[32] Researchers Edward Donnerstein and Daniel Linz report that while "research over the last decade" demonstrates that sexual images in themselves don't seem to facilitate aggressive behavior, the impact of *"aggressive pornography"* and *"sexually violent mass media images"* is quite different.

Research shows that "exposure to aggressive pornography increases aggression against women in a laboratory context."[33]

Even if this were not so, even if the worst that could be said of pornography was that it provided "young males" with "sexual information," it would still be a danger to women; for the information it provides is that sex is violent and violence sexy, and the total control of another person is sexiest of all. And it is this intoxicating concoction of violence and sex and tyranny that misguides "young males" and provides both a violent scenario and a sexy justification for the batterer, or indeed for the average man. For example, in 1981 when Bernadette Powell appealed her conviction for the murder of her husband, the prosecuting attorney admitted that the dead man had in the past repeatedly assaulted Powell, but this fact, he wrote in his legal brief, *"regardless of her acquiescence or lack of it,"* was "not any proof of . . . violence toward her" or grounds for her to have any "reasonable fear" of injury because the man's assaults were *"sexually motivated."*[34]

To see things as the district attorney did in this case, you have to see them from the point of view of the dead man—which the justices did—and *not* from the point of view of the woman who, if the act of shooting her husband is any indication, saw his sexually motivated assaults quite differently. (Her view didn't count; her appeal was denied and her sentence of fifteen years to life confirmed.)[35] But how could she have expected to be heard? The pornographic conflation of sex and violence is a product of the male imagination—("men producing images for men to consume")—a version of sexuality that overrides the desires of women, threatens our integrity, restricts our choices, demeans our humanity, endangers our lives, and silences our protests. Civil libertarians, of course, defend pornography as free speech, but it is a peculiar kind of free speech by and for men which can exist only by silencing the speech of women.

I call particular attention to the many ways in which pornography impinges on women's lives because it is all the more difficult for women to secure freedom from bodily harm when our free speech is silenced on the very subjects we must shout about. The speech of Bernadette Powell, for one, was silenced when her husband tied her up and raped her, and again when the prosecutor labeled that assault *sex*, not *violence*, and again when the judge discounted her evidence and sentenced her to prison, and again when the justices of the New York State Supreme Court upheld that conviction. Somehow sexual motives make violence okay—which must be what the Milwaukee cops thought, too, when they returned a dazed, naked, and bleeding fourteen-year-old boy to the custody of his "lover" Jeffrey Dahmer. Konerak Sinthasomphone became Dahmer's thirteenth murder victim.[36]

Young people learn from other sources, too, that sex and violence go together. TV, movies, videos, the latest mainstream ads for jeans or perfume, pop songs and rap (with their pornographic record jackets) all help to construct a world of sexy violence and violent sex. Take, for example, this heavy metal "love" song recorded by "Sarcofago" on the Kraze label:

> Tracy you hurt me and broke my heart . . .
> Putting my lust and feelings apart
> Tracy i loved you and didn't wanna do it.
> Your rotten flesh is now so sweet
> Too cold you are driving me to a intense orgasm
> Licking your body i realize my dream
> Why did you force me to kill?[37]

Or consider a 1991 NWA (Niggas with Attitude) album which includes songs such as "Findum, Fuckum & Flee," "She Swallowed It" (lyric: "If you've got a gang of niggas, the bitch will let you rape her"), "To Kill a Hooker," and "One Less Bitch," the last a song about tying a "bitch" to a bed, fucking her, then blowing her away with a forty-five.[38] Or this 1990 rap from The Geto Boys:

> Her body's beautiful so I'm thinking rape,
> grabbed the bitch by the mouth, drug her back 'n
> slam her down on the couch, whipped out my
> knife, said if you scream I'll cut you, opened her

legs and commenced to fuckin', she begged me not
to kill her, I gave her a rose, then slit her
throat and watched her shake 'til her eyes closed,
had sex with her of course before I left her, and
drew my name on the wall like helter skelter.[39]

Disc jockeys at the radio station of Mount Holyoke College, the oldest women's college in the country, told me that record promoters are amazed and angry when the women refuse to play these songs on the air. "All the other schools play 'em," the promoters say.[40]

Whatever our sources of information or entertainment, it seems, we can't escape the peculiar amalgam of sex and violence that is now widely regarded as normal love. Expressing this "love," men batter and rape and kill women. When Alan Matheney broke into Lisa Bianco's house in 1987 to beat and rape her, he told her he was doing it because he loved her. At a sentencing hearing, Matheney's attorney explained his client to the judge this way: "Mr. Matheney, I don't know why, could never let go of this woman. . . . Just to call it love would be wrong. Although I'm sure that's what Al perceives it as. I perceive it as an obsession. A love obsession."[41] When Matheney beat Lisa Bianco to death two years later, he did it because he still *loved* her.

After Michael Cartier gunned down Kristin Lardner in Boston in May 1992 and then killed himself, a friend of his told a reporter: "He loved her a lot and it was probably a crime of passion." Lardner had ended what the friend called "their relationship" because she wanted to date other people; she had known Cartier two months and was afraid of him. "He was in love," said Cartier's friend. "He didn't do it because he's nuts."[42] Kristin Lardner's roommate and best friend said that Lardner had done just what abused women are advised to do: she stopped dating Cartier after the first incident of abuse, and when he persisted, knocking her down in the street and kicking her into unconsciousness, she got a restraining order. Yet even Lardner's friend still bought the "romantic" view of Cartier's violence. She said that Kristin Lardner "cared" about Cartier, "and she was the only one who ever did. That's what pushed him over the edge . . . when he lost her."[43] But Rose Ryan, Cartier's former girlfriend, had cared about him too and tried for months to redeem him with love and kindness and Christmas presents before she brought the assault charges that got him jailed for six months. Rose Ryan is a valuable witness to the "lovemaking" of Michael Cartier. "After he hit me several times in the head," she said, "he started to cry." He would say, "I'm so sorry. I always hit the people I love." And the hook: "My mother, she never loved me. You're the only one."[44] It's a confusing and powerful message for a woman—when two things we believed to be incompatible, "love" and violence, become inextricably snarled.

It's a confusing message for journalists, too, whose job it is to describe clearly to us what's going on in our world. The muddling of sex and violence has knocked the meaning out of so many perfectly good words—or "gendered" them—that these days when crimes of violence against women are reported in magazines and newspapers, women have to read between the lines. Rape, assault, and even murder are crazily described in the language of "love"— as though Miss Lonelyhearts were working the police beat. This is not merely a semantic problem. It has measurable consequences in the lives—and deaths—of women.[45]

Take, for example, this item reported in the *Baltimore Sun* in June 1989: "Kevin Lee Kern received the maximum 10-year sentence yesterday for strangling his wife in what he said was a *fit of jealous rage* last year, after he *collected* her from a bar, punched her, *made love* to her in the woods near their home, then was told their youngest child wasn't his." The euphemism "made love" is currently so commonplace a term for rape as to be unremarkable. But what degree of force is masked by that odd, innocent word "collected"? Batterers very often display pathological jealousy, accuse "their" women of infidelity, and force them to "confess" that children were fathered in adultery; and it's impossible to tell from the newspaper account of the courtroom proceedings whether Denise

Kern's revelation was either voluntary or true.[46] In any event, Kevin Kern choked Denise Kern for "five minutes or possibly longer," which, as the judge observed, "is a very lengthy period of time." Time enough, one would think, for even the most impassioned and jealous "lover" to collect his wits, but the jury was remarkably generous. They declined to convict Kevin Kern of murder, opting for simple manslaughter instead. "This is a very fine line that was drawn between second-degree murder and manslaughter," the judge said, "as fine a line as I can conceive a jury ever drawing."[47]

Doubtless the jury was influenced by the defense attorney's argument that "Kevin Kern *loved* his wife, Denise. His support for his wife, his *love* for his wife, his *willingness to stay with her* were evident in his life." All this although he was "devastated by his wife's drinking and broken promises to quit." The judge, in possession of a presentence report which revealed that Kevin Kern had had "a serious drinking problem since his teens, several drunk driving arrests and drug use, including LSD, PCP, amphetamines and marijuana," was less charitable; he handed down the maximum ten year sentence.[48] And when Kern sought in 1991 to have his sentence reduced so that he might spend more time with his motherless children, the court turned him down. (Like so many other intensely controlling men, however, Kern is a model prisoner, eminently respectful of those who temporarily have power over him; his "good" behavior will almost certainly win him early parole.)[49] At the time of sentencing, Kern was still living with his three children, eight, five, and three years old. Apparently it occurred to no one to suggest that an alcoholic drug addict who assaulted and killed the children's mother might be an unfit parent, especially for the child whose very existence had made him mad enough to kill. But why should anyone think him a murderer, and why should anyone think him an unfit father when his *problem* is defined as an excess of *love* and his murderous rage as only a normal *passion?*

What could be more useful to "aggressive" men than this confusion of sex/love and violence? It gives a man an excuse for assault: "I did it because I love you so much." It gives a woman an explanation—"He did it only because he loves me so much"— which snares her in forgiveness, understanding, compassion: staying on. (Writer John Stoltenberg observes: "Forgiveness from a woman represents her continued commitment to be present for him, to stay in relationship to him, enabling him to remain by contrast *male*."[50] Forgiveness is the visible sign of his total control.) The confusion of sex/love and violence gives all of us— newspaper readers, television viewers, jurors, voters, taxpayers— an *understanding*: things happened that way because he loved her so much.

All these misconceptions and self-delusions persuade us that "a certain amount" of "fighting" is "normal" in relationships, just as a certain amount of swatting and shaking children passes for "discipline." But if *some* physical violence is acceptable, how much is too much? Where is the line? Are we to draw it as we do in the boxing ring—no punches below the belt? No jabs to the kidneys? Or shall we follow the rule so many batterers use: body blows only, where the bruises don't show?

On this question—how much is too much?—the battered woman is as confused as everyone else, and with good reason. She lives in the gaslit zone of doublespeak. The rapist/batterer says to her: "I wouldn't do this if I didn't love you so much." Or: "You made me do it." Or: "Where did you get that black eye?" Or: "What black eye?" Then the cop looks straight into her bloody face and says, "What seems to be the trouble here?" The marriage counselor suggests: "Why don't you help him get his anger out?" The clergyman asks: "What did you do to make him angry?" Meanwhile, to keep the peace, to get through, she gives way here and there. She compromises. She tries to understand, to be loving, to be strong, to care, to cope. Faced with what seems the hard prospect of being a woman alone, or a woman alone with her children, she submits—not in spite of the violence but because of it. Then the abuse becomes too much, and although she knows it's not her fault, she knows she's implicated. She hears about "victims of domestic violence," but she can't think of herself as a *vic-*

tim. Because she *did* provoke him. She *did* get angry with him. She *did* refuse to do what he wanted. She hears about "battered women," but surely she is not *that*. *They* are "passive" and "helpless"; but she is a strong woman, trying to hold her own. *They* get hit because they're "passive"; but she gets hit because she doesn't do what he wants. She keeps trying as best she can to work out her "marital problems." After all, he loves her.

Actress Robin Givens tried to work out "marital problems" with heavyweight champion Mike Tyson in what reporters jokingly referred to as "The Tyson-Givens fight." After they "broke up," Tyson, who had just knocked out a challenger in ninety-three seconds flat with a punch he said "wasn't that hard," allegedly stalked Givens, turning up at her home, sometimes to tell her he loved her, sometimes to "whack her around." (Referring to an attack in May 1989, "a source close to Givens" told a *TV Guide* reporter: "He didn't break anything—just injured her.") Givens tried to describe Tyson's stalking to the reporter. She said, "The phone rings night and day . . . and it's him." She said that when she worked, he would come to the location, wait "patiently" until she was finished, and take her back to her hotel. He showed up unexpectedly at her house. "I never know when he's going to be there," she said. "He might be there now." The reporter wrote that Givens spoke of these things with "a mixture of fear and longing on her face."[51]

Mike Tyson, as the world now knows, is a dangerous man—dangerous to women precisely because sex and violence seem to be all the same to him. When he was brought to trial in January 1992, charged with rape, confinement, and "criminal deviate conduct," Miss Black Rhode Island told the jury that Tyson had pinned her on a bed with his forearm, stripped her, and raped her. She testified: "I said, 'Please, you're hurting me! Please, stop!' And he started laughing, like it was a game."[52] It was her word against his, of course: her word "rape" against his word "sex." (He claimed she was a "one night stand" who got mad because he was too tired to walk her downstairs after the "lovemaking.") But Tyson was convicted on all three counts, largely because the jury found his eighteen-year-old victim an unimpeachable witness—a remarkably pretty, outgoing, and intelligent high school honor student and college scholarship winner who taught Sunday School, coached the youth softball team, assisted the mentally retarded as a volunteer, and served as an usher at her church.[53] She was everybody's idea of what a "nice" young lady ought to be, and she was absolutely clear about what Mike Tyson had done to her. Tyson was sentenced to six years, and with good behavior will probably serve three.[54]

Robin Givens, on the other hand, was never taken seriously because she had spoken so often in the early days of her relationship with Tyson about the "romantic" notions that got her into the marriage: "The thrill . . . the danger." She said that when she talked "too much," Tyson told her to shut up. When she didn't want to get in the car, Tyson picked her up and put her in. "Wow!" she said, "I was definitely attracted to that." (This drama is an updated version of *Gone With the Wind*.) "I think what people don't realize with a certain type of woman," Givens said, "is that there are times when she wants the man she is with to be . . . a man." Then again, there apparently are times when even Robin Givens would rather *not* shut up, *not* get in the car. Who gets to decide? Where is the line? And who draws it? Givens talked about the way Tyson tracked her, and the *TV Guide* reporter wrote: "Every confusing emotion of Robin Givens' own internal struggle is evident, even in the twinkle of her eyes."[55]

But the "struggle" is not Robin Givens's alone. It's a struggle imposed on all women by a culture that muddles sex and violence, considers "hostility" and "blows" in marriage both "natural" and "civilized," pronounces the angriest among us the most "healthy," calls terrorism "love," and then projects this monumental obfuscation onto individual women, labeled "crazy" for "love."

Not that men don't go "crazy" for "love" too—like Kevin Kern—but when they do, it's a *tragedy*. We're supposed to understand and sympathize with them. (Imagine how poor Kevin Kern must have felt, being told the child wasn't his!) And poor Donnie Moore. On July 18, 1989, he shot his battered wife Tonya three times and then killed himself. That "tragedy," like Mike Tyson's rape, was covered in the sports pages because Donnie Moore was the former California Angels' pitcher who gave up a home run that cost the team a decisive game in the 1986 American League playoffs. Tonya Moore had left her husband a month before the shooting, complaining to the neighbors that he beat her; and miraculously she survived, thanks to her seventeen-year-old daughter who drove her to the hospital. A reader could learn the condition of Tonya Moore from the wire service accounts, *after* wading through all the details of that crucial eleven-inning game against the Red Sox *and* the two subsequent games that put Boston in the 1986 World Series. Donnie Moore's "friends and teammates" mentioned that he had "marital problems" and "financial strains," but his real problem was said to be this: "He could not live with himself after Henderson hit the home run. He kept blaming himself." The *New York Times* headlined this tragedy: "A Ballplayer's Life Turns on a Home Run."[56] (And his wife's life?)

And what about poor Felix Key, the New York City cop who on May 19, 1989, dragged his "girlfriend," Jean Singleton, into the street in front of police headquarters, shot her four times, killing her, and then killed himself. Jean Singleton reportedly had been trying to end the relationship, saying that Officer Key was "too jealous and overprotective," and the police had "disciplined" Officer Key before for threatening another woman at gunpoint; yet the Police Department's official spokesperson (a woman) described the killings as "a lover's quarrel between the two of them."[57] Nobody used the term "murder." And the *New York Post* ran a banner headline on the front page: "Tragedy of a Lovesick Cop."[58]

Surely the fact that people lost their lives in these incidents gives them greater significance than the "Tyson-Givens fight." Yet isn't there a curious imbalance here? Why is a man "crazed" by love tragic, a woman merely crazy? Why is it that even when a man murders a woman, or tries to, the tragedy is somehow *his*? And when the heavyweight champion of the world whacks his wife around, why is it her responsibility and a great joke besides? This double standard alone is enough to make women crazy.

One of the most popular films of the last decade, *Fatal Attraction,* reverses typical sex roles; "nice guy" Michael Douglas, trying to end an adulterous fling and keep his wife in the dark, is stalked by Glenn Close, a woman who won't be flung out. She practices many of the batterer's favorite techniques: harassing phone calls, unexpected appearances at home and work, killing pets, abducting children, faking suicide, assault with deadly weapons. And theater audiences scream with terror and sympathy for poor Michael Douglas, haunted by this deranged bitch from hell. Formerly battered women, watching the film, rarely scream in the right places, for they are watching *their* experience and *their* terror—with the gender turned upside down. One bewildered woman I interviewed asked, "How come when I was going through shit like that nobody saw it from my point of view?"[59] Good question.

The point is that as long as "a certain amount" of sexual and physical "fighting" is thought natural, civilized, desirable, or necessary in marriage, violence will always be thought to occur with the woman's consent, the woman's provocation, the woman's solicitation, the woman's pleasure, just as rape was once thought to be provoked, solicited, consciously desired, and subconsciously needed by women victims of rape. Battering (which commonly includes marital rape), like stranger rape, is a crime of power and control committed mainly by men against women, a crime in which the perpetrator does not consult the victim's wishes and from which he will not let her escape.

But rape and battery are different crimes. Stranger rape is an isolated act of violence, while battery recurs within a continuing relationship in which the woman appears to be a full participant, a consenting adult, a collaborator.[60] So it seems, but in any relationship with a violent person, there can be no such thing as full and *equal* participation. What the battered woman participates in, as best she can, is an effort to regain the relationship she once had and hopes to have again—(Didn't he promise?)—the relationship *without* the violence. Trying to save a marriage, or save her life, or save her children, a battered woman may submit to violence, just as a rape victim may submit to rape for fear of being killed. But submission is not *consent*.

Still, to some, the distinction seems a fine one; and it's confusing precisely because we still accept that "certain amount of fighting" in marriage. Think of the messages a battered woman receives: A good marriage is worth fighting for. You can't just walk out at the first sign of trouble. It's up to you to make it work. He needs you. Stand by your man. For better or worse. Til death do us part. Love means never having to say you're sorry. A good man is hard to find. Good husbands are made by God, good marriages by women. Children need their father. You owe it to him to help him through this. And so on, ad nauseam. And don't forget, he *loves* you.

How much is too much? It's *never* the battered woman who gets to decide. A violent man backed up by all the coercive force of our male-defined world tells her to stay, and if she complains, we say: "She's a participant, a consenting adult, a collaborator." An African-American woman I interviewed, the mother of four boys, was convinced by her family, her church, and her black pride that she had to make her marriage work. She was determined not to fall into what she called "the white folks' stereotype" of the black family: "mama on welfare and a bunch of delinquent fatherless children." She said, "I put up with violence all those years trying *not* to be that welfare mother white folks hate, and then those same white folks had the nerve to turn around and tell me I should've left my husband and applied for welfare." Black or white, that's always the kicker. The all-purpose question: "If she doesn't like it, why doesn't she leave?" The final obfuscation. Designed to make us think that she too finds "a certain amount of fighting" just fine.

And when a woman does try to escape, do we help her? Rose Ryan, the young woman who escaped Michael Cartier, told a reporter: "They can pass as many laws as they want, but until people decide to get involved, nothing's going to change. Michael beat me around the corner from where he killed Kristin, people were there in the street, kicked me in the face with steel-toed boots when I was on the ground. Nobody did a thing. He punched me in the mouth in the subway, in front of all kinds of people. Again, nothing."[61]

For battered women, it's damned if you do, damned if you don't. And it will be so, until we can say—as we now say of rape—battering is *always* wrong, no matter who the woman is or what she does, no matter what she provokes or solicits or submits to or consents to or consciously desires or subconsciously needs, and no matter how much the assailant *loves* her. Robin Givens's "internal struggle" is one private version of what has become, as battered women compare notes, an external, public, political struggle for recognition of what they have learned the hard way: all women have an absolute right to be free from bodily harm, the language of love notwithstanding.

Why Doesn't She Leave?

When we look again at the facts—millions of women battered every year, a woman battered every few seconds, thousands of women murdered every year by the men they live with—and when we consider what a fundamental right it is to be able to live, just to *be*, free of harm inside one's own skin, then the next question should be obvious: why hasn't this violence been stopped? Any reasonable person has to ask: What can we do to prevent it?

But as it turns out, that's not the question reasonable people ask. We ask instead: *Why doesn't she leave?*

Take Dan Rather, for example. For the CBS network show "48 Hours" he interviewed Tracey Thurman in her kitchen in Torrington, Connecticut, in 1988. Charles Thurman, who had been sentenced to twenty years for his attempt to kill Tracey, was scheduled to become eligible for parole in 1990, and Tracey Thurman explained to Rather how she felt about the possibility of his release. "I know that he's going to come back after me, and that frightens me," she said. "And it just scares me to think that I'm going to have to live like I lived for eight months, when I was going through the separation. I mean, a nervous wreck; my child I didn't allow to go outside . . . for his own protection. And I know one day I'm going to have to go through all that again. Hopefully this time they'll be there on time, and they'll be able to protect me. Hopefully. But I know that he's determined, and

I know he has stated right in the courtroom, and his father got on the stand and said that he said that he will finish the job. And he has stated in several things that both of us can't live in this world, and he's not going to be the one to go. What frightens me most is the fear that—him ever hurting my child. That scares me. Just the thought of . . . If he was ever to get to me, I would rather him just—I mean, then finish the job then, because I could never deal with another beating like this. You know, I mean, I—how much more handicapped could I be?"[1]

Since that interview Tracey Thurman has learned to live with fear, for Buck Thurman was released in April 1991 to a Connecticut halfway house, having served seven years and ten months of his twenty year sentence. He was placed on closely supervised probation for five years.[2] His parental rights were terminated. Tracey Thurman, who still lives in Torrington, has become a compelling and articulate voice for battered women in Connecticut, but she can no longer travel freely around the state as she could when Buck was behind bars. Testifying before the Senate Judiciary Committee in December 1990 on behalf of the proposed Violence Against Women Act, Tracey Thurman said, "Because of what I've experienced with him, I know he's going to find me."[3] Now, day in, day out, with her second husband and her son, Tracey Thurman Motuzick must plan always for her safety.[4]

But when Dan Rather interviewed Tracey Thurman, he had a suggestion, one he perhaps guessed would occur to thousands of his viewers. "Why not move away?" he asked. "Why not get a long, long way?"[5]

The familiar question. Why doesn't she just walk away?—this disfigured and terribly handicapped woman whom the television viewers have watched struggling with her physical therapy exercises and the monumental task of frying an egg? Why doesn't she take her little boy and just leave? Again.

Tracey Thurman had an answer. She said: "Why should I? You know . . . I grew up here. . . . My family is here, my support is here. . . . I can go to another state, but even if I was in Hawaii and I had heard that he was getting out, my son would still be glued to me. I mean I would be scared to death. I mean, if he really wants me that bad—it's awful morbid—but if he really wants me that bad, he's that determined, he's going to find me no matter where I go. And I feel as though here, the Torrington police department don't want to mess up again. They don't want to look like they made themselves look the first time."[6]

But of course it's the question, not the chilling and sensible answer, that sticks in the mind. It suggests that Tracey Thurman's life is entirely in her own hands, that the violence of the man she once married, the man she left, is *her* problem, *her* responsibility. What does it mean to "leave"? How far does a woman have to go? And how many times?

Despite the immense achievements of the battered women's movement in the past fifteen years, those who work to stop violence against women—those who staff the hotlines and the shelters and the legal service centers, those who press to make law enforcement and criminal justice act responsibly, those who lobby for legislative reform—know that the next time a woman is battered in the United States (which is to say within the next twelve seconds) few people will ask: What's wrong with that man? What makes him think he can get away with that? Is he crazy? Did the cops arrest him? Is he in jail? When will he be prosecuted? Is he likely to get a serious sentence? Is she getting adequate police protection? Are the children provided for? Did the court evict him from her house? Does she need any other help? Medical help maybe, or legal aid? New housing? Temporary financial aid? Child support?

No, the first question, and often the only question, that leaps to mind is: *Why doesn't she leave?*

This question, which we can't seem to stop asking, is not a *real* question. It doesn't call for an answer; it makes a judgment. It mystifies. It transforms an immense social problem into a personal transaction, and at the same time pins responsibility squarely on the victim. It obliterates both the terrible magnitude of violence against women and the great achievements of the movement against it. It simultaneously suggests two ideas, both of them false: that help is readily available to all *worthy* victims (which is to say, victims who leave), and that *this* victim is not one of them.

So powerful and dazzling is this question that someone always tries to answer it. And the answer given rarely is the simple truth you find in the stories of formerly battered women: She does leave. She is leaving. She left. No, so mystifying is the question that someone always tries to explain why she doesn't leave even *after she has left.* This exchange takes place remarkably often on television talk shows and news programs—as it did on "48 Hours"— heavily influencing the way the public thinks about battered women. Let me give you another example.

In October 1987 the local New York City affiliate of the CBS television network included in the nightly news a segment on the case of Karen Straw, a twenty-nine-year-old woman about to stand trial for murder. Karen Straw had left her husband Clifton in 1984, after a three-year marriage, and moved with her two children to a welfare hotel. She wanted a divorce, but she couldn't afford one. For more than two years, her husband harassed and beat her although she obtained orders of protection from the court and tried at least ten times to have him arrested and prosecuted. In December 1986 he broke into her room, beat her, raped her at knifepoint in front of the children, and threatened to kill her. She got hold of a kitchen knife and stabbed him. She was charged with second degree murder, the heaviest charge the state could bring against her since New York reserves first degree murder charges for murders of police officers and prison guards.[7] The WCBS report filed by reporter Bree Walker, a woman, showed footage of Karen Straw, the Queens courthouse where she was to be tried, and short bites of three interviews prerecorded separately with Michael Dowd, a prominent attorney who had volunteered to defend Straw; Madelyn Diaz, a woman previously acquitted of all charges after killing her assaultive husband (a police officer);[8] and me. Introduced by Jim Jensen, the anchorman, the segment went like this.

JIM JENSEN: This is a problem society has never really learned to deal with: women who are physically abused by their husbands. This evening we take a closer look at this problem and the way some women are finally getting some help. Bree Walker has more.

BREE WALKER (*REPORTER*): Jim, it's a painful closer look at this black eye on society, how the cuts and bruises suffered by women with abusive husbands are usually overlooked, but when women finally stop suffering in silence and turn to desperate measures like murder, no one can overlook that, especially in court where once again the plea of self-defense will be tested.

Tomorrow this woman, Karen Straw, faces the trial of her life. The charge: second degree murder. The penalty: life in prison. Karen Straw allegedly killed her husband after escaping to a shabby welfare apartment where she lived with her two children. She says she turned a knife on him after he broke in and raped her at knifepoint. After two years of repeated attacks, her attorney says she had no other way out.

MICHAEL DOWD (*ATTORNEY*): She went to the family court. She had him arrested in the criminal court. She called the police numerous times. She moved away from him. And nothing that she did stopped him from coming back, beating her, threatening her, hospitalizing her, raping her.

ANN JONES: She'd done everything a battered woman can do to get out of that situation and to get the criminal justice system to be responsive and responsible for her safety. But it still didn't work. They still didn't protect her.

WALKER: . . . Both [Jones] and Straw's attorney agree: the only protection our society provided Karen was a flimsy paper shield.

DOWD: She was given a piece of paper—what we call an order of protection. It's as if we gave her a crucifix to defend herself against a vampire.

WALKER: The story of Karen Straw begins to unfold here tomorrow at her trial in Supreme Court. But it's a story that's hardly unique. She's only one of many battered wives who turn to violence as a last defense. A common thread ties many of these women together. They are victims not only of abusive husbands but of weak criminal justice, of a system that again and again failed them until finally it was too late. We've seen it in newspapers and on television. A movie called "The Burning Bed" told the story of Francine Hughes, a Michigan housewife who poured gasoline around the bed of her husband and lit a match, leaving him to die in the flames. And two years ago a Bronx woman said her husband left her no alternative.

MADELYN DIAZ: I just remembered what he had threatened me. He said if I didn't change my mind in the next few hours that he would kill me and the baby.

WALKER: Sympathetic juries in both cases found these women not guilty, but experts say cases like these shouldn't have to even go that far.

JONES: Battered women are denied protection. Battering men are not arrested. They're not locked up for any substantial length of time.

DOWD: There's no question in my mind that Karen Straw was acting justifiably. She defended herself in her own home. Hopefully twelve honest people will give her something that the professionals couldn't—and that's some fairness and justice and a chance to live her life.

WALKER: The one positive note to this tragic song that plays too often is that support [systems] like victim service agencies, hospitals, and church outreach groups seem to be making a difference. The numbers show women murdering husbands and boyfriends is the only type of homicide that has in fact decreased in the last ten years. So perhaps we can say that where the courts have left off, individuals have picked up.

That ended Walker's prerecorded report. Wrapping it up, anchorman Jensen leaned toward reporter Walker, sitting beside him in the studio, and asked the standard question, the one everybody always asks: Why didn't she leave? Jensen phrased it this way: "Why would one murder her husband instead of just walking away?" The question was particularly remarkable, for it didn't match Bree Walker's report or the circumstances of Karen Straw's life at all.

But even more remarkable was reporter Walker's reply. As though the facts lay not in her own report but in the anchorman's irrelevant question, Bree Walker began to explain why Karen Straw, a woman who *had* walked away, had not. "There are a lot of different reasons psychologists say—helplessness, dependence, a lot of different reasons. A lot of women feel . . . "

Jensen interrupted: "Well, if they're dependent on them, when they kill 'em, they've lost their dependence, haven't they?" He sounded angry, as if he were scolding Walker for her point of view. Walker, looking startled, responded, "Well, certainly. Yes. It's an ugly, ugly confusing problem." There was a moment's awkward airspace before anchorwoman Carol Martin jumped in. "Well, from that subject we'll move on," she said. "Still ahead, we'll talk about the rain . . . ."[9]

But Jensen's question still hung in the air: "Why would one murder her husband instead of just walking away?" It enveloped the story in a fog of mystification. Clifton Straw's violence and terrorism disappeared in that puff of rhetoric, utterly overlooked. Vanished too was the public issue reporter Walker had presented, magically replaced by the personal problem of another dumb woman. Viewers did not have to question the failure of the police and courts to protect this woman; they could think instead that

Karen Straw might simply have walked away. Just when viewers were beginning to feel indignant on her behalf, they could say to themselves instead: "How stupid of her. Why didn't she think of that?"

I told this story about the TV program to a very smart, very successful network television producer, a woman, of my acquaintance. "Don't you think Jim Jensen's comments were outrageous?" I asked.

"You're too hard on men," she said. "You can't expect men who've never been that scared of another person to understand why battered women can't leave. You have to be patient and explain to them that it was fear, not just dependence, that made her stay with him."

"Wait a minute," I said, taken aback. "You didn't *hear* the story either. The point is that this woman *didn't* stay. She was outta there. Gone. Goodbye. She *left*."

My friend looked puzzled. "Then how did she get raped?"

Karen Straw was acquitted of all charges against her by jurors who heard the whole story; and she was released to gather up the tatters of her life.[10] But that familiar, trivializing question—the question that obscures both the extent of violence against women and the immense individual and collective efforts of women to overcome it—doesn't go away. It contains the whole history of woman beating in America. And our response to it shapes the future.

In 1966 Dr. William Ryan, a psychologist who'd taught at Harvard and Yale Medical Schools and Boston College, wrote an impassioned book which has rightfully become a classic. Its title—*Blaming the Victim*—is now a phrase tossed about in everyday conversation, but because it has been cut loose from Ryan's careful analysis, it's helpful to look again at what he wrote—especially because so many of the social problems he noticed have only grown worse. Ryan was concerned about America's "oppressed," by which he meant the underclass of black and poor people, and about the way America typically approached "solutions" to "social problems" that seemed to afflict them—problems of education, health care, housing, crime, unemployment and the like. We assume, Ryan said, "that *individuals* 'have' social problems" because of some "unusual circumstances" such as "illness, personal defect or handicap, character flaw or maladjustment" which prevent them from getting ahead as other people do.[11] Because we "cannot comfortably believe that *we* are the cause" of social problems, we've developed a habit of locating the problem in the victim.[12] The "dominant style in American social welfare and health" policies, he said, is "to treat what we call social problems . . . in terms of the . . . deviance of the special, unusual groups of persons" who have them.[13]

This convoluted habit of mind has grotesque implications for social policy. As Ryan pointed out, the process of developing social programs "happens so smoothly that it seems downright rational." The process goes like this: "First, identify a social problem. Second, study those affected by the problem and discover in what ways they are different from the rest of us as a consequence of deprivation and injustice. Third, define the difference as the cause of the social problem itself. Finally, of course, assign a government bureaucrat to invent a humanitarian action program to correct the differences."[14]

Ryan elaborates:

[Victim blamers] turn their attention to the victim in his [or her] post-victimized state. They want to bind up wounds, inject penicillin, administer morphine, and evacuate the wounded for rehabilitation. They explain what's wrong with the victim in terms of social experiences *in the past*, experiences that have left wounds, defects, paralysis, and disability. And they take the cure of these wounds and the reduction of these disabilities as the first order of business. They want to make the victims less vulnerable, send them back into battle with better weapons, thicker armor, a higher level of morale.

In order to do so effectively, of course, they must analyze the victims carefully, dispassionately, objectively, scientifically, empathetically, mathematically, and hardheadedly, to see what made them so vulnerable in the first place.

What weapons, now, might they have lacked when they went into battle? Job skills? Education?

What armor was lacking that might have warded off their wounds? Better values? Habits of thrift and foresight?

And what might have ravaged their morale? Apathy? Ignorance? Deviant low class cultural patterns?

This is . . . Blaming the Victim. And those who buy this solution . . . are inevitably blinding themselves to the basic causes of the problems being addressed. They are, most crucially, rejecting the possibility of blaming not the victims, but themselves.[15]

Ryan was certainly not thinking of battered women. It was still possible in 1966 to write about targets of discrimination in America without thinking of women at all, and Ryan mentions wife beating only once in passing as a "crime." Seven years were to pass before the first American shelter for battered women opened and articles about the issue, giving some startling statistics, began to appear in national magazines—seven years before "battered wives" became a "social problem"—but already the search for the victims' "vulnerability" and "deviance" was underway. In 1964, one of the first American studies of battered women, conducted by three men and significantly entitled "The Wife-Beater's Wife: A Study of Family Interaction," studied women in Framingham, Massachusetts, who had charged their husbands with assault, and found the women "castrating," "aggressive," "masculine," "frigid," "indecisive," "passive," and "masochistic." What's more, the authors concluded, the husband's assaultive behavior served "to fill a wife's need even though she protests it."[16] As Ryan described the usual practice of victim blaming, Americans looked for the roots of a problem in the individual's "unusual circumstances." But the neo-Freudian psychiatric researchers who studied the wife beater's wife found her "deviance" deep within her own distressingly "masculine" psyche, feminine only in its profound "masochism." Thus they redefined a universal crime as a personal psychological aberration. They blamed the wife beater's wife not simply for falling victim to battering but for *causing* battering, and then lying about it afterwards. Without the wife beater's wife there would be no wife beating. The reasoning is indeed so smooth it almost sounds rational.

Today such sexist "reasoning" in the scientific literature is better concealed, but it's often there nonetheless, lurking about the premises.[17] The conclusions of the Framingham study are repeated without qualification in a recent book of pop "scholarship" on the subject, *Intimate Violence*, billed as "The Definitive Study of the Causes and Consequences of Abuse in the American Family." The authors are Richard Gelles and Murray Straus, two sociologists who have turned the dispassionate, objective, scientific, mathematical inspection of victims and the superficial statistical survey into a busy, profitable academic industry. They conclude that, "There is *not much* evidence that battered women as a group are more masochistic *than other women*."[18] These authors are the most prominent of the band of academic researchers who after nearly twenty years of government supported research have still not turned their attention from the victims to the violence of men. No wonder this "reasoning" still dominates popular thinking about women who are battered. And this ingenious application of psychiatric diagnosis to social problem leads to social policy more irresponsible than Ryan could have imagined: the ultimate evasion—no policy at all. If the wife beater's wife causes the problem, then there's really nothing the policy makers can do, is there? President Jimmy Carter established a federal Office of Domestic Violence in 1979, but President Ronald Reagan quickly closed it down the following year.[19] For this social problem no government bureaucrat is assigned, no humanitarian action program planned.

If the problem is her fault and the solution her responsibility, then neither the criminal justice system, which we might expect to come to the aid of crime victims, nor other social institutions can do anything about it. And that's exactly what they've been saying all along.

The police, for example, say that wife assault is a "family matter." They also maintain—somewhat inconsistently it would
seem—a false but astonishingly durable myth that these little
family matters are the most dangerous situations police officers
can face, far beyond the call of duty. The myth implies that police
should not be expected to go up against potentially deadly men
for the sake of women who maliciously create this danger to the
police in the first place.[20] Evidence for this bit of police folklore
comes largely from two sources. Firstly, FBI statistics on police
casualties during "disturbance" calls are often taken to apply to
"domestic disturbance" calls only, when in fact the category also
includes far more dangerous street and barroom brawls and "man-
with-a-gun" calls. Secondly, old policemen's tales about particularly explosive domestic situations are taken to be the general
rule, when in fact the bulk of "domestic disturbance" calls involve
"minor assaults" which pose a danger to the victim, but little or
none to police.[21] Obviously it's a peculiar logic that excuses cops
from duty just when the trouble starts and leaves it up to women
to deal single-handedly with men too dangerous for armed police
to handle. Nevertheless, for decades the myth of police endangerment has justified to a sympathetic public the do-nothing policy of cops who consider themselves more precious than the female
citizens they are paid to assist. That in itself tells you how much
we value women, how much we blame women for their predica-
ments, and how easily we abandon them.

This is not to say that police policies haven't changed in the
course of the last twenty years. They have, and in some communities dramatically so. During the 1960s, under the influence of
pop psychology, law enforcement officials took up mediation as
the best way to deal with criminal assault in the home. Psychologists said that arresting batterers "exacerbated the violence,
broke up families, and caused the abuser to lose his job," so up-
to-date police departments trained officers in "crisis intervention
techniques," converting cops to social workers handling not crime
but "interpersonal crisis."[22] One goal of such programs was to re-
duce the number of arrests; and by 1977, 70 percent of the nation's

large police departments were training officers in crisis intervention.[23]

At the same time, however, under pressure from battered women and their advocates, law enforcement officials began to reconsider. In 1976, legal aid attorneys filed suit against the Chief of Police of Oakland, California, on behalf of "women in general and black women in particular who are victims of domestic violence" (*Scott v. Hart*), and police agreed to make arrests when they had probable cause to believe a felonious assault had occurred, or when a misdemeanor occurred in their presence.[24] On the other coast, battered women sued the New York City police commissioner for failing to enforce laws against assault (*Bruno v. Codd*); the trial judge told cops that they could not automatically decline to make an arrest simply because the assailant was married to his victim.[25] In the same year, 1976, the International Association of Chiefs of Police distributed two "Training Keys" on wife beating that instructed cops to treat assaulted wives as crime victims and not to protect batterers from prosecution.[26] By 1980 a national organization of police chiefs, the Police Executive Research Forum, had studied the problem and concluded that police should be trained to arrest wife beaters.[27] Then in 1985, as I have mentioned before, Tracey Thurman's courtroom victory reminded police of their civil liability and prompted widespread adoption of the new pro-arrest policy. The value of the policy was underscored when a highly publicized experiment in Minneapolis demonstrated to the satisfaction of then-Police Chief Anthony Bouza the "efficacy" of arrest in deterring batterers.[28]

With new pro-arrest policies in place, cities such as Duluth, Minnesota, and Alexandria and Newport News, Virginia noted dramatic decreases in domestic assault and homicide.[29] But policy is not practice. Follow-up studies in Minneapolis and other pro-arrest cities revealed that while police made more arrests shortly after the new pro-arrest policy was adopted, they soon backed off and resumed their traditional "discretionary" methods. Surveying "big city police agencies" from 1984 to 1989, criminologist Lawrence Sherman, one of the principal designers of the Minneapolis

experiment, found the "almost universal" pro-arrest policy ne-
gated by "widespread circumvention by police officers on the
street."[30] Chief Bouza points out that in police departments, the
people in the lowest ranks actually hold the most power, for they
determine on the spot how laws are (or are not) enforced. But who
polices the police? Unless cops fear that their chief will punish
them severely for disregarding departmental policy, Bouza says,
"they will handle calls according to their prejudices, convenience,
or personal perspective."[31] They will continue, in other words, to
abet the batterer and deprive his victim of her safety, her freedom,
and her constitutional rights.

Thus, despite dramatic changes in state and municipal law enforcement policies, many cops still conduct business as usual, enforcing not the law but the do-nothing policy they know best.
Many police chiefs, including Chief Bouza, have had to bring disciplinary actions against their own officers to persuade them to
comply with departmental policy and arrest batterers. To put
teeth in the new pro-arrest policy, many state legislatures made
arrest *mandatory*; Oregon was the first in 1977. Eight states subsequently had to amend their mandatory arrest statutes, however,
to call for arrest of the "primary aggressor" only; compelled to
arrest battering men, many cops arrested battered women as well,
on the grounds that he and she were "assaulting" each other.[32] At
least fifteen states have passed laws to make arrest *mandatory* in
cases of domestic assault, yet in much of the country, many a cop
continues to be—as one judge described Detective Felix Grabowski, the cop who refused to help Deborah Evans—an "inert
spectator to an unfolding tragedy."[33] A tragedy in which the victim is to blame.

Police also argue that there is little point in arresting batterers
when battered women won't follow through with prosecution. In
the finest blame-the-victim tradition, police shift the burden of
arrest to the battered woman who, in most cases, is in no position
to press them to arrest the man who assaulted her and threatens
to do so again. Yet the cops do have a point. As the Attorney General's Task Force on Family Violence noted in 1984, "the prose-

cuting attorney . . . generally does not issue criminal charges or routinely prosecute these cases."[34] That is still the case; a recent study in Milwaukee found that 95 percent of assaultive men arrested were not prosecuted, and only 1 percent were convicted.[35] Instead, prosecutors too shift the burden and the blame to the battered woman. They say battered women don't press charges. They say this to women who are trying, like the wife beaters' wives of Framingham, like Tracey Thurman, like Karen Straw, like Deborah Evans, to press charges. And they go on saying it, even though studies done fifteen years ago demonstrated that given the slightest help with complicated legal procedures, women follow through with remarkable tenacity. As long ago as 1977, studies in California found that with the help of Victim Assistance programs, only 10 percent of domestic assault victims in Los Angeles refused to cooperate with the prosecutor, and in Santa Barbara only 8 percent.[36]

Many prosecutors, however, say that there is little point in prosecuting batterers when judges simply release them, and they too have a point. A 1991 study in Charlotte, North Carolina, for example, found that among assaultive men arrested, convicted, and sentenced, less than 1 percent (0.9%) served any time in jail.[37] Yet judges who dispense "justice" so lightly to assaultive men have been known (as we've seen) to castigate women for wasting the court's time, to *order* battered women to make up with their husbands, and to laugh women out of court. They have been known to set free on minimal bail men who have already attempted to kill their wives or girlfriends, and then to say when the murder is done, "There's just no way of predicting these things."

And judges, too, shift the burden and the blame to women. It's a waste of time to issue temporary restraining orders against batterers, many judges say, because battered women don't show up for the hearing to extend the order anyway; once again, women don't "follow through." And there the judges too have a point. A Massachusetts study found that 71 percent of women who got temporary restraining orders in the Brockton District Court in

1982 did not appear at a hearing ten days later. But this study, for once, found fault with the court, not the women; for in the Quincy District Court, where there is a separate office for restraining orders, daily briefing sessions for women seeking restraining orders, and support groups run by the prosecutor's office, only 2.8 percent of the women failed to show up for the hearing. Again, given a little help to negotiate a complicated and hostile system beset with obstacles, women follow through.[38]

But why, you may ask, should battered women be afforded all this extra "help"? Why can't they just use the system like anybody else? Think of Mary Baumruk, shot and killed in May 1992 by her estranged husband Ken Baumruk in a St. Louis courtroom during a divorce hearing. (Ken Baumruk then shot and wounded his wife's lawyer, his own lawyer, a court bailiff, and a security officer before he was shot by police.)[39] Think of Shirley Lowery, a grandmother of eleven, stabbed nineteen times by ex-boyfriend Benjamin Franklin in a Milwaukee courthouse in March 1992 when she came out of hiding to attend a hearing on a restraining order. In her application, Shirley Lowery had said that Franklin raped her and held her at gunpoint. "He follows me 24 hours every day and threatens my life," she wrote.[40] Think of Danielle Almonor, shot to death by her estranged husband, Max, in the Brooklyn Family Court in March 1992 as she waited to be called for a child custody and support hearing requested by her husband. (Max Almonor also critically wounded another woman awaiting a hearing who happened to be seated next to his wife.)[41] For women trying to get free of violent men, going to court can be far more difficult, lonely, and dangerous than it is for any other class of complainants. One way courts can facilitate justice is by making their own processes easier, safer, and more accessible. Instead, police, prosecutors, and judges who believe that the "typical" battered woman gives up give up on her. And if a woman perseveres despite the obstacles they place in her way, they may pronounce her "vindictive," a crafty manipulator of the system, using the law to get back at a man. This catch-22 is no accident. When blame for a "social problem" falls on its victims, the victims look blame-worthy, no matter what they do.

Each branch of the criminal justice system, then, evades its duty by blaming another branch. Police say there's no point in making arrests when prosecutors won't prosecute, and prosecutors in turn say they can't prosecute when (a) police don't arrest, or (b) judges won't sentence anyway. Judges say that women waste the court's time. Blaming the victim allows everyone in the system to pass the buck; and buckpassing conveniently enables individuals within the system to acknowledge a problem without doing anything about it. They'd like to help, but, hey, what can they do? Besides, when you come right down to it, isn't it really up to a woman to follow through? Why doesn't she just leave?

Many women assaulted by husbands or boyfriends never do call the police, or having found them no help on one occasion, never call them again. But more than half the women assaulted are injured, and at least 25 percent of them seek medical treatment.[42] (Undoubtedly this figure would be higher if more Americans had access to affordable health care.) Despite their injuries, many assaulted women have no contact with the police or courts at all. But 10 percent of the injured visit hospital emergency rooms and many others visit private physicians to have their wounds dressed, their broken bones set, their injuries treated.[43] One in five women who visits an emergency room—some studies say one in three—does so because of "ongoing abuse."[44] Of women requiring emergency surgery, one in five was battered, according to one study; one in two, according to another.[45] Battering accounts for half of all cases of alcoholism in women. It accounts for half of all rapes of women over age thirty.[46] From 33 to 46 percent of women who suffer physical assault also report sexual assault—rape—and a "wide range" of resulting injuries, "from superficial bruises and tearing to internal injuries and scarring," not to mention psychological consequences which, according to the American Medical Association, can be "extreme."[47] Battering is a cause of one quarter of suicide attempts by all women, and one half of suicide attempts by black women.[48] And the *Journal of the American Medical Association* reports: "Approximately 37 percent of obstetric patients, across class, race, and educational lines, are physically abused while pregnant." Among the results: "placental separation, antepartum hemorrhage, fetal fractures, rupture of the uterus, liver, or spleen, and preterm labor."[49] Preterm labor, of course, may mean spontaneous abortion or miscarriage.

All this adds up to almost 100,000 days of hospitalization, 30,000 emergency room visits, and almost 40,000 visits to physicians each year.[50] Yet physicians manage to identify perhaps no more than one battered patient in twenty-five.[51] One reason may be that fewer than half the medical schools in the United States and Canada provide any training on domestic assault, and those that do typically cover the topic in one ninety-minute session.[52] Dr. Carole Warshaw, a Chicago psychiatrist and emergency physician, studied the records of fifty-two battered women treated at the emergency room of a large urban hospital in 1987 for injuries resulting from domestic assault, injuries ranging from a fractured ankle to a gunshot wound. In three out of four cases physicians did not inquire about the woman's relationship to the assailant. Nine times out of ten physicians failed to ask about abuse at all. They referred only 8 percent of the cases to a social worker, and although every case involved at least assault and battery, nurses reported fewer than half of them to the police.[53] (Medical personnel didn't report child abuse either, until the law required it.) Instead, doctors typically patch up wounds, prescribe tranquilizers, and discharge patients, with no arrangements made for their safety, to return to the same life-threatening situation they came from. Warshaw reports that doctors fill out forms in "passive, disembodied phrases," rendering the assailant invisible: "Hit by lead pipe." "Blow to head by stick with nail in it." "Hit on left wrist with jackhammer."[54]

Dr. Mark Rosenberg, of the Centers for Disease Control, observes: "It's striking that physicians almost never ask their patients about violence. The only physicians who ask about violence are psychiatrists, and they're only interested if it occurs in a dream."[55] Faced with victims of the real violence of battering, psychiatrists often mislabel patients, mistaking the after-effects of prolonged trauma for personality disorder. Like the three men who brought us "The Wifebeater's Wife," psychiatrists find women *inherently* dependent, passive, self-defeating, or masochistic when they should be diagnosed as suffering from post-traumatic stress. Psychiatric victim-blaming reappears in quasi-psychiatric labels routinely attached to battered women by other medical personnel. Doctors observed in one study of emergency room practice, for example, routinely designated battered women "hysteric," "neurotic female," "hypochondriac," or simply "crock."[56]

This situation has been an open secret for as long as family physicians have treated "families." But in 1985, then-Surgeon General C. Everett Koop told health professionals that "domestic violence is a public health menace that police alone cannot cope with."[57] He suggested that hospitals and trauma centers might prevent further violence by intervening, especially since they see many of the same patients repeatedly. Mental health and counseling centers might play a similar role. But a 1987 survey of trauma centers in the San Francisco area found that more than half of them still had no protocols for dealing with domestic assault victims.[58] A study of Massachusetts emergency rooms found 80 percent still without protocols in 1991.[59] In 1989 Koop tried again, kicking off a campaign to alert the 27,000 members of the American College of Obstetricians and Gynecologists, often women's primary care providers, to what Koop called "an overwhelming moral, economic, and public health burden that our society can no longer bear."[60] The success of that campaign can be judged by the fact that in October 1991 the American Medical Association announced the start of "a campaign" to combat a "public health menace": Family Violence. At a press conference in Chicago, AMA leaders handed out an informational packet identifying family violence as "America's Deadly Secret." *Secret?*

Koop's successor as Surgeon General, Dr. Antonia C. Novello, commended the AMA for "bringing this topic of domestic violence to light."[61]

Novello recommended that medical personnel be required to report domestic violence, as they are already required to report suspected child abuse; but the AMA settled for writing up "guidelines" for physicians to use in dealing with the "menace" that's been there, right under their stethoscopes, all along. Like police "policies," medical "guidelines" are not practice. A 1991 study of health professionals found that "Family violence is recognized as a major problem at the health care systems level," but "little and inadequate attention is given to the prevention, identification, treatment and follow-up of cases." The problem seems to be not ignorance but indolence. The study suggests one explanation: "Physicians have 'an unfortunate prevalence' of sexist, racist and ageist attitudes that helps them overlook the causes of their patients' cuts and bruises."[62]

Most studies of health care for battered women, as we've seen, study the victims, not the health care system; but in doing so, they've uncovered the fact that health care in America can be positively dangerous to an abused woman. When physicians and nurses do nothing, even when the victim/patient knows they *know*, they magnify the victim's anxiety, hopelessness, fear, and shame—her sense that she alone is responsible for her safety, that she alone is perhaps, after all, to blame. One study rightly concludes: "the current pattern of medical response contributes to the battering syndrome."[63] Another confirms that "Failure to acknowledge the woman's abusive experience is often psychologically damaging in itself."[64] And another stresses that "disconfirmation of abuse by a care giver is an important factor in the development of subsequent psychopathology.[65] In other words, the way doctors and nurses and counselors treat battered women—as though nothing happened—drives them *crazy*. But health professionals too ask: isn't she a grown-up? Didn't she get herself into this? Why doesn't she just leave?

If the problem is her fault, no one else need help either. Ministers, priests, and rabbis admonish the battered woman to try harder, to be a better wife. Marriage counselors, family therapists, and mediators counsel her to consider her husband's point of view, practice "interpersonal communication skills," and work diligently (often in long-term therapy) to raise her self-esteem. To illustrate "the absurd level that victim blaming reaches," a handbook published by the Duluth Domestic Abuse Intervention Project recounts what happened to a woman named Janice:

"My husband shot at me twice but he was so drunk he missed me. I locked myself in the bathroom and crawled out the window. I ran through a field in knee-deep snow with no shoes on. The neighbors took me to the hospital. The next day I was admitted to the psych ward for anxiety. I took several tests. When the psychiatrist met with me he said I scored very high on the paranoia scale. I asked what that meant and he said, 'It means you have an irrational fear that someone is out to get you.' My anxiety turned to depression. I was released to go back home a week later with a prescription for Valium."[66]

Privately, the representatives of social "services" and the members of the "helping professions" *know*. Privately, they may fear and despise the battered woman for being the victim she is. They grow impatient with her and angry that she presents herself to them, wanting something from them, wanting *help*. Why doesn't she help herself? (If she were anyone else, with any other kind of problem, they would see that asking for help *is* a way to help oneself.) Sometimes they say to her: keep the house cleaner, don't be so nervous, lose weight, be agreeable, don't answer back, make the kids behave, take Valium, wear lipstick, smile, pray. Sometimes they say: Why don't you just leave?

And if she does leave? And he comes after her? Perhaps she'll be maimed and crippled, like Tracey Thurman. Perhaps she'll defend herself and then be tried for murder, like Karen Straw. Perhaps she'll be convicted and sent to prison for a long term—fifteen years, maybe, or life—as are so many battered women who kill.

Or perhaps she'll be murdered—as four women every day are murdered by their "partners." Lisa Bianco's mother told a television reporter: "People ask 'Why don't battered women leave?' They get killed. That's why."[67]

The pattern is so commonplace that law professor Martha R. Mahoney has coined the useful term "separation assault" to describe the "varied violent and coercive moves" a batterer makes when a woman tries to leave him. Mahoney writes: *Separation assault is the attack on the woman's body and volition in which her partner seeks to prevent her from leaving, retaliate for the separation, or force her to return. It aims at overbearing her will as to where and with whom she will live, and coercing her in order to enforce connection in a relationship. It is an attempt to gain, retain, or regain power in a relationship, or to punish the woman for ending the relationship. It often takes place over time.*"[68] As Mahoney points out, the battered woman whom we think of as "staying" with a batterer, or returning to him, is usually a woman held captive by the force of separation assault. And as we have seen time and time again, when a woman perseveres in her struggle to get free, the grand finale of separation assault is often her own death.

But even an abused woman's death does not put an end to the blame we customarily heap upon her. Think of Carol Irons, who made history in 1982 at age thirty-three by becoming the first female judge in Kent County, Michigan. She was reportedly a great asset to the bench: a judge who took domestic assault seriously and conveyed that attitude to battered women and battering men as well.[69] In 1984 she married Clarence ("Rat") Ratliff, a policeman, on the lawn of the Hall of Justice in Grand Rapids. Before long, he accused her of infidelity, and for months he secretly tapped her telephone, trying to gather evidence against her. In June 1988 Carol Irons left Ratliff and started divorce proceedings. The newspapers called it "a rancorous separation."[70] On October 20, 1988, Ratliff stopped for a few drinks when he got off work in the morning, then went to the courthouse and shot Judge Irons in the chest. He fired at her again as she tried to get away, and he popped off three shots at fellow officers who came to aid the dying judge. When he was subdued, he explained: "I just couldn't take the bitch anymore."[71]

Clarence Ratliff apparently was a tough, macho guy. One of his pals in the Dilleywackers Motorcycle Club told reporters, "If there were 10,000 Clarence Ratliffs, the communists would start digging holes and burying themselves in."[72] Ratliff's first wife, Olga Ratliff, said that he repeatedly hit her during their marriage and that after she left him he broke into her house and pistol-whipped her. Carol Irons's divorce attorney reported that Irons had applied for a restraining order after Ratliff harassed her and threatened to kill her.[73] But when Ratliff went on trial for first degree murder, the judge excluded information about his previous threats and violence lest it prejudice the jury (nine men and three women) against the man. The jurors heard instead Ratliff's sordid suspicions about his wife and his complaint that she refused to continue paying the mortgage on his cottage after the divorce. They heard how hard it was on a man when his wife was "a judge and a whore at the same time."[74]

After that, the jurors simply could not find it in their hearts to pronounce Clarence Ratliff guilty of first degree murder. Or second degree murder either. They convicted him of voluntary manslaughter. They felt that Ratliff was under too much "stress" and too full of alcohol to have intended murder. Besides, as one juror said: "Everybody felt he was provoked by his wife to do this. First of all, she went out with other men. Then he was having trouble sexually, and I imagine she rubbed that in to him. Then he went to his lawyer's office and found out she wouldn't agree to the settlement. All of that provoked him into doing it."[75] Judge Irons's outraged friends called this "the-bitch-deserved-it defense."[76]

Given the manslaughter conviction, Clarence Ratliff might have been out of prison within six years, as most men who kill their wives and girlfriends are, but the jurors had not taken kindly to his shooting at the cops. They found him guilty of two counts of assault with intent to commit murder, and one count of assault with a firearm, and one count of felony firearm (that is, using a firearm in the commission of a felony).[77] Thousands of citizens protested the dangerous message the verdict sent to batterers: that shooting at a cop is serious, but killing your wife . . . well, that's not so bad. But the prosecutor said he was "gratified" that the jury "realized how serious the attack on the police officers was."[78] In June 1989 the judge sentenced Ratliff to ten to fifteen years for killing his wife, two life terms for the assaults on two police officers, up to four years for assaulting a third officer, and two years for using a firearm in the commission of a felony. That makes Ratliff eligible for parole in 2000 and means, in practice, that he'll be in prison about twice as long as he might have been if he'd settled for "manslaughtering" his provocative wife.[79] And it left the friends of Carol Irons to rehabilitate her name. "She was a gifted and brilliant person," said one, "a far better person than was portrayed in the trial."[80]

Historian Elizabeth Pleck notes that the inevitable question, or its variant "Why does she stay?," was first asked in the 1920s, coincidentally with the rise of modern psychology, and experts have been "answering" it ever since. "The answer given then," Pleck says, "was that battered women were of low intelligence or mentally retarded; two decades later, [as we have seen] it was assumed these women did not leave because they were masochistic. By the 1970s, an abused woman stayed married, the experts claimed, because she was isolated from friends and neighbors, had few economic or educational resources, and had been terrorized into a state of 'learned helplessness' by repeated beatings." As Pleck observes, even this "modern answer" is "far less revealing than the persistent need to pose the question."[81] What that need reveals is our refusal to *do* anything to stop violence against women.

Instead, "experts"—psychologists, psychiatrists, and sociologists mostly—fortified with government grants, busily study why women stay. Naturally they study the question, and the whole problem of male violence, by studying women, thereby managing to blame women while turning "their problem" into a tidy profit, generously provided by your tax dollars and mine. The experts have examined the personalities of battered women, their education, their family history, their previous experience with violence, their physical health, their mental health, their employment record, their use of alcohol and drugs, their sexual history and attitudes, their religious beliefs, their child-rearing practices, their veracity, their verbal skills, their problem-solving skills, their "interpersonal tactics" (which means mostly what they do when a man hits them), and—endlessly—their self-esteem.

In 1978 the National Coalition Against Domestic Violence, a coalition of grass-roots women's groups struggling on shoestring budgets to shelter and provide services for battered women, recommended that federal research grants "be limited to those helping local groups meet particular programmatic needs."[82] But those local groups were made up mostly of formerly battered women, uncredentialed and clearly on the side of women; so the substantial grants—from the National Institute of Mental Health, the Department of Justice, and other federal agencies— went instead to psychologists and sociologists, mostly men, with academic credentials and affiliations, who could be counted on to be "objective"—that is, to *not* take the side of women. So adept have the experts been at studying women while hiding women's complaints, blaming women while silencing them, that two male "experts" who reviewed the heavy body of "standard literature" in the field in 1986 remarked: "The search for characteristics of women that contribute to their own victimization is futile. . . . It is sometimes forgotten that men's violence is men's behavior. . . . What is surprising is the enormous effort to explain male behavior by examining characteristics of women. It is hoped [presumably by the authors] that future research will show more about the factors that promote violent male behavior and that stronger theory will be developed to explain it."[83]

Don't count on it. Gender bias oozes from the very methods of the academics: quantitative, statistical, "objective," and as distant as possible from the real experiences of real women. (Researchers who "use" battered women as experimental "subjects" commonly present them with a list of predetermined questions, designed to elicit the information the researchers want, and keyed for quick reduction to faceless numbers—a "scientific method" very different from *listening* to what women have to say for themselves.) When not busy finding out what's wrong with women, researchers investigate what's wrong with "families."

In the 1970s, while psychologists studied women's "helplessness" and passivity (instead of men's violence and aggression), sociologists tried to measure the exact "magnitude" of "family" violence, spending money that might have gone to fund shelters and save lives. At the University of New Hampshire Family Violence Research Program, professors Murray Straus and Richard Gelles, assisted by Suzanne Steinmetz, devised a "Conflict Tactics Scale" to score fights in violent "families" on a convenient numerical basis, regardless of context, intention, relative size of the contenders, or real damage done. The experts then conducted a large survey, and in 1977 pronounced the battle between the sexes a statistical draw.[84] This finding, that women are just as violent as men, seemed ludicrous to workers in the battered women's movement who saw at firsthand that the damage inflicted by violent men had no parallel. But the study was among the first on "family violence." It was big and official, backed by the weight of academia and the National Institute of Mental Health. And it conveniently deflected attention from male violence against women by recasting "family violence" as an unfortunate but egalitarian problem. For all these reasons, the study was taken seriously and widely reported in the popular press. Ever since, pro-feminist academic researchers have engaged themselves year after year in doggedly deconstructing the shoddy studies based on the "logical positivism and abstract empiricism" of the Conflict Tactics Scale.[85] (To cite examples of the Scale's failings, and of the general idiocy of trying to evaluate complex issues in simplistic statistical terms, on the Conflict Tactics Scale hitting your "partner" with a pillow counts the same as hitting him or her with a sledgehammer, and two slaps on the wrist count the same as two knife attacks.)[86]

Straus and Gelles met this criticism by ignoring it, and in 1986 they repeated their statistical survey, using once again the handy Conflict Tactics Scale. To no one's surprise, they discovered anew that in using violence, the sexes are "equal."[87] This study was just as ridiculous as the first one, but it was also just as big, just as official, just as well funded, just as warmly received, just as well publicized, and just as often quoted. So the professors go on producing what they call "definitive" studies of "family violence," and they retain their reputation as the leading academic "family violence experts" in America, enjoying the prominence reserved for those scholars whose findings best fit the misogynist temper of our times.

Their results—that women and men abuse each other in equal numbers, that the battered "spouse" is as often as not a "battered husband"—have made headlines for more than a decade. One recent example is yet another article in the *New York Times* on "battered husbands" seeking "equal rights."[88] Their research continues to mislead the public and policy makers alike and to mask the real nature and severity of male violence against women. (It also saddled us with verbal fakery like "family violence" and "spouse abuse" and the "violent couple.") R. Emerson Dobash and Russell P. Dobash, co-directors of the Institute for the Study of Violence at the University of Wales point out that: "In Britain, Europe, Canada, Australia, Asia, Africa, South and Latin America, and the Soviet Union the problem [known in the United States as Family Violence] is believed to be and research findings show it to be *violence against women*." They conclude: "One must ask if there is something peculiar about society in the USA, or about its social science."[89]

More important, little or none of this peculiar research has had any application to the real experience of survivors and advocates trying to help real abused women and children. Just the reverse. Susan Schechter notes:

> The shelter movement has never had the time or money to conduct its own research, documenting how battered women are active on their own behalf, how they creatively avoid and survive the violence, and the conditions under which they ultimately leave. Few researchers have documented the complex steps through which women pass as they make positive changes in their lives. Nor do we know enough about those interventions that stop assailants and those that prevent further violence. The shelter movement has found most academic researchers in the field of family violence to be indifferent, if not hostile, to its posing these questions.[90]

Worse, organizations that shelter and support battered women and children find it harder and harder to find funding when "experts" lead policy-makers and the general public to believe that "there are no clear cut victims or assailants, only violent couples in need of psychotherapeutic transformation," and that when women complain of "family violence," they have only themselves to blame.[91]

So thoroughly have "experts" in psychology and social science taken over the problem of woman assault that criminologists have next to nothing to say about it. Only one major theoretical study of crime in the United States even names as a *crime* what is now the leading cause of injury to American women. In *Confronting Crime: An American Challenge*, Elliott Currie writes, "Violence against women is . . . one of the most serious and deadly forms of criminal violence in America."[92] Until very recently, of course, there was no record of domestic crime for criminologists to think about: no arrests, no police reports, no numbers, nothing. Look through sixty years of FBI *Uniform Crime Reports*, crime statistics gathered unsystematically from 16,000 law enforcement agencies across the country, and you'll find that domestic violence doesn't *exist*. The FBI started gathering and publishing crime statistics in

1930, but it has *never* collected information about the victims of aggravated assault. Attorney General William French Smith acknowledged in 1983 that the "insidious criminal problem" of domestic violence has "never received the kind of national attention it deserves," and it still hasn't.[93] Elliott Currie says that "conservative criminologists have, with few exceptions, been oddly silent on the entire issue of domestic violence," perhaps because they "may be more concerned with upholding 'traditional' norms, at whatever cost, than with reducing violence, inside or outside the family."[94] Traditional norms, of course, include the sanctity of the family and the "right" of every man *privately* to maintain "order"—which is to say, his own supremacy—within his own household. Indeed many of the most prominent "thinkers" in criminology uphold precisely the same patriarchal, authoritarian, and punitive values in society that the batterer literally fights for in "his" family. They would be the last to interfere with his tyrannical project—or with the psychologists and sociologists who are still trying to pin the blame on the victim.

A few criminologists concerned with police work, however, took up in the early 1980s the question of how police should respond to domestic violence calls: whether to mediate as psychologists urged, arrest as battered women and their advocates demanded, or do nothing, as police tradition dictated. As criminologists, however, their concern was not the safety of women but the *deterrence* of crime, which seems to mean mainly reducing the number of annoying domestic emergency calls to the police.[95] The story of the police experiments is complicated, but its moral is simple: there's more than one way to blame the victim.

The results of the Minneapolis Domestic Violence Experiment conducted by Lawrence Sherman and Richard Berk, published in 1984, suggested that batterers arrested by police were far less likely to repeat violence within the next six months than those who were merely "advised" or sent away from the scene.[96] Sherman and Berk recommended that police be empowered to make warrantless arrests in domestic assault cases, confirming the trend of law enforcement agencies, already underway, to adopt a policy of arresting batterers. But Sherman and Berk recommended *against* another trend: passing mandatory arrest laws to compel cops to arrest batterers. The researchers warned that police, who cherish their power of discretion—their power *not* to arrest— would circumvent mandatory arrest laws.[97] As we've seen, they were right about cops circumventing the law. Mandated to arrest, many police officers refused, or they arrested battered women as well as, or instead of, batterers. Nevertheless, more and more states accepted the advice of law enforcement officials and women's advocates, and they enacted statutes mandating arrest.

Criminologist Sherman then led a small group of researchers in spending about four million taxpayer dollars to replicate the Minneapolis experiment in five other cities, but because the researchers conducted each experiment a little differently, the results were predictably conflicting and inconclusive.[98] In all six cities studied, arrest seemed to deter batterers in the short run; that is, it kept them from battering again for at least the first thirty days after arrest. (That is often all the time a woman needs to make good her escape.) In three cities, including Minneapolis, arrest seemed to deter batterers for up to six months, while in three other cities—Omaha, Charlotte, and Milwaukee—it seemed not to.[99] These results led different members of the research group to different conclusions. Researchers in Omaha recommended more research.[100] Researchers in Charlotte said that even if arrest didn't have a deterrent effect, it was still "a more conscionable choice than non-arrest," because nonarrest "legitimated" abuse and left women "on their own."[101] But Lawrence Sherman, who led the study in Milwaukee as he had in Minneapolis, made a remarkable leap. Not only does arrest *not deter* battering in the long term, he said, but in some groups it actually *causes* it.[102]

Sherman found that after arrest, "employed, married, high school graduate and white suspects" were less likely to repeat violence. But arrest a "marginal" man—an unemployed, unmarried, high school dropout and/or black suspect who has "nothing to lose"—and *"arrest will backfire by causing increased violence."*[103] This much is probably true, especially in Milwaukee where most of the arrested men were freed in a couple of hours and almost never prosecuted. (Men arrested in Minneapolis were jailed for twenty-four hours and arraigned before a judge.) But there's a big difference between *failing to stop* escalating violence and *causing* violence to escalate, as feminist legal scholars, busy dismantling Sherman line by line, have pointed out.[104]

But if it's true, as the data show, that "marginal" men are undeterred by arrest, should we bring heavier punishments to bear to make them desist? No, says Sherman, "the evidence fails to justify . . . greater severity."[105] What the evidence justifies to Sherman—and here he makes another dazzling leap, writing social policy for all in terms of the alleged behavior of a few—is the repeal of mandatory arrest laws. Better, says Sherman, to have police choose from a list of "options" such as offering to take the victim to a shelter or "mobilizing the victim's social network to provide short term protection."[106] Police, exercising their famous discretion, can treat those Sherman calls "different folks" differently.[107] And just in case they don't get it right, Sherman also recommends: "Police should not be held civilly liable for failure to prevent future domestic homicide or serious injury because of failure to make arrests in . . . prior misdemeanor assaults."[108]

You'll recognize the notion that arrest backfires, making violent men more violent, as the longstanding excuse of cops. But now, since Sherman, it's "science." (Sherman likes to compare his "controlled experiments" to biochemical research.)[109] It's "unfortunate," he says, that the battered women's movement has paid so little attention to his "evidence that arrest positively harms black women."[110] Be it on *their* heads, he suggests, when black women are battered by those poor black men with nothing to lose, infuriated by arrest. But law professor Cynthia Grant Bowman questions the male perspective that draws conclusions about violence against women solely in terms of the socioeconomic circumstances of the men involved. Looked at from the woman's perspective, it's clear that poor inner-city women, who often have no support services and can't afford to leave public housing, may be sitting ducks for further assaults. Such women need more law enforcement, not less.[111] As for Sherman, he carries us back, by a circuitous route, to an old paternalism—though he calls it "smart" policing for the "twenty-first century."[112] He comes down squarely on the side of a universal do-nothing (but the same old "options") "domestic violence" policy. And why? In order *to protect women*.[113]

What are we to call this kind of double whammy by which "controlled experiments" lay both the problem and the nonsolution at woman's door? (And leave her to guard the door all by herself.) Victim blaming squared, perhaps? Complex victim blaming syndrome? Post-feminist stress disorder? (The *Milwaukee Journal*, in a strong editorial upholding Wisconsin's mandatory arrest law, called it "missing the point.")[114]

To feminist critics the significant thing about this research is not simply that it kept another band of academics, mostly men, happily employed for a decade in defense of the status quo ante, but that it is so relentlessly male in its design and interpretation. Here again, as in the work of "family violence" researchers, are "objective" studies that try to isolate one behavior (arrest) from a complex context and measure its effects in a broad statistical survey. (One might question the ethics of studies that answered *real* women's *real* calls for help with cops engaged in an academic experiment.) Here again are social scientists studying a "problem" which primarily injures women without consulting injured women in designing the study. (Any battered women's advocate could have told them that arrest alone, without other serious consequences such as prosecution, conviction, sentencing, and jail time, leaves batterers laughing at their victims and at the police, too.) The studies objectify the women studied as statistics classified by race, employment, and socioeconomic status, and deprive us of valuable information their voices could provide.[115] In fact, one of the most interesting things about the police experiments is that whenever women were asked about the repetition of assaults, their reports differed from official police records; women reported, for one thing, "better results from arrest."[116] Sherman, however, focused on the official police data which he found "far more reliable" than the "expensive and troublesome" victim interviews.[117] But then, he didn't actually talk to victims. In Milwaukee, he hired female interviewers to do the job.[118] One can only guess that Sherman intended to be sensitive to women victims in dispatching other women to question them. Still, he might have learned something by doing it himself.

Cynthia Grant Bowman points out: "The perspective from which neutral statistics are analysed clearly makes a difference both in the conclusions to be drawn and in the policy implications which emerge from those conclusions."[119] From Sherman's perspective, "What prevents police from preventing repeat violence is the deep reverence for privacy in American life."[120] The underlying cause of "domestic violence," he thinks, is not male dominance, but things like "adultery, alcoholism, or just plain argumentativeness"; and these matters, he says, drawing upon the familiar assumptions of ventilationist psychology, are related to the "intimate emotions of a *sexual* relationship." "Given a choice between privacy and prevention," he says, "Americans choose privacy."[121] We must ask, *which* Americans? *Whose* privacy? It doesn't seem to occur to Sherman that women and "Americans" see things differently.

In the course of all this expensive, redundant, and obtuse investigation, psychologists have pinned "the problem" on various permutations of the battered woman's psyche from her "low self-esteem" to her "self-destructive behavior." Psychiatrists have done their utmost to get her "syndrome" officially classified as a "mental illness," and have slipped into the official psychiatric diagnostic canon a brand new "Disorder"—"Self-Defeating Personality Disorder"—dreamed up by a committee of white male psychoanalysts.[122] Pop therapist/writers have added "co-dependency" and "addictive personality," which is/are either one new "disease" or two, depending upon which pop therapist you read. Sociologists have manufactured that monumental problem—"battered husbands"—which all at once trivializes wife beating and blames battered women not only for being victims but for victimizing men. (Every time this reactionary notion is relaunched it gets great play from male TV "personalities" who mistakenly apply "the fairness doctrine" to gender, balancing every story of battered wives with another about battered husbands.) And the victim-blaming "re-search" encourages the criminal justice system in its well-established do-nothing policy, so that the battered woman who tries to blame the man battering her—who tries, in fact, like Karen Straw and Tracey Thurman, to get him arrested and locked up—finds she gets no help at all.

All this can be discouraging to a woman. It can—if you will put yourself in her shoes for a moment—make her terribly upset or depressed. It can fill her with rage or despair. It can even give her a case of "low self-esteem," creeping like mildew over her soul. Once she comes down with these "mental health problems," the experts rush in again to blame the victim for the violence. "We cannot tell," say Professors Gelles and Straus in their most recent "definitive" text, "whether, in fact, the violence came before the problems or whether the problems produced the violence. It is certainly plausible that health or psychological problems create stress in a home. This can lead to violence."[123]

Thus we come full circle. *Her* mental health problems magi-cally "*produce* the violence" (an abstraction, perpetrator unspeci-fied) and once it starts coming down on her head, we know what the next question is.

The huge pile of data about battered women which the victim blamers have amassed reveals one critical fact: one battered woman is as different from the next as night from day. Taken all in all, the studies show that all battered women have only one significant characteristic in common—they all are *female*.

Some battered women were abused as children; others were not. Some battered women never got past grade school; others hold advanced degrees. Some battered women have never held a job; others have worked all their lives. Some battered women were married very young, others in middle age, others not at all. Many battered women are very poor; many are well-to-do. Many bat-tered women have "too many" children, others none at all. Many battered women are passive introverts; others are active extroverts. Some battered women drink too much or use drugs; others never touch the stuff. Many battered women are black; many others are white, yellow, red, brown. Many battered women are Catholic; many others are Protestant, Jewish, Hindu, Muslim, agnostic, atheist, Buddhist, Mormon. In short, there is no typical battered woman. Or to put it another way, any girl or woman might be battered.

This is not a comfortable thought. And it helps to explain why even women blame women for being battered. (In the studio audience of every TV talk show there are two people who seem to be sent from central casting: the cop who says, "These women don't really want 'em arrested," and the woman who says, "I wouldn't stand for that. I would never let that happen to me.") If there is something wrong with *her*, then we can feel safe. And if she doesn't leave the assailant, then we are absolved of responsibility to help her and guilt for our failure to do so. The thought that we are safe only by chance or luck, and perhaps only for the time being, temporarily ahead in some cosmic lottery over which we have no control is too disturbing to take in. And the thought that she isn't leaving because she *can't* without help, and no one will help her, and she could be *me*—well, what woman wants to think about that?

The psychological "experts" like to say that even battered women blame themselves for the abuse they suffer, but I haven't found that to be true. All the survivors I meet know perfectly well who did what to whom: they blame the batterer for his abuse. They blame themselves mainly for sticking around as long as they did; and they take responsibility for specific acts which "set him off." They say things like, "I should have known better than to go back for my clothes." "I should have kept my opinion to myself." "I was an idiot to think he wouldn't follow me." Implicit in such remarks, of course, is the desire to be in control of one's own life, the need to believe that one can be safe by not repeating the same "mistake." The same desire helps to explain the enormous popularity, even among battered and formerly battered women, of books like *Women Who Love Too Much* and *Co-Dependent No More*, self-blaming, "self-help" handbooks full of advice to help a woman "work on" herself, "take charge" of her life, realize her "potential," "grow." If I love him less, or better, or differently, if I don't do *this*, if I don't do *that*—then I will "change" and maybe he will "change" and our relationship will change and everything will be different and I will be safe. It will take a lot of "work," of course, but all the advice is so very helpful, and so self-absorbing, so time-consuming, so apolitical, so doomed. This is victim blaming at its most pernicious.

Just as any woman may fall victim to any form of male violence, any man may become a batterer. A man beats up a woman not because there is something wrong with her (though he says so) or even because there is something wrong with him (though women say so) but because he *can*. He can because nobody stops him. On the contrary, many individuals and institutions—including pornography, popular media, police, prosecutors, judges, physicians, mental health professionals, clergy, and academic "experts"—encourage him. Even Congress abets him through its unwillingness to fund any social programs that do not foster the "Family Ideal" which is, as historian Elizabeth Pleck has noted, "the single most consistent barrier to reform against domestic violence."[124] Lest Congress neglect the "Family Ideal," the political right wing issues reminders. When the House first passed a Domestic Violence bill in 1980 to provide some emergency services, the *Washington Star* urged the Senate to vote it down and keep "the long arm of Washington bureaucracy" out of "private life." Shelters for abused women, the editorial said, would "weaken the traditional family." Emergency counseling for abused women would "break down the emotional ties that make a family unit strong."[125] Jerry Falwell's Moral Majority mobilized against the bill and flooded Senators with mail warning them not to "meddle with family matters."[126]

Even more horrifying to the *Star* was the prospect that "domestic violence shelters would be staffed by a good many far-fringe feminists," a fear that roused the opposition, prompted Senate majority whip Alan Cranston to withdraw the bill, and held up legislation for years. (First introduced by Representative Barbara Mikulski in 1978 and every year thereafter, a "Family Violence Prevention and Services Act" finally slipped through in October 1984, not in its own right but as a watered down amendment to the "Child Abuse Prevention and Treatment Act" which was up for renewal.)[127] New Hampshire Senator Gordon Humphrey agreed with the *Star*, inserting his opinion in the Congressional Record: "The Federal Government should not fund missionaries who would war on the traditional family."[128] It's *those* women—those far-fringe feminists and lesbians—who are to blame, the right wing says, for causing domestic violence in the first place. How? The *Star* explains: "Rejecting traditional female roles and attitudes, they are . . . rejecting a profound part of themselves. And out of their unrecognized self-hate comes a bitterness that detonates real wars of the sexes, complete with black eyes and bruises that send women out into the night looking for help."[129] The *Star* probably was right about that "real war of the sexes," for the rise of feminism certainly did detonate the deepest fears of many terrified men and inspire them to more vigorous authoritarianism at home, just as it inspired a public backlash (well chronicled by Susan Faludi) of which the *Star's* editorial is an example: a new wave of blaming *everything* on the victimized woman, and on feminist women trying to help her.

Think again of Karen Straw. The indelible paper trail she left through the records of hospitals, police, courts, and social services proves that she made every possible appeal for help to "the system." For women's advocates, Karen Straw became a textbook case: a woman who followed through on everything the criminal justice system told her to do, only to find the system worse than worthless. Karla DiGirolamo, Executive Director of the New York State Governor's Commission on Domestic Violence, told the press, "It's a crime of the system that we allow people to live this way, without public intervention, until they feel they have no alternative but to kill." Ronnie Eldridge, former Director of the New York State Division for Women, commented, "Obviously this system doesn't work at all."[130] But in fact, considering that the system was designed by men for men, it worked perfectly—at least until the murder trial when the jury refused to cooperate by convicting Karen Straw. Karen Straw, all by herself, had to stop the man who terrorized her. Why should men, who had no quarrel with her assailant, have done it for her? What *right* had she to ask?

But men don't like to come right out and say *that*. Think about it—how would it sound? So they say instead, as anchorman Jim Jensen did: Why didn't she leave? And then someone, someone like reporter Bree Walker, begins to explain—all about dependence and helplessness and low self-esteem and masochism and psychological problems and what the experts say and . . . Well, you see how neatly that works.

And you see what battered women, individually and collectively, have been up against all this time.

6

A Woman to Blame

On December 12, 1988, Hedda Nussbaum made the cover of *Newsweek*. There had been other "battered women" on the covers of other magazines—*Ms.* for one—pretty, posed models, delicately bruised with makeup in subtle tones of mauve and heliotrope, their eyes cast down in simulation of shame or sadness. But nothing like this. Hedda Nussbaum was the real thing. The photo was shot as she testified against her companion of twelve years, Joel Steinberg, who was charged with murder for beating to death the six-year-old girl the couple had illegally "adopted." (Hired as an attorney to place the child, Steinberg simply took her home.) Hedda Nussbaum's bruises had healed and the discolorations faded, but her face remained permanently scarred and misshapen, remodeled first by Joel Steinberg and subsequently by Dr. Monte Keen, plastic surgeon—the man-made face of America's most famous battered woman.

On the cover of *Newsweek* that face is contorted by grief or remembrance; the jaw sags away as though she were just recoiling from a blow. A tear slides from her left eye, though it is impossible to know whether this tear wells up from emotion or merely leaks from the tear duct that Joel Steinberg shredded beyond repair. In the photo her eyes are cast down or closed; readers can look at her without risking the terrible blank stare of those spent eyes looking back. Day after day in December 1988 that face came into our homes on our television sets, and there in the privacy of our living rooms, our kitchens, our bedrooms, Hedda Nussbaum stared at us. That face made some people weep. It made others want to destroy her. Especially women. Put her on trial, they said. Lock her up. Get rid of her. Just look at what she let him do to her. Look at what she let him do to her *child*.

At first, reporters could find a point of reference for that face only in the arena. Jimmy Breslin wrote in *Newsday*, "She looked as if she had just fought Fritzie Zivic in Pittsburgh. Fritzie used to get his thumb into an eye and turn it like he was dialing a phone number."[1] Pete Hamill of the *New York Post* was "most shocked by the nose." He wrote: "This is the nose of an old pug, some club-fighting veteran of the St. Nicholas Arena or Eastern Parkway, battered and hurt and healed and hurt again, until it is no longer the nose worn when young."[2] *Newsweek* too led off with that "boxer's face—the nose flattened, the left eye distorted, the upper lip still showing signs of a cleft so severe that nearby tissue was used to fill it."[3] The difference, of course, is that fighters earn their faces. Boxing is a sport, while wife beating is merely a national pastime. In the ring, boxers give as good as they get, and afterwards they get paid. For them the face comes with the job. For Hedda Nussbaum, it came with "love."

She should have died. All the specialists and advocates called in to the case after Nussbaum and Steinberg were arrested on November 2, 1987, said they'd never seen a woman so badly battered yet still alive. A doctor from New York University Medical Center who examined Nussbaum "from head to toe" on November 3, 1987, described the forty-five-year-old woman to the jury as anemic, debilitated, malnourished, wasted, limping, and hunchbacked from osteoporosis. He found "old and new lacerations on her scalp, chunks of hair torn out from the right side of her head, an old ulceration and a new fracture on her nose, a black eye, lacerated upper lip, three- or four-month old fractures on both cheekbones, a scar on the abdomen, bruises on the abdomen and back, eight fractured right ribs, seven fractured left ribs, a very large new bruise on the right hip with many scarred areas around it, old abrasions on the left leg, and two deep, three-inch-wide ulcers on the right leg, which was infected, partly gangrenous, and red and swollen from foot to knee.[4] The ulcerated lesions on Nussbaum's lower right leg were "potentially fatal" injuries, the doctor said, which if untreated "could have led to blood poisoning and cardiovascular collapse."[5]

But Joel Steinberg was a skilled and calculating batterer, until the end when cocaine got the better of his judgment; then, being less practiced in assaulting the fragile child, he underestimated the impact of his attack upon her. So it was six-year-old Lisa who died while Hedda sat by, unable to call for help, unwilling to show "disloyalty" to Joel. She wasn't supposed to use the phone unless Joel was present, listening in on the speaker phone, to tell her what to say. She wasn't supposed to open the apartment door to anyone, not even her own family, unless Joel was present. "Should I call 911?" she asked him. Only then, with his okay, did she telephone. Only then, did she "run," as best she could on those ruined legs, to open the apartment door to the emergency team—and after them the police, the reporters, and all the world.

A neighbor who saw Lisa carried away said later, "I always thought it would be Hedda who'd be carried out of here."[6] If it had been Hedda—if *she* had died—we would have had nothing so terrible as the death of Lisa to forgive her for. At least, if Hedda Nussbaum had been carried out, the victim of gangrene or blood poisoning or a deadly blow, we would have been spared the ordeal of Hedda Nussbaum on the stand telling her terrible story.

Newsweek called it "a chilling tale of drug abuse, systematic beatings and a life of squalor hidden behind a middle-class facade."[7] But what's "chilling" is the very ordinariness of that "life of squalor." It's true that the Steinberg apartment held some drugs and drug paraphernalia and a stash of cash and travelers' checks not found in the average American home, and it hadn't been cleaned in a very long time. (Police and reporters who saw it described it as "filthy," "a pigsty," and "a cave.") But mostly the two rooms seem to have been cluttered, like any too-small New York apartment. Steinberg maintained a law practice of sorts out of his home and apparently kept his files on the only bed, *his* bed, and an accumulation of electronic junk in the living room. But the details that leap from every printed description are commonplace ones: a clean fishtank, a pet rabbit, ironing, Sunday afternoon family "quality time" with Mommy and Daddy and little Daughter cooking in the kitchen (little Daughter with her own small knife) while Baby watches from his "little seat" and the football game drones on the TV in the background.

In the courtroom men talked over Hedda Nussbaum's injuries. Prosecutor Peter Casolaro wanted Nussbaum to tell the jury about some of Steinberg's assaults, but because Steinberg was on trial for killing Lisa, not for assaulting Nussbaum, Judge Harold Rothwax had to decide how much the jury could hear—and which incidents should properly be excluded as "merely cumulative" or "inflammatory." Under the law, which is supposed to temper excessive vengeance, it was considered unfair to Steinberg to give the jury the impression, however true, that he had a long-time habit of assault. At a hearing preceding Nussbaum's testimony, without the jury, Casolaro outlined thirty-two "incidents"— some of them clusters of multiple assaults—and Rothwax decided which to let in. The newspapers printed summaries, like this list adapted from *Newsday*'s "Catalog of Abuse":

1. March 17, 1978. The first time Steinberg struck Nussbaum, hitting her in the eye with an open hand. She required hospital treatment. Admitted into evidence.

2. In 1978. Steinberg gave Nussbaum at least ten black eyes.

3. Feb. 4, 1981. Steinberg ruptured Nussbaum's spleen in a beating. She had to go to St. Vincent's Hospital to have it removed. Admitted into evidence.

4. In 1982. Steinberg beat Nussbaum and she sought treatment at St. Vincent's for broken ribs.

5. In 1983. Steinberg used a broomstick to beat her on the feet, causing injury and scars.

6. Late 1983 through 1984. Steinberg beat her severely and repeatedly during this period. Her face was disfigured, her nose broken, and her ear cauliflowered. Steinberg restricted her movements, presumably so her injuries would not be noticed. Once, when she phoned her father for help, Steinberg threw her down. This point admitted into evidence. Feb. 11, 1984. Her knee was broken in a beating and she limped to Bellevue Hospital for treatment. April 14, 1984. She was beaten and ran away.

7. In 1984. Steinberg kicked Nussbaum in the eye, producing serious injury.

8. In 1984. Steinberg hit Nussbaum in the eye, leaving her with a swollen eye.

9. In 1984. Steinberg beat Nussbaum after she refused to take a cold bath and then threw her into the bath with her clothes on. She ran away.

10. In 1984. Steinberg choked Nussbaum, damaging her vocal cords.

11. August 1984. Steinberg gave Nussbaum a black eye. She lost her job with Random House while staying home to recuperate. Admitted into evidence.

12. Late 1984 to early 1985. Steinberg used a blowtorch used for freebasing to burn Nussbaum, leaving scars.

13. In late 1984. Steinberg took a bath with Nussbaum and then beat her "brutally."

14. Late 1984. Steinberg used a broomstick handle to beat her hands, leaving them permanently injured.

15. In 1985. Steinberg used a stick to beat Nussbaum's sexual organs, causing them to swell for several months. In a subsequent beating, she hemorrhaged.

16. and 17. In 1985. Steinberg urinated on Nussbaum twice after throwing her to the floor.

18. September, 1985. Steinberg handcuffed Nussbaum in the bathroom and forced her to sleep there.

19. In 1985. Steinberg handcuffed Nussbaum to a chinning bar in the bedroom and told her to sleep.

20. In 1985. Steinberg struck Nussbaum, chipping or knocking out teeth.

21. Late 1985 to early 1986. Steinberg knocked her down and she cut her wrist by falling against a filing cabinet, causing severe injury and scarring.

22. In 1986. Steinberg hit Nussbaum, knocking out more teeth.

23. In 1986. Steinberg beat up Nussbaum in a car on the way to visit his mother.

24. In 1986. Steinberg hit her head against a wall, causing her to bleed.

25. Late 1986 through 1987. Steinberg beat Nussbaum repeatedly with a metal exercise bar, especially during the two months before Lisa Steinberg's death on Nov. 5, 1987. Admitted into evidence.

26. In 1987. Steinberg struck Nussbaum with his open hands, splitting her lip repeatedly.

27. In 1987. Steinberg broke her nose again in a beating.

28. October 1987. Steinberg grabbed her by one ankle and one wrist and bounced her on the floor, severely bruising her buttocks.

29. Late 1987. When Nussbaum refused to take a cold bath, Steinberg threw her into the bathtub with her clothes on.

30. In 1987. Steinberg pulled her hair out numerous times.

31. October 1987. Steinberg repeatedly poked his fingers in Nussbaum's eyes, lacerating her nose once.

32. During the last nine years the couple lived together the

physical abuse continued with regularity, "a persistent tool used . . . to control Miss Nussbaum, or . . . to break her will."[8]

No wonder even Steinberg complained that for some time before Lisa's death, Hedda wasn't the woman she had been. He told one journalist that Nussbaum was "in a state" which he described as "trancelike"—though he attributed Nussbaum's "state" not to physical or mental trauma but to "posthypnotic suggestion" made by someone else. Assistant District Attorney John McCusker described Nussbaum's behavior at the time of her arrest as having a "total zombie-like quality."[9] When Child Welfare Worker Joseph Petrizzo went to the Steinberg apartment on the morning of November 2 to take away a second illegally "adopted" child, the sixteen-month-old boy then known as Mitchell Steinberg, he found Nussbaum "a mass of black and blue marks." "Her nose was caved in," he testified. "Her face looked like it was swollen. . . . She looked a bit dazed and confused. . . . She just seemed out of it." Her daughter had been taken away in a coma to the hospital, and as Petrizzo prepared to take away her second child, "she never said anything."[10]

When she took the stand herself, Nussbaum spoke like a woman who had forgotten how. The monotony of her voice, the lack of emotional timbre, the "flat affect" marked her as a severely traumatized woman, afraid to reveal anything in her speech and manner for fear it might be, as always, wrong. That was only to be expected, but Nussbaum kept lapsing into silence. Columnist Pete Hamill noticed that it happened when she tried to speak about the times Steinberg beat her. At those moments, Hamill wrote, "she stops, the eyes stare at nothing, and it's as if some other image has scribbled across her consciousness, filling her with such fear and trembling that only stillness can ward off the fear."[11]

Thirteen months after she hobbled out of that apartment for the last time, Hedda Nussbaum, encouraged by psychiatrists and advocates and teams of lawyers, was just learning how to speak again. Silence, for all its terrors, still was self-protection. To speak was to risk everything. And if she had never spoken, many would have found in their hearts more sympathy; for when she spoke she condemned herself. Then you could feel the public mind set like wet concrete, and harden in judgment, as sympathy for the battered woman evaporated.

At first, as Nussbaum testified, all New York seemed fascinated, and the *Times* explained why. "Most Can Identify," said the headline. "Quite simply, people wonder what separates her from them. Her very ordinariness, experts in human behavior say, is the attraction, a reminder that even a life with all the trimmings of stability can slide into disarray. . . . 'She crossed the line, and we all know that we have the capacity to cross that line, too,' said William B. Helmreich, a professor of sociology at the City College of New York and an expert in group responses to public events. 'That's frightening. But at another level, it's reassuring because we know that we didn't cross that line.' "[12] The formula is neat: not "There but for the grace of God go I," but "There, thank God, goes someone who is most decidedly not me."

But it leaves unanswered the more critical question: how does a life *slide*? How does one happen to cross the line? "People may ask themselves," the *Times* said, " 'Could it happen to me?' " The answer (which the *Times* didn't give) is *yes*. Judith Lewis Herman reports flatly that "under extreme duress anyone can be 'broken.' "[13] And survivors of severe trauma—combat soldiers, prisoners of war, rape victims, disaster victims, hostages, battered women—*universally* attribute their survival largely to good luck.[14] But who wants to believe that our well-being hinges upon chance? Instead we trace the root of trouble from where it flowers. As we saw in the last chapter, we search the *victim* for those peculiarities of psyche and circumstance that made the life give way, or, worse, impelled the victim to step across the line herself, deliberate and heedless. Herman says that we try "to account for the victim's behavior by seeking flaws in her personality or moral character" because, having no knowledge of terror and coercion, we presume that in similar circumstances we "would show greater courage and resistance than the victim."[15] Certainly, as Hedda

Nussbaum testified, observers in the courtroom and the enormous television audience sought out the flaws in *her*.

District Attorney Robert Morgenthau had determined that on November 1, 1987, the night Lisa was taken to the hospital, Nussbaum was too physically and mentally incapacitated herself to be capable of either injuring the girl or taking action to save her; and in July 1988 he had arranged to drop murder charges against Nussbaum in exchange for her cooperation in prosecuting Steinberg.[16] But until she took the stand, no one knew whether Hedda Nussbaum would be able to speak at all.

And who knew that when she spoke she would say unspeakable things? She said she had worshipped Steinberg as "God." She said he had the power to heal. She said he was a wonderful man. She said he had left her alone with the unconscious Lisa for three hours, and during that time she hadn't called 911 or the pediatrician who lived in the neighborhood because she "trusted" Steinberg; he had said that *he* would get Lisa up and heal her, and she didn't want to show "disloyalty" to *him*. She said that when Steinberg returned she prepared cocaine for him and smoked a little herself, and then for hours worried about Lisa as she half-listened to Steinberg talk. She said that in effect she had let Lisa die. And she said, weeping, that she didn't know why.

Reporters had a new story. To columnist Gail Collins, writing in the *Daily News*, Nussbaum's inaction was "unforgivable." Weighing one victim against another, she concluded: "Not even Nussbaum's 32-part itinerary of abuse can make up for her failure to save that dying child on her bathroom floor."[17] Columnist Judy Mann of the *Washington Post* found "sickening" the "collusion between the state and its key witness *to use victimization as an excuse* for the most reprehensible behavior."[18] Michele Launders, Lisa's birth mother, who had sympathized with Nussbaum before the trial, told reporters she found her as contemptible as Steinberg.[19] Columnist Murray Kempton thought it "shameful" that the D. A. had "let her go free" with "an official certificate of innocence."[20] Commentators began to inquire pointedly about who was *ultimately* responsible for Lisa's death, and talk shows addressed the thorny question of Nussbaum's "culpability."[21] Author Susan Brownmiller, whose novel based on the Steinberg case was already in the stores, argued on the op-ed page of the *New York Times* that Nussbaum, "an active participant in her own—and Lisa's—destruction," should have been brought to trial.[22] *Daily News* columnist Bob Herbert noted that Nussbaum, "in no danger of criminal prosecution," was "home free."[23]

The question of Hedda Nussbaum's culpability became the subject of heated debates in the press and in private, especially among feminists. Susan Brownmiller, best known for her book *Against Our Will*, a history of rape, told reporters that when it comes to domestic assault, " 'classic feminist movement' theory is wrong." A battered woman is not simply a victim of a batterer, she said, but a participant in "a sustained relationship between two people," a relationship in which "a woman *decides* to stay."[24] Most advocates for battered women, on the other hand, saw Hedda Nussbaum as a victim: a woman so badly assaulted, psychologically and physically, that *decision* was beyond her. They were dismayed at the sudden wave of "Hedda bashing."[25] Sympathizing with Nussbaum, Gloria Steinem tried to explain the disagreement among women: "Either you allow yourself to realize that it could have been you or you're so invested in making sure it couldn't have been you that you reject the victim."[26]

Everyone seemed to agree that Nussbaum had a *moral* responsibility to act for the good of her child, and that no circumstance could make her any less accountable to a higher authority, or if you will, to God. It was all the more tragic then, many thought, that Steinberg's abuse had rendered her incapable of taking the action she was morally bound to perform. But others, when they spoke of culpability, meant a narrower *legal* responsibility; they believed her guilty of specific criminal acts, the exact nature of which was also at issue. Reckless endangerment? Criminally negligent homicide? Murder?

Culpability, however, is not a term the law uses. Any person may be *culpable*—that is, to blame for doing an act (or failing to)—and yet not be legally *guilty* of a crime; for legal guilt is not based solely upon the commission (or omission) of an act. The law considers other circumstances, such as whether the culprit acted in self-defense or under duress or under the handicap of some mental disease or defect. Thus a person can be both *culpable* and *not guilty* at once. So it happened that the District Attorney considered bringing criminal charges against Nussbaum, concluded that no jury would convict a woman so badly victimized herself, and decided not to press for her indictment. Then all at once, as writer Marilyn French observed, Hedda Nussbaum became "really the one on trial, at least in the court of public opinion."[27]

In the end, the same disagreement split the jury. When they started deliberations, Judge Rothwax dismissed five alternate jurors, and four of them, all women, spoke to reporters. Three said they would have voted to convict Steinberg of "something," but it was Nussbaum reporters asked about and Nussbaum the alternate jurors talked about. "I just feel she was to blame," one said. "I don't think she should get away with everything." Nussbaum was "partly responsible," said another.[28] "She's a very sick woman," said the third. "She should be convicted of something."[29]

The twelve deliberating jurors were divided from the start. When they entered the jury room on January 23, four jurors were reported to be "strongly convinced" that Steinberg was guilty of murder, five "in the middle," and three holding out for lesser charges because they believed that Hedda Nussbaum had killed the child.[30] They emerged on January 30 with a verdict: *Not Guilty* of murder—but *Guilty* of manslaughter in the first degree.[31]

To many legal scholars and reporters, the verdict was mystifying, for the language of the manslaughter charge was a poor match for the circumstances of the crime. Clearly the verdict was a compromise—ending what the *Times* called "a long wrangle over the technical language and . . . the relative culpability of Mr. Steinberg and Ms. Nussbaum."[32] After reviewing testimony of medical experts, all twelve jurors finally agreed that Hedda Nussbaum "could not have delivered the deadly blows" to the child. Yet juror Anne Marie King said, "She should have been charged too." And juror Helena Barthell agreed that Nussbaum should have been charged with "some crime."[33]

As for Steinberg, Barthell explained that the jurors "felt there was a lack of proof of his depravity."[34] And "certain jurors," took the attitude: "'Poor Joel. Joel's a victim. We have to send a message to the system: 'You don't make victims out of nice men like Joel.'"[35] Even though he'd beaten Lisa into unconsciousness, gone out to dinner, then freebased cocaine and talked through the night, he might not have realized, in his coked-up state, that the girl was *dying*. The jury apparently disregarded what it had been told about New York State law: that because ingesting drugs or alcohol is a *voluntary* act, a person "under the influence" *is* legally responsible. A person with a mental disorder or defect, on the other hand, is not responsible in the eyes of the law because mental deficiency is a condition for which one does not volunteer. The Steinberg jurors, however, thought Hedda guilty of "something" *because* of her "sickness," while Joel's drug abuse, legally a criminal act in itself, relieved him of legal responsibility for worse crimes. And with such a crazy "wife," Steinberg came in for female sympathy. Juror Barthell said: "I feel sorry for Joel. He's been through a terrible ordeal."[36] At his sentencing, Steinberg agreed. "I have remorse about losing my life," he said. He maintained—and does to this day—that he hadn't hit anyone. "It's my loss," he said. "I'm the victim."[37]

People still ask me if I went to the "Nussbaum trial." Watching the *Steinberg trial* from Boston, David Douglas who counsels batterers there, understood why Steinberg was "not the focus." Douglas said it reminded him "of the way the guys we see are so good at pointing the finger at the woman. . . . These guys are scary, so it's much easier to confront someone who's not that scary, which is the woman. Social agencies do that all the time. Battered women get treated like it's their problem and their fault. There's something wrong with them for not leaving."[38] That's what happened in "the Nussbaum trial." The jurors, the press, and the public ran shy of Steinberg and beat up on Nussbaum. "She's despicable," said one reporter.[39] "An absolute schmuck," said a self-described "feminist lawyer."[40] We focused on *her*. We blamed *her*. We called *her* names. We made excuses for him. And somehow, like these neglectful parents, we forgot about the child.

But Hedda Nussbaum—this bad mother, this revolting and culpable creature, this gray and desolated woman—was described perfectly by psychiatrist Elaine Hilberman in a now-classic study of sixty battered women published in *The American Journal of Psychiatry*—thirteen years ago. Hilberman writes:

> These women were a study in paralyzing terror that was reminiscent of the rape trauma syndrome, except the stress was unending and the threat of assault ever present. Agitation and anxiety bordering on panic were almost always present. Events even remotely connected with violence— sirens, thunder, a door slamming—elicited intense fear. . . . The women remained vigilant, unable to relax or sleep. Sleep, when it came, brought no relief. Nightmares were universal, with undisguised themes of violence and danger. In contrast to their dreams, in which they actively attempted to protect themselves, the waking lives of these women were characterized by overwhelming passivity and inability to act. They were drained, fatigued, and numb, without the energy to do more than minimal household chores and child care. They had a pervasive sense of hopelessness and despair about themselves and their lives. They saw themselves as incompetent, unworthy, and unlovable and were ridden with guilt and shame. They thought they deserved the abuse, saw no options, and felt powerless to make changes.[41]

A few women Hilberman says, became "frankly homicidal" and a few fought back verbally or physically, but "passivity and paralysis of action more accurately described the majority of these women. Aggression was most consistently directed against themselves, in the form of suicidal behavior, depression, grotesque self-imagery, alcoholism, or self-mutilation." It's either that, or kill the batterer, as Hilberman concludes: "Passivity and denial of anger do not imply that the battered woman is adjusted to or likes her situation. These are the last desperate defenses against homicidal rage."[42]

I quote Hilberman at length because although her work has been known for more than a decade, it doesn't seem to have filtered into public consciousness. Rather, with our perverse habit of blaming the victim, we assume that when a victim does not rescue herself, she *chooses* not to; she chooses instead to stay because she *wants* or even *needs* to be where she is: looking like, but not truly, a victim. Further, when a victimized woman is unable to protect her children from her "partner"—as happens in perhaps half of all cases of child abuse[43]—we conclude that she chooses not to, that she chooses rather to betray them, to collude in their abuse, or worse, to abuse them herself, and that she claims falsely to be a victim merely to escape punishment for her dereliction.[44]

As a rule, when we contemplate the victimization of our fellow human beings, we have the least sympathy for the worst case. Psychologists know that this is just another common defense by which we distance ourselves from disaster, but it's curious and disturbing nonetheless, violating at once the laws of logic and the leanings of the heart. No wonder that when the worst case becomes a public spectacle it sets us against one another, loudly defending our views against adversaries who seem bereft of common sense on the one side and compassion on the other.

We set victims against one another, too, in a contest of authenticity or worthiness. Think of the factions of the unfortunate: the "deserving poor," for example, distinguished from the poor who presumably deserve nothing; *bona fide* refugees, as opposed to "economic opportunists"; "innocent" AIDS victims, as opposed to those who "asked for it." And now "real" battered women who have no money or job skills or family, as opposed to Hedda Nussbaum who had all three. "Heroic" battered women who flee. Heroic battered women who save their children. As opposed to Hedda Nussbaum who stayed. Hedda Nussbaum who let the child die.

Illogical though it may be, *the greater the abuse, the less our sympathy for the sufferer.* We are inspired by those who gallantly pass through hardship, but we despise those who succumb. We admire those who triumph over adversity, but we condemn the full-blown victim. Thus, for many complex reasons, many who followed the Steinberg case—in the jury box, in the press rows, in the papers, on television—came to see Hedda Nussbaum as a "willing" victim, which is to say, really not a victim at all. And by focusing on the victim, they managed to lose sight of the criminal, and the crime.

Women and men on both sides of the divide described Nussbaum either as an active woman willingly participating in "the violent relationship," and hence no victim, or as a passive and helpless victim of violence, and hence no active woman. In fact, she was something far worse than either side cared to contemplate: an active person reduced *against her will* to powerlessness, a woman reconstructed as a victim.

We can trace that terrible process in the history of Nussbaum's relationship with Steinberg. But as we do so, it's important to remember the distinction between powerlessness and passivity. Powerlessness is a political condition, while passivity is a strategy adopted by the powerless to survive. The process of victimization consists of (1) first putting the victim in a position of powerlessness relative to the victimizer, and then (2) repeatedly impressing the victim with his or her powerlessness, including the powerlessness to escape, until the victim eventually adopts passive and compliant behavior in order to stay alive. Once you recognize the process, you can see the importance of offering help to battered women early on, and if it comes to that, intervening. With some empowering help from the outside, a relatively powerless woman can get free, as most battered women do. Even a woman who *seems* to be passively complying may be biding her time, waiting for the right moment to escape; she holds her own by *acting* with extreme caution, and she too needs empowering outside help to get free.[45] But once the victim is coerced to believe that resistance is futile, she may surrender voluntary action and judgment, and escape into a detached state of consciousness. Once she is "out of it," she may no longer be able to seek help herself, or even to respond to it.[46] Then, without decisive outside intervention—from neighbors or police or medical personnel, for example—she and her children will be trapped.

In the Steinberg household, where she lived for more than a decade, Hedda Nussbaum was more powerless than most: not a legal wife, not a legal mother, not even a legal tenant—legally she did not exist. But she was *not* passive. Only later, after her attempts to escape failed, did she try to survive by being passive: by doing nothing that Joel Steinberg did not approve or demand. Her final test came as Lisa lay in a coma on the bathroom floor and Nussbaum, alone with the child for three hours, *thought* of calling 911, *thought* of calling the pediatrician, and did not. Life posed her a cruel dilemma, and she *chose* inaction. "I was trying to be loyal to Joel *and* save Lisa," she said in court. "I was trying to do *both*."[47] But how is a woman brought to the point at which the only possible action is not to act at all?

Batterers share a common aim—to control—but they use whatever tools come to hand. Joel Steinberg was a lawyer. He used words. "He was a fantastic orator," Nussbaum said. "He was very intelligent, and I loved listening to him talk."[48] They had endless "conversations," Nussbaum said. "He talked, I listened." When they met at a party in the spring of 1975, she was thirty-two, good-looking, a rising editor of children's books at Random House, and he was thirty-three, good-looking, a lawyer, and (like Nussbaum) Jewish. She was drawn to him, she said, by his "bright, shining, alive eyes" and by the attention he paid her.[49]

They dated for two months, and Hedda broke it off.[50] Joel wanted to talk to her every day, spend every moment of every weekend together. Hedda wanted time to herself. But soon Joel came back. Hedda wasn't busy. They went to dinner. This time he impressed her more—with his brilliance, his success, his friends in high places. He took her to Lincoln Center. He introduced her to the author of a book she was reading. "I couldn't believe that this special man cared so much for me," she said. In that respect he was different from other men she'd dated. She used the cliche: "He swept me off my feet."[51] And in all the years they spent together, he never stopped talking.

In the beginning, when "everything was so wonderful," she was intensely "flattered" by the attentions of this "wonderful" man. But his attention monopolized hers and focused it on him. He monopolized all her free time. He monopolized her career: he took an uncommon interest in her work, coached her on how to get ahead, and when she did get ahead, he reminded her that she couldn't have done it without him. To Hedda, Joel's interest came to seem not only "helpful," but necessary to her continued success.

He monopolized her life: she moved into his apartment in January 1976, and although she held on to her own place for a few months, Steinberg angrily persuaded her to let it go. He monopolized her mind: he let her know she "wasn't functioning at the level he liked" and set about "helping" her to "improve." She dropped a therapist she'd seen for a couple of years and accompanied Steinberg to a Reichian "relationships" group. Steinberg himself undertook to "spend hours, usually almost every night, trying to work on and improve" Nussbaum's "problems." At his suggestion she took up jogging and dancing; she lost weight and started wearing high heels.[52]

"He built me up," she said, but he also criticized her more and more "for her own good." He criticized especially her failure to be "spontaneous" and to "give" herself sexually. She said she had a lot of "evidence that he was on my side," but she began to live under threat, anxious that she "couldn't live up to his standards."[53] The nightly psychobabble sessions increased her anxiety and wore her down. More and more he isolated her: he was rude and overbearing to her family, friends, and coworkers, who predictably avoided the couple, blaming Hedda for having chosen a partner they didn't like. More and more he made the decisions, he set the standards to an increasingly fine gauge—his complaints were always about "little things," she said—and he barked out snappy backhanded put-downs, especially in public.

A glance back at the Amnesty International chart of coercive methods (see chapter 3) will confirm that Joel Steinberg's "help" was textbook brainwashing. *Isolation, monopolization, induced debility, threats, occasional indulgences, demonstrating omnipotence, degradation, enforcing trivial demands*—Steinberg did it all. Certainly a Greenwich Village apartment seems nothing like a jungle prison camp, but equivalent effects can be produced in any place where a diligent controller can hold his victim in relative isolation—in a religious cult, for example, or a brothel, or a family.[54] Typically the effects of brainwashing are capitulation, compliance, dependence upon the interrogator, anxiety, and despair. On Hedda Nussbaum, the effects were predictable and grim.

On December 7, 1977, after two years of Steinberg's attention, she wrote in her diary: "I must have Joel's love and approval to survive. I'm worthless and helpless. I am a piece of shit."[55] This capitulation is not "willed"; it is what happens when, under relentless pressure, resistance gives way—when the will is vanquished. "Willing capitulation" is a contradiction in terms—as is "willing victim." Hedda Nussbaum didn't volunteer to become a zombie. Against her will, at the expense of her will, Hedda Nussbaum was victimized. *Victimize*: *to make a victim of, especially to make a victim of by deception*; *to dupe*; *cheat*; *gull*.[56] Afterwards, as facts were revealed to her, Nussbaum said in astonishment: "Everything he told me was a lie!"[57] She should have seen it coming. But she didn't. That's what it *means* to be a victim. On March 17, 1978, three months after Nussbaum wrote in her diary, "I am a piece of shit," Steinberg hit her for the first time—not to gain control, but to *demonstrate* it.[58]

Like most battered women, Hedda Nussbaum was "shocked." Steinberg said he was shocked too, but he "didn't apologize."[59] Like so many of the most lethal batterers, Steinberg never used "remorse," insisting either that he beat Nussbaum "for her own good" or that someone else did it; but he routinely followed violence with indulgence. "Afterwards he was very affectionate," Nussbaum said, referring to that first blow. "We both thought it would never happen again."[60] Actually Steinberg had every reason to think it *would* happen again, for he had a habit of assaulting people, including a business associate, a colleague's wife, and two former girlfriends; but that was one of the facts about Steinberg that Nussbaum didn't know.[61]

In February 1981, after a beating, Nussbaum sneaked out to St. Vincent's Hospital where her ruptured spleen was removed in emergency surgery. Steinberg, no doubt sensing he'd gone too far, became indulgent. What followed, Nussbaum testified, was "the best number of months in our whole relationship and in my whole life."[62] In May 1981, Steinberg brought home Baby Girl Launders, to be known as Lisa, and perhaps because the child now kept Nussbaum in place, he stopped the violence for six months. Everything was "wonderful" again.

Nussbaum was thoroughly "in love" in that peculiarly tenacious way that psychologists call "traumatic bonding." It can happen, they say, when there is a power imbalance in a relationship. The person without power feels increasingly worthless, anxious, and depressed. The person with power feels increasingly self-important. The powerful one comes to depend utterly upon the power*less* one for his relative sense of omnipotence—(which explains why batterers usually won't let "their" women go)—and knowing she doesn't like the abuse, he treats her nicely when he has to, to keep her from going away. The powerless one, clinging to the big shot as her last hope of affection, "bonds" to the "nice" side of his personality and overlooks the rest.[63] The traumatically bonded battered woman "dissociates" one violent episode from the next, seeing no *pattern* of battering but only an occasional shocking "aberration" having nothing to do with the basically "nice" character of her powerful abuser.[64] Hedda Nussbaum put it this way: "I didn't see myself as being battered. To me, the beatings were isolated incidents. I always thought each one was the last. I loved Joel so much. I always felt there was much more good between us than not."[65]

After months of intensive psychotherapy (following Lisa's death), Nussbaum concluded that her own "fear of abandonment," induced by her grandmother's death, and her imperfectly developed "sense of self," the result of her unusually close child-hood bond with her sister, made her an easy mark for Steinberg.[66] That may be true—the reasonableness of it apparently comforted Nussbaum—but such fears and imperfections can be found ret-roactively in all of us, to explain almost anything. Interestingly enough, both Nussbaum's friends and her detractors diagnosed characterological problems contributing to her fate—different di-agnoses, different problems, same fate. What we saw of Nuss-baum's character, however—in interviews, in court, on televi-sion—was the *product* of that fate, not its cause. The effects of traumatic bonding, like the effects of brainwashing, do not de-pend upon the *character* of the victim, but upon her *situation*.[67] As Judith Lewis Herman writes: "The most powerful determinant of psychological harm is the character of the traumatic event itself. Individual personality characteristics count for little in the face of overwhelming events."[68]

Successful brainwashing enables the interrogator to exercise ex-traordinary, if not total, mind control of the subject; and it is usually accomplished, as it was in the case of Hedda Nussbaum, without violence. Put brainwashing in the context of an intimate relationship where traumatic bonding is likely to occur, add phys-ical violence, sexual coercion, sexual abuse, and drugs—and the subject's world rapidly collapses inward. She restricts her move-ments, censors her thoughts, silences her opinions to match the demands of her increasingly powerful controller. Options disap-pear. Choice becomes dangerous. She is captive.

Not that Nussbaum didn't try to find a way out. But when she reached for help, she met only denial, indifference, and blame. What seems extraordinary in this story is the failure of *every* per-son who might have helped her. It seems that sheer chance should have produced at least one helpful person among the many to whom Nussbaum turned. On the other hand, the murders of so many abused women and children remind us that there are thou-sands, like Nussbaum, abandoned by the world.

Late in 1981 Steinberg resumed the physical assaults with greater intensity. He completed Nussbaum's isolation by beating her so badly so often that in August 1982 she lost her job. Then he destroyed the free-lance work she brought home, so that her employers judged her incompetent; as a result, she lost all paid work and contact with colleagues. Steinberg put her to work himself, as a paralegal, in his service, without pay, at home. (As Lisa lay dying, Nussbaum was dutifully straightening Steinberg's files.) He induced her to stop seeing her friends; and in 1983, claiming her parents had "a terrible effect on her," he barred them from the apartment. Once when Steinberg was out, she called her father to come and get her; but Steinberg returned while she was packing, beat her up, and, when her father arrived, ordered her to send him away. Steinberg made a rule after that: Nussbaum couldn't leave the apartment without his permission. ("I missed my parents," she said, "but I was actually relieved when they stayed away because I began to believe the things Joel told me about them.")[69] Towards the end, he told her they weren't her *real* parents anyway.

In 1983 and 1984 Steinberg took to freebasing almost nightly and stepped up the violence. In February 1984, feeling she couldn't take any more, Nussbaum escaped and walked to a shelter for homeless women, which referred her—because she had a broken knee—to Bellevue Hospital. Although she made up a cover story about a mugging, Bellevue doctors recognized her as a battered woman—and called Steinberg. They held her a few days in the psych ward where she repeated to them as "fact" Steinberg's obsessive fantasy: that she was involved with, and had been beaten by, a pornographic sadomasochistic cult on Long Island.[70] Then they told Steinberg to take her home.

Two months later she escaped again to the office of an old friend's brother. She asked to stay with his family for a while, but he told her she "owed" something to Joel. He phoned Joel to come and get her. Some time later she took a train to New Haven and spent two days with a former Random House colleague; the woman turned her over to a social worker who telephoned Steinberg and sent her home. Later in 1984, after a beating and a prolonged ice-water "bath," she ran in her nightclothes to a doorway down the street; someone sent her in an ambulance to St. Vincent's Hospital. And there *she* telephoned Steinberg so he wouldn't "worry."

The very first time she fled to a hospital, after Steinberg first hit her in 1978, she told the doctor (a woman) that her boyfriend hit her; then, fearing legal consequences and Steinberg's wrath, she asked the doctor to change that part of the report—and the doctor did. So Nussbaum learned right away that the authorities didn't particularly want to hear how she got injured. Nevertheless, each of her subsequent escape attempts carried her a little farther, lasted a little longer—until someone to whom she had turned for help notified Joel Steinberg and sent her *back*. On that last sad trip to St. Vincent's she called Steinberg herself, exactly like a child who wants to run away, but knows she will be punished for crossing the street. In December 1985 she got all the way to LaGuardia Airport, planning to flee to another ex-colleague in St. Louis, but she telephoned Steinberg, again so he wouldn't worry, and never got on the plane.[71] During that period, when Nussbaum was trying to flee, someone reported the couple to the Child Abuse Hotline. Caseworkers who visited the apartment found nothing wrong with the family, and Nussbaum never tried to leave it again.

Steinberg increased "disciplines"—such as the ice-water baths—to reinforce her habit of compliance and increase her debility. He deprived her of food; her weight dropped from 125 to 100 pounds.[72] He deprived her of sleep. He assigned her the floor, often without a blanket; and in the last months, as his cocaine habit rocketed out of control, he kept her up most of the night—on her feet, so she wouldn't doze off—listening to him talk. (He slept during the day, while Nussbaum looked after the children.) He degraded her more and more—urinating on her, beating her sexual organs—and now she lived constantly under the threat of his violence. The beatings "hurt a lot," she testified. "I hated it and I told him that I didn't want him to keep doing it," she said. "But I had a problem getting angry then."[73] "He always warned me just before he'd hit me," she said. He listed one by one the offenses for which he was about to beat her. She testified, "That was the time I was most afraid of him."[74]

Paradoxically the threat of violence bound her to Steinberg even more closely. "I was very connected to him," she testified. "Not like someone who hurt me."[75] Psychologists studying hostages and terrorists find similar bonds. One study observed that hostages in life-threatening situations may experience "spontaneous identification under stress" and "become satellites of the person who threatens their life."[76] Other studies of hostages describe "traumatic psychological infantilism," a condition which amounts to being "scared stiff." One expert calls it "frozen fright," a state common to hostages and to battered women "brainwashed by terror."[77] The victim may appear to be behaving normally, albeit without much animation, but is in fact totally focused on survival, concentrated utterly on the terrorist or abuser. As the experts put it: "The condition of traumatic psychological infantilism causes the victim to cling to the very person who is endangering her or his life."[78] (Nussbaum said of Steinberg: "I needed him and wanted to please him.")[79] Psychologists studying hostages also describe a characteristic attitude shift, technically a "pathological transference." The victim sees that the terrorist has the power of life and death over him, sees that so far the terrorist has let him live, and comes to think gratefully of the terrorist as a "good man." ("I always believed he *meant* to help me," Nussbaum said of Steinberg.)[80]

Taken together, these two phenomena—traumatic psychological infantilism and pathological transference—comprise the Stockholm Syndrome, that peculiar psychological somersault by which a hostage aligns himself with his captors and their concerns, and against his rescuers. The Stockholm Syndrome may account for attitudes and behavior which to onlookers can only seem inexplicably bizarre—such as Patty Hearst's "enlistment" in the Symbionese Liberation Army. Such as the promise of an American male hostage upon his release from the 1985 TWA hijackers: "I will be coming back to Lebanon. Hamiye [one of the captors] is like a brother to me."[81] Such as the sentiments Colleen Stan expressed in notes to Cameron Hooker, the man who kidnapped her and for years raped and tortured her and kept her locked in a box under his bed: "You know how to make me feel good about my-

self. And I love you so much for it." And "my love for you is growing with every changing day. You fill my life with happiness and
love. And I pray that that happiness and love will never end."[82]
Such as the answer Hedda Nussbaum gave, when asked what she
thought about bringing a baby into the violent Steinberg household: "My perception of Joel was that he would be a good father
and not continue to hurt me or certainly hurt a child."[83] Such as
Hedda Nussbaum's belief that Joel Steinberg "had supernatural
. . . godlike powers." Such as Hedda Nussbaum's hope: "to spend
the rest of my life with *him*."[84]

This is not to suggest that Hedda Nussbaum was simply a victim of the Stockholm Syndrome. There are too many differences
between the experience of hostages and those of battered women
for such a tidy comparison. Most hostages are male, for one thing,
men still being more "important" in the world, more likely to
lead consequential public lives. Hostages usually are held in
groups in which they can support one another, or at least infer
from the presence of other adult victims that their victimization
is not their own fault, while battered women are isolated individually. Hostages usually are held briefly, often a matter of hours or
days; battered women usually are held longer. Hostages are rarely
subjected to serious physical violence or abused sexually; while
battered women (and some female hostages) regularly suffer physical violence, sexual abuse, and rape. Hostages know that authorities are working to free them, while battered women learn
that no outsider is likely to intervene, even when they ask for help.
Hostages know they'll be treated with sympathy when they're released, perhaps even as heroes, appearing on television, lunching
at the White House. Certainly they'll never be *blamed* for having
been taken hostage. But battered women know they're likely to
be found at fault.

In short, battered women are so much *worse* off than hostages,
that it seems unfair to compare them—except perhaps in the effects of captivity under threat.[85] When they can't get away, when
they feel the threat of death over their heads, battered women,
like hostages, may be scared stiff; trying to survive, they may fo-

cus completely on the abuser, and in extreme cases, like that of Hedda Nussbaum, they may come to think of the abuser as "a good man," even perhaps a "god."

The threatened hostage instinctively focuses on the captor. The brainwashed subject, focused *by* the interrogator, focuses *on* the interrogator. And if ever one human being focused on another it was Hedda Nussbaum on Joel Steinberg. Like the god she thought he was, he issued "commandments" and she wrote them down. "If he was displeased with some of my behavior," she said, "we'd have long talks about it and he'd have me write ideas that were beneficial to me. I would write them repeatedly. I would write things about how to improve myself so I could look back at the book and improve as a person."[86] She was a writer. She wrote.

But all she wrote was what he dictated. For example, an assignment introduced in evidence at Steinberg's trial was headed: "My goals in terms of Joel's interest." They included: "Give myself sexually," a rule always prominent in Steinberg's program. "Be more direct. Learn to really care for Joel and show it. Learn to take risks. Be honest. Be spontaneous. Be responsive. Be alert and aware. Get bedroom cleaned up. Get kitchen cleaned up." She wrote pages and pages of loopy script listing things she should and would care about, all of them boiling down to Joel. "I want to care about Joel's hair," she wrote. "I will care about Joel's hair." Next line: "I want to care about Joel's clothes. I will care about Joel's clothes." Next line: "I want to care about Joel's work. I will care about Joel's work." And so it went, through Joel's "shaving," Joel's "feelings," Joel's "shirts," Joel's "dinners," Joel's "health," Joel's "happiness," Joel's "problems," Joel's "diet," Joel's "future," Joel's "teeth," Joel's "legal malpractice insurance," Joel's "goals," Joel's "image," Joel's "concern," Joel's "recreation," Joel's "bike riding," Joel's "fun."[87]

There were "punishment lessons" too, in which Hedda had to write Joel's instruction ten times. Most of these lessons were upbeat and inspirational, aimed at instilling in Hedda the drive she needed to get the kitchen cleaned and to go on caring about Joel's teeth despite her depression and her flagging health. "Can do."

"Will do." "Spontaneity creates energy." "I feel better when my energy is up." The rest were clear lessons in compliance, which apparently even then was not sufficient, not quite perfect. "Anger is destructive, not constructive." "Self-defense is regressive, not progressive." "Arguing, being defensive and negative, reinforces bad habits." And another frequent assignment: "I will not resist Joel."[88]

To survive, powerless Hedda kept active and busy being passive: busy denying what was really happening, busy paying attention to Joel, busy caring about Joel and showing it, busy giving herself sexually, busy being afraid, busy being anxious, busy trying to see everything Joel's way, busy—when she could think of it—taking care of the children. Busy writing. Busy improving as a person. "Adoption of these submissive postures is an instinctive response to a life-threatening situation from which the victim cannot escape," the experts say.[89] Diplomats and international businessmen who may not trust their submissive instincts can now get behavior training for survival from expert psychologists, just in case they should be taken hostage. They're taught *not* to be aggressive or hostile or angry or "to develop any negative transference." They're taught to be passive and submissive and docile without lapsing too far into active and annoying obsequiousness. They're taught to behave in a "feminine" way. They're taught to behave like Hedda Nussbaum. Hedda Nussbaum apparently figured it out for herself, or did it by instinct, and for a long time, it worked.

Certainly no one helped her. Not her co-workers, who said impatiently that they'd *told* her to leave. Not her parents or her sister, who when ordered by Steinberg to stay away, stayed away. Not her friends, one of whom talked endlessly to reporters about what a wonderful woman she'd been years ago, and about how he'd noticed, when he called on Steinberg in recent years, the strange way she lurked, half-hidden, in the background, looking like a bag lady. Not the school administrators, who didn't seem to note Lisa's bruises and matted hair and disheveled appearance, even when teaching assistants pointed them out. Not the child welfare worker who in 1984 found nothing wrong with the Steinberg "family." Not the doctors at one hospital or another who patched up Nussbaum and sent her back to Steinberg, like a wounded soldier back to the lines. Not the neighbors, some of whom listened for years to Nussbaum's cries. (One said: "Ten years ago it was unbelievably loud—screaming and yelling. . . . in the last couple of years it got much more quiet, but she was still getting beaten up very badly.")[90] They told reporters they'd called police time and time again for a decade, but the precinct records showed only one call, less than a month before Lisa's death.[91] Not the police, who responded to that anonymous domestic violence call on October 6, gave Nussbaum some printed information about Family Court, and left without making an arrest. Not the State Police, who, having been alerted by a toll collector that a child in a car was being abused, possibly kidnapped, stopped the car, talked to Steinberg, photographed Lisa, and waved them on their way together—and later reprimanded the alert toll collector for having sent them on a wild goose chase.

To be fair, Joel Steinberg could be an intimidating man. Nobody wanted to tangle with him. "He was big, he had connections," said a woman from Random House.[92] "He was a lawyer," said the state patrolman. "What could we have done?" asked Nussbaum's sister.[93] The New York City Police, when they went to the apartment on October 6, had both the power and the authority to arrest Steinberg, like any other perpetrator of assault, on probable cause—that is, if *they* had cause to believe an assault had taken place—but instead they left it up to *Hedda Nussbaum*. A police Department spokesman first reported that Nussbaum had been "hit in the face," had *only* a "slight injury," and "refused" to press charges; but Police Officer Glenn Iannatto later testified that when he and his partner finally got inside the apartment—after talking for half an hour with Steinberg through the door and summoning a sergeant to back them up—they found Nussbaum "covered with bruises." "We observed that her face was pretty battered," he testified. "She had bruises, a swollen lip, a bruise about her eye. We couldn't see much of her body. She was holding [her] housecoat up around her neck. She kept saying she was okay."[94] They took her word for it. (Why is it that so many male police officers, notoriously skeptical when a woman reports rape or battering or threats of violence, take a bruised and bleeding woman at her word when she says she's "okay"?) They left Hedda Nussbaum to take care of her bruises, and the man who bruised her, all by herself.

That's how it happened that everything came down to Hedda Nussbaum's choice. Lisa, neglected, abused, terrorized, and finally pounded or shaken into a coma, lay on the floor, and Hedda Nussbaum had to decide what to do. She didn't know what was wrong with the child, who "seemed unconscious." (She asked Steinberg, "What happened?" And Steinberg replied: "What's the difference what happened?")[95] Nussbaum checked Lisa's eyes, her neck pulse, her breathing. She pumped her chest and gave her mouth-to-mouth resuscitation. She testified that when Steinberg went out for dinner, leaving her alone with the child, she did "nothing"; but in fact she continued to do quite a few things, dabbing at details in the feeble, ineffectual way of a person who fears the consequences of a mistake. (Much later, trying to help Steinberg, the "healer," she tried to look up the problem in a medical dictionary, but she passed over the word "coma" as "too permanent.") Lisa drooled. Hedda wiped her face. Lisa soiled her underpants. Hedda took them off and washed them. Lisa lay still. Hedda sat still and watched her. When Hedda figured out that her constant watchfulness had no effect on Lisa, she decided she could safely do something else. That's when she went to work on Joel's files. But she kept checking Lisa's breathing and her pulse. And she thought about making a phone call—to 911, or to the doctor.[96]

There seemed to be a choice involved, between helping Lisa and being loyal to Joel. As she said, she wanted to do both. Who knows what *thought* she was capable of at that moment? We know she didn't want to anger Steinberg. We know she counted on *him* to help. And we know that nobody else *ever* had helped her. So there was a certain cruel logic to her decision, though it looked as though she simply failed to act, too passive to *do* anything; and perhaps that's all there was to it. In any event, Hedda Nussbaum's failure was a measure of Joel Steinberg's success. It was also a measure of society's failure to help either the woman or the child.

Yet we resist the thought that what happens to others may be out of their hands, and that it may consequently fall to *us* to protect them. For that would imply that what happens to ourselves may be out of our hands, that things may befall us, that in the face of deliberate evil, we may go under. Far better then, despite all we know of terrorism and victimization, and of the collusion of those who look away, to blame the victim. To that end, journalist Daphne Merkin assured readers that somewhere in Nussbaum there were "needs being met."[97] And writer Joyce Johnson reported that Hedda Nussbaum definitely had an "appetite for self-annihilation."[98]

To that end too, it's useful to postulate another party, a secret or subconscious inner being, to take the rap. Thus, Merkin wondered "if somewhere in Hedda Nussbaum is a woman waiting to be beaten—to be pummeled out of her senses."[99] And Joyce Johnson, discovered in Hedda Nussbaum a "dangerous, second self" who "pressed to be released," a Hedda "underneath" who "burned to violate taboos, to do things and let things be done to her that were impermissible."[100] Murray Kempton detected the same struggle, but with the players reversed: Hedda Nussbaum (the visible one) "in active pursuit of the destruction of her inner self."[101] And Susan Brownmiller, writing in *Ms.* about Hedda Nussbaum on the witness stand, saw "what was left of her shriveled soul" fly across the courtroom "to the defense table to rest at Joel's side"—figuratively speaking, you understand.[102]

But such literary excess is not innocent. It practices a deception upon readers by presenting as a kind of observed fact something the writer has entirely *imagined*. Worse, it fabricates a *blameworthy* woman and passes her off as a resident in the body of a real woman who suffered real harm. This is the worst kind of psychological second-guessing, suggesting guilt by association: the inner woman is guilty, so the outer woman must be too. Readers thrilled by the titillating prose may forget that the guilty inner woman lurks not in the real woman but in the minds of the writers. This kind of ill-informed commentary has other dangerous implications as well. It privatizes a political act—the domination of three people (a woman and two children) by another. It represents a long series of (male) criminal acts as a (female) psychological problem. It reduces a social problem to an individual one. By recasting forcible domination as romance, life-threatening assault as eccentric love, and sexual abuse as sophisticated consensual kinkiness, it draws the musty nineteenth-century curtain of privacy again over woman beating, precluding altogether the public discussion of social policy and social change. And it obscures the fundamental point that because women have an *absolute* right to be free from bodily harm, aggravated assault is aggravated assault, even in the odd case where a woman's perverse second self feels the need to be bludgeoned into oblivion.

To be sure, in the wake of Lisa's death, many commentators and public officials raised issues of social policy and practice, suggesting communal responsibility for children like Lisa, and even women like Hedda Nussbaum. They raised disquieting questions about the role of schoolteachers, neighbors, doctors and hospitals, police, and child welfare workers. But the *Times*, the "newspaper of record," which had joined New York City's more flamboyant papers in weighing the "culpability" of Hedda Nussbaum, warned against such fruitless "speculation." In a remarkable editorial writing *finis* to the Steinberg case, the *Times* said: "to speculate too much about society's failure to protect this child is to miss the message of the Steinberg case. Lisa Steinberg died because she was living with brutes." What we have to learn from this case is that "we remain fascinated by the abominable."[103] So much for wife and child abuse. Hedda Nussbaum and Joel Steinberg become abominable together, a partnership of "brutes," joint victimizers of a "pretty little girl"—whose death seems as inevitable as it was sad and "fascinating."

Still, commentators went on about Hedda Nussbaum—and

the second Hedda Nussbaum and the inner Hedda Nussbaum—
and we forgot all about the simple, obvious questions like: How
come Officer Iannatto didn't arrest Steinberg, like he's supposed
to? And: How can you protect a child if you won't protect her
mother? Joel Steinberg's assaults on Hedda Nussbaum were criminal, *no matter what the character of the woman and no matter what the
nature of the relationship between them*, just as his assault on Lisa
amounted to murder; but because we don't hold him fully accountable for one, we don't hold him fully accountable for the
other. In the end Steinberg got off with a manslaughter conviction
and a sentence of 8⅓ to 25 years for killing the child Lisa—and
no punishment of any kind for what he did to Hedda
Nussbaum.[104]

A few weeks after the Steinberg trial, reviewing an historical
study of family violence for the *New York Times Book Review*, sociologist Kenneth Keniston observed that "the fact of wife beating . . . was once acceptable if it conformed to 'the rule of thumb'
(no rod thicker than the husband's thumb could be used). Today,
the same fact is morally (and legally) unacceptable."[105] So reasonable men and women would like to believe. But these days, it
seems, even the rule of thumb does not apply. Joel Steinberg
bludgeoned Hedda Nussbaum with a steel exercise bar as thick as
a man's arm, and when we learned this fact, reasonable people,
influential people, "feminist" people, said the fault was hers, or
at least that being bludgeoned was no excuse for being a bad
mother.

Steinberg used to beat up Nussbaum, then make her sit down
with him to watch television as though nothing had happened.
Thus is violence fastened to the victim alone, subsumed in the
fairy tale of the loving American family, and "normalized." For
months we watched that woman with the boxer's face battered
again and blamed, not only for failing to protect her child, but
for her own battering. (Steinberg used to say to her: "Just look at
what you've done to yourself!")[106] Then academicians, journalists,
and government and criminal justice authorities reassure us that

our society regards wife beating as morally and legally wrong. It is as though nothing has happened. Although one of Nussbaum's neighbors, who remembered that years before "she was an attractive human being," said that watching the woman go downhill was almost "like watching the disintegration of a *person*."[107]

What Can We Do?

To measure change, it helps to take the long view of history. Then one can see that in the last century and a half, public opinion about battered women has undergone a fundamental shift. During the nineteenth century and a good part of this one, when a woman left her husband, the public asked: Why did she leave? The question was not merely inquisitive but judgmental, suggesting other loaded questions: What kind of woman walks out on her husband and family, the sacred duty entrusted to her by God and nature? How could she abandon her obligations, her destiny? Throw away her life? Her children's happiness? Is she deranged? Irreligious? Unnatural?

Today, family, friends, clergy, courts, and counselors still urge a woman's duty upon her, but when a woman complains too loudly, or some "real" trouble occurs—a homicide perhaps, or the battery of a child—the public wants to know: Why *didn't* she leave? A century ago a dutiful woman's place was with her husband, even a brutal one, though she herself was blameless. Today she is still supposed to stand by her man, but only up to a point— a point always more easily discerned in retrospect, and by others. Then, as we saw in the case of Hedda Nussbaum, if he is "really" abusive and she stays, whatever happens is said to be her own fault.

It is also clear that today in the mainstream culture of this country a woman's duty to her child is supposed to take precedence over her duty to her husband. This judgment too represents a fundamental shift away from an older, purely patriarchal order which valued nothing as much as the privilege of the patriarch himself. Marilyn French tells an old story from India, one of those instructive moral tales designed to teach women how they are supposed to *be*. French writes: "The story presenting an exemplary Indian wife tells of a woman sitting with her sleeping husband's head in her lap, watching over him and her baby playing in front of the fire. The baby wanders near the fire, but the woman does not move lest she disturb her sleeping lord. When the child actually enters the flames, she prays, begging Agni not to harm the baby. Agni rewards her wifely devotion by letting the child sit amid the flames unscathed." As French observes, the Indian wife is "a model for Hedda Nussbaum."[1] But as we've seen, the model no longer applies—except perhaps in the minds of men like Joel Steinberg who still feel entitled to all the powers and privileges of the sleeping lord. Today, in this country, the exemplary wife is supposed to stand up and rescue her child from the flames, and if need be, from her "lord" himself.

Thus it happens that the big question—Why didn't she leave?—cuts two ways. On one hand, it shifts the blame from the "nature" of men in general and the societal attitudes and institutions that abet male violence to the character of the individual victim; it blames the victim for the abuse she suffers. On the other hand, it suggests that women now have more options and should make use of them. It implies a widespread belief that women *should* leave abusers, that living with brutality (or, as some would say, "excessive" brutality) is no longer a good wife's duty. Taken in the context of a century and a half of struggle, this is progress.

Yet nothing makes it easy for a woman to leave. Many factors—from low wages and inadequate child care to the unresponsive criminal justice system and a Congress unwilling to fund victims' services—conspire to keep the abused woman in her place within the "traditional" family. Abused women leave anyway, but often they are strictly on their own. Many flee one problem—battering—only to become part of another: "the feminization of poverty." Today 65 percent of black children live in a family headed by a single mother, and 45 percent of all American families headed by a single mother live in poverty.[2] Dan Quayle pointed to abortion, divorce, and these single parent families as grievous *causes* of "the disintegration of the American family." But we can attribute this "disintegration" in part to violence, just as we can attribute the "feminization of poverty" in part to woman and child abuse, a cause economists and politicians never cite. Today, experts name battery as a "major cause" of homelessness; large numbers of the nation's growing band of homeless are women on their own with children—women and children who, despite the social and economic obstacles, ran from male violence at home.[3] (Reflect for a moment on conventional explanations for the feminization of poverty—*her* youth, *her* lack of education, *her* lack of job skills, *her* sexual activity, *her* insistence upon becoming a single mother, heedless of Quayle's righteous admonitions—and you'll see that we blame the victim for poverty too. Men, especially men of color, are blamed for "abandoning" women and children—but not for the violence that drives women and children away.) Today most people recognize that women have a right—even a responsibility—to leave abusive men, but we don't yet recognize our responsibility as a society to help: our duty as a society to protect the right of every woman to be free from bodily harm.

Our public attitude—damned if you don't leave, damned if you do—is not simple hypocrisy. Two conflicting views come down to us from nineteenth century debates, and we've never sorted them out. To radical women in the mid-nineteenth century, questions of marriage and divorce were, as Elizabeth Cady Stanton put it, "at the very foundation of all progress" on women's rights.[4] After all, as Stanton wrote in 1860, "We decide the whole question of slavery by settling the sacred rights of the individual. We assert that man cannot hold property in man, and reject the whole code of laws that conflicts with the self-evident truth of the assertion."[5] How then can man hold property in woman? Has woman no sacred rights as an individual?

As Stanton and her colleague Susan B. Anthony saw it, marriage was an institution devised by men, and backed by all the authority of church and state, to give husbands absolute authority over wives. Worse, no matter how "unfortunate or ill-assorted" the marriage, society and government compelled it to continue. Stanton believed, however, that marriage and divorce were private matters, not properly subject to civil or canon law, and should be transacted by simple contract. "There is one kind of marriage that has not been tried," she said, "and that is a contract made by equal parties to lead an equal life, with equal restraints and privileges on either side."[6] Fundamental to Stanton's "radical" view, of course, is the assumption (never shared by American law) that women and men are equal beings in the eyes of God and should enjoy equal rights and responsibilities in all things.

For women in the nineteenth century the catch was this: the marriage made in heaven maintained on earth the rights and privileges of the man, as Stanton correctly said, and so did all other social institutions. Divorce might be the way out of domestic tyranny, but for most women it looked like a dead end, depriving them as it did at the time of their children, home, livelihood, reputation, and prospects. Consequently, more conservative advocates of women's rights tried not to get women out of marriage but to protect them within it. Temperance leaders battled drunkenness, always considered a cause of brutality and violence, while moral reformers sought to curb male "animal" lust and to "improve" men with an infusion of female "purity." More to the point, Lucy Stone and her husband Henry Blackwell campaigned in Massachusetts from 1879 to 1891 for legislation modeled on laws already passed in England in response to Frances Power Cobbe's revelations about "wife-torture." The new legislation provided legal separation (not divorce) and financial maintenance for wives whose husbands were convicted of assaulting them; but even that modest proposal, seen as an attack upon the family, failed.[7]

The same attitudes persist today, both within the family and outside it. Some battered women are as dedicated as any conservative congressman to keeping the family together; they want only to stop the violence. Other battered women are ready to strike out for freedom and self-determination, for themselves and their kids. All these women, whether they struggle under the banner of *The Family*, the flag of *Woman's Rights*, or the colors of *Women's Liberation*, need protection from violence, and institutional supports to help them.

In the public arena, "radical" feminists go on arguing for the rights of women, though we live in what conservatives wishfully call a "postfeminist age." Never mind that for a pile of economic and social reasons the "traditional" family is as scarce these days as the blue whale. Never mind that, as Elizabeth Cady Stanton observed, "A legislative act cannot make a unit of a divided family."[8] Legislators and policy makers, backed by custom, the church, "modern" psychology, and twelve years of Republican administrations beholden to the far right, still try to keep "the family" alive. Consequently, our economic and social arrangements still impede a woman's departure, especially if she has children. Under federal reimbursement programs that require child protective agencies to try to keep "families" intact, abused women are pressured to enter counseling or mediation with their assailants, while their abused children are left at his mercy, sometimes in his household. And if a woman reports that her husband or boyfriend abuses the children, she may see them removed not only from his custody but from hers to be placed in a *family* of foster parents. If she and the kids set up their own household, they may get poorer, while the abusive husband gets relatively richer. And even the prospect of that supposedly inevitable financial decline, much trumpeted in the media, serves to intimidate the woman who considers setting out on her own.[9]

Nevertheless, today's battered woman has options her sisters struggled in the last century and in this to win for her. She may not be formally married at all. If married, she can divorce, provided her religion and her pocketbook permit. She may get custody of her children, if she can afford the lawyers she'll need to persuade a judge that a violent man is not fit to be a custodial parent. She can work, albeit for lower wages than a man doing the same job—if she can find a job. She may even get some public assistance. And she hears, as her nineteenth century sister did not, the nagging question: "Why doesn't she leave?"

The danger today is that we overestimate society's changes. Implicit in the question, "Why doesn't she leave?" is the assumption that social supports are already in place to help the woman who walks out: a shelter in every town, a cop on every beat eager to make that mandatory arrest, a judge in every courtroom passing out well-enforced restraining orders and packing batterers off to jail and effective reeducation programs, medical services, legal services, social services, child care, child support, affordable housing, convenient public transportation, a decent job free of sexual harassment, a living wage. The abused woman, wanting to leave, encouraged to think she will find help, yet finding only obstacles at every turn, may grow disheartened and doubt herself. If it's supposed to be so easy, and it's *this* hard, she must be doing something wrong. What seemed to be a social problem—judging by all the reports about "domestic violence" in the news—becomes just a personal problem after all. For the abused woman, it's just one more turn of the screw.

Public opinion too, can easily turn backward—without even changing the dialogue. When we ask "Why doesn't she leave?" do we mean to be helpful, encouraging, cognizant of her rights, and ready with our support? Or do we mean once again to blame her for her failure to avail herself of all the assistance we mistakenly think our society provides? Lucy Stone and Henry Blackwell thought wife abuse would cease when women got the vote—because women would vote off the bench judges who failed to punish wife beaters.[10] That didn't work. The battered women's movement has organized for more than fifteen years against "domestic violence," yet the violence continues. Could it be that individual women are to blame after all?

Or could it be rather that battered women play some indispensable part in this society that we've overlooked? Could it be that battered women have some function, some role or social utility we haven't taken into account? Thus far in this book we've looked at the problem from the point of view of battered women—women who almost invariably ask for help. But perhaps we should look again from the point of view of "society"—if we can try for a moment to imagine that this many-headed abstraction has something like a point a view. Perhaps we should put a different question: What are battered women *for*?

Asking a different question puts a new light on the problem right away: battered women are *for battering*. The battered woman is a woman who may be beaten; she is a *beatable* woman. If you doubt that society views battered women as, by definition, "beatable," then how do you explain the fact that we almost always put responsibility for woman beating on the woman? Why else would we probe her psyche to reveal the secret self within, yearning for abuse, if not to set her apart as a *beatable* woman, unlike ourselves? In our society there are millions of these beatable women. Many of them live within "the family" which entitles only the "head" of the family to beat them. Many others live outside "the family"—in which case anyone may beat them who will. Many live and work in industries that rent or sell beatable women and children to the male "public"—prostitution, for example, and pornography. A few beatable women, like Hedda Nussbaum, become public figures whom everyone can assail.

In the aggregate, battered women are to sexism what the poor are to capitalism—always with us. They are a source of cheap labor and sexual service to those with the power to buy and control them, a "problem" for the righteous to lament, a topic to provide employment for academic researchers, a sponge to soak up the surplus violence of men, a conduit to carry off the political energy of other women who must care for them, an exemplum of what awaits all women who don't behave as prescribed, and a pariah group to amplify by contrast our good opinion of ourselves. And for all their social utility, they remain largely, and conveniently, invisible.

Consider this story. In the early hours of March 25, 1990, a social club in the Bronx went up in flames and eighty-seven people

died. New York City Mayor David Dinkins called a press conference to discuss an important public policy issue raised by this disaster. The issue, he said, was licensing and inspection of private
social clubs, like the one that incinerated its patrons. But there
was another issue, an invisible issue, unmentioned by the mayor
or the police or the press. It lurked between the lines of the press
reports on the fire and its aftermath.

The arsonist was thirty-six-year-old Julio Gonzalez, a refugee
who'd left Cuba ten years earlier for the Bronx. For most of the
previous eight years he'd lived in the housing project apartment
of forty-five-year-old Lidia Feliciano together with Feliciano's
three grown children and various other members of her extended
family. Lidia Feliciano worked nights, keeping the cloakroom at
the Happy Land Social Club. Two months before the fire, Lidia
Feliciano accused Gonzalez of "making sexual advances" to her
nineteen-year-old niece, Betsy Torres, who lived in the household.
Feliciano threw Gonzalez out. But Gonzalez wouldn't go away. A
few days before the fire he tracked Feliciano to a beauty shop, and
there he publicly swore to "love" her forever. Then he showed up
at the Happy Land Social Club, still vowing his undying love. But
he was drunk. Feliciano sent him away. He picked fights with
patrons. It took a bouncer to hustle him out the door. He got some
gasoline and returned to burn the place down.[11]

This is a typical story of "domestic violence": a typical story of
a typical abusive man who will not let "his" woman go. Predictably, reporters told it in the language of love. New York's *Newsday* called this a "Love Story" that "Ends in Hate"—"an eight-
year love story" that "erupted in jealousy, rage and death." The
"love" in question, according to all the papers, was the love of
"young" Julio Gonzalez for "older woman" Lidia Feliciano. And
the jealousy and rage were *hers*, prompted by Gonzalez's "attentions" to her niece. Feliciano "rejected" him. She "turned him
down." She "threw him out."[12] Columnist Jimmy Breslin got the
inside word from a guy named Popo, one of Julio Gonzalez's
drinking buddies, that Lidia Feliciano "dominated him" and "got

him mad." "She went out to the club and made him stay home," Popo said. (The club, of course, was where she worked, checking coats.) Another of Breslin's informants, a guy named Jesus, said: "She never should have told him to go away when he came to the club." According to Breslin, Lidia Feliciano was so clearly in the wrong, so clearly asking for trouble, that "people in the Bronx" wondered why Gonzalez hadn't just borrowed a gun and shot her.[13]

Lidia Feliciano compounded her sins by being one of only five people to survive Julio Gonzalez's bonfire at the Happy Land Social Club. (Betsy Torres, the niece she had tried to protect from Julio Gonzalez, was killed.) Like the newspapers, many of Feliciano's neighbors blamed her for the fire, blamed her for the eighty-seven lives lost, blamed her for surviving. Some told her that she shouldn't have left the burning building. To save her from her friends and neighbors, the police had to move Lidia Feliciano and her children out of the apartment she had lived in for twenty years and place her under special protection.[14]

Why, when a man burns down a building, killing eighty-seven people, does a woman become the scapegoat of the neighborhood? Isn't the answer clear? Lidia Feliciano failed miserably to do her *duty*: to absorb the violence of the man who claimed her, and by so doing to keep her neighbors safe. Instead she turned him out and unleashed his violence on the whole community.

Years ago Simone de Beauvoir reminded us that some women are meant to be "sewers," safeguarding the "wholesomeness" of lovelier parts of society. "It has often been remarked," she wrote in *The Second Sex*, "that the necessity exists of sacrificing one part of the female sex in order to save the other and prevent worse troubles." She was thinking particularly of prostitutes, a caste of "shameless women" who make it possible for "honest women" to claim respect. "The prostitute is a scapegoat," she wrote. "Man vents his turpitude upon her and rejects her."[15] In just the same way the battered woman is a scapegoat. Man vents his violence upon her and blames her for it. And so do we. How else can we explain this curious fact: that when a man commits an act of unspeakable violence, public blame falls upon the woman who failed to prevent it?

This, then, is what battered women are for. Like prostitutes (who commonly are battered women themselves), battered women serve to drain away excess male violence and assaultive sexuality. Admittedly, I employ here a peculiar theory of social relations based on the notion that violence and assaultive sexuality well up in men of their own accord, like floodwaters, and must find an outlet lest they drown us all. This hydraulic theory of human behavior is perhaps a projection onto social life of the mechanics of the male orgasm. Whatever its origins, it has been a popular theory for at least a century, probably because it gives men an excuse for excess, positing an inexplicable and uncontrollable force to blame for the violence and sexuality that are, in fact, simply behaviors men *choose* to act out. Hydraulics provided de Beauvoir with a theory of social relations that explained the social utility of prostitutes. And the theory serves as well for battered women who, like prostitutes, must be sacrificed to preserve the "family" and "society."

No wonder then that social institutions and policy makers are so reluctant to put a stop to either prostitution or battering. Imagine if prostitution were stopped. Where would all those men go with their kinks and aberrations and "needs"? Where would they expend them? And if battery were stopped? In this country, we've learned, a man beats up a woman every twelve seconds. That's 7,200 outbursts of violence every day, 50,400 every week, 2,620,800 every year. If battering were stopped, where would all those men go with their obsessions and jealousy and rage and despair? With all that "love"?

The potential consequences of stopping battery are terrible to think about. Perhaps that's why we've gone on for so long saying we disapprove of "domestic violence," yet blaming the victim whenever it occurs. But the consequences of battery are terrible as well: the pain and suffering, the lives lost, the time and resources and human potential squandered; the way it spills over into our streets, killing bystanders, and into the next generation, wounding the future. Four more women every day, dead. We *could* make it stop.

We might make a start by passing the Equal Rights Amendment. Amending the U.S. Constitution to provide equal rights for women won't stay the hand of the batterer, but it will affirm the constitutional, philosophical, and moral underpinnings for woman's right to be free from bodily harm. At the moment, women seem to have no such right, either in popular sentiment or under the law as it is currently enforced. In fact, as a social contract, the Constitution does not even include women as citizens. More than a century ago John Stuart Mill argued: "That the principle which regulates the existing social relations between the two sexes—the legal subordination of one sex to the other—is wrong in itself, and now one of the chief hindrances to human improvement; and that it ought to be replaced by a principle of perfect equality, admitting no power or privilege on the one side, nor disability on the other."[16] The principle of perfect equality was *not* adopted in Mill's time because, as he observed, "the generality of the male sex cannot yet tolerate the idea of living with an equal."[17] It has not been adopted in our own time for much the same reason. Yet Mill's argument still holds.

As things stand now, because neither our sentiments nor our laws as they are currently enforced recognize freedom from bodily harm as a fundamental right for women, we judge instances of bodily harm to women case by case, and we assess the victim's "rights" in the matter on the basis of her status or her character or her behavior. We condemn the "bad" victim, like Hedda Nussbaum, and occasionally we pity the "good" victim, but fundamental *principles* and human *rights* do not come in to our calculations. It was John Stuart Mill again who pointed out our bad habit of paying lip service to the principle of individual freedom. "If the principle is true," he wrote, "we ought to act as if we believed it."[18]

It is now long past time to admit that the right to be free from bodily harm, the right that belongs to all men under the constitution, belongs to *all* women as well. It is (or should be) an absolute right. A fundamental *human* right. Not contingent upon the status, character, or behavior of the individual. That means that *no* woman anywhere should be subjected to bodily harm at any time for any reason. Today, given our immense burden of sexism and racism and class bias, our tendency to blame victims and to whitewash violence in the language of love, the *only* way to combat violence against women is to acknowledge this fundamental right of every woman—every "masochist," every "narcissist," every neglectful and abusive and "unfit" mother, every prostitute and junkie and drunk, every mother of an "illegitimate" child, every "bimbo," every "slut," every "bitch" and "fox" and "whore" and "cunt" and "piece of trash." Women are just women, after all: no better than we should be, and often a good deal worse. But rights do not have to be earned. Human rights, by definition, are ours by virtue of our humanity.

It's true that men often seem to have trouble recognizing the humanity of women. Representative Pat Schroeder points out that our government, so keen to defend human rights around the world, most often views oppression of women in other countries not as a violation of human rights but as a "custom" or "tradition"—another quaint example of "cultural difference."[19] And individual women everywhere face that blindness every day—the blindness of men who simply can not *see* that women are human beings too. Sarah, for example, was held captive by a pimp when she was twelve years old and used in prostitution; her "clients" were New York City businessmen. "I was a little kid," she says, "with black eyes and bruises all over my body, crying in pain and fear, sometimes bleeding, but it didn't seem to diminish the pleasure of the johns one bit. Nobody ever complained or offered to help me or even seemed to notice that maybe I wasn't totally happy to be doing what I was doing."[20] Nevertheless, despite this blindness, most men and women today would grant in principle at least that women *are* human beings. And as Mill said, if the principle is true, then we ought to act as if we believe it.

Institutional Change

R. Emerson Dobash and Russell P. Dobash, directors of the Institute for the Study of Violence at the University of Wales, point out that different cultures respond to social problems in terms of their longstanding habits of mind. Britain, for example, brings its tradition of leftist and Labour politics to bear on the *social* problem of battery; it emphasizes the role of the state in creating the *material* conditions that enable women to escape male violence and become independent. Help for battered women comes in the practical form of refuge, housing, social and health services, adequate welfare benefits, child care, and jobs. The United States, on the other hand, emphasizes the *individual* and the "politics of the mind."[21]

In the United States, "domestic violence" is addressed in terms of the personal psychology of individual victims and (far less often) perpetrators. "Domestic violence" is a "social" problem only in the sense that it affects an aggregate of those supposedly aberrant individuals. Hence, all that research into the pathology of victims, "mediators" in courtrooms, "conflict resolution" training for cops, support groups for victims and assailants alike, endless self-help books for women, and so on. When problems long left unattended threaten to overwhelm us, we send in the cops or the National Guard or the Marines, as though imprisoning aberrant individuals in sufficient numbers will achieve social justice. But if we are to make progress against battering and child abuse, we must understand that neither the problems nor the solutions lie in the individual psyche, and that the material conditions necessary for women to become free and equal and independent will not be found in our heads.

When the material conditions of women's lives change—when women have access to shelter, housing, child care, adequate welfare benefits, job training, and living-wage jobs—most women can free themselves and their children from violence. But we must change the way our institutions operate as well, to combat male violence and to aid women and children still victimized, always keeping in mind, however, that no institutional change can "save" women and children set up by economic dependence and poverty, real or threatened, to be easy marks for male violence.

Susan Schechter points out that almost all activist/researchers in the last fifteen years have identified as a primary source of the "continual epidemic" of battering and child abuse "the failure of institutions to intervene properly." She writes:

> In the last fifteen years of testimony before Congress and state legislatures, in newspaper accounts, in proposals to foundations and state agencies, the same problems have been identified again and again: judges fail to hold offenders accountable or to take victims' fears seriously, doctors patch wounds and send women back to their assailants, clergy tell women to try harder, courts issue visitation orders requiring children to see fathers who sexually assault them. The result of this institutional response is an almost guaranteed escalation of assaults. Other outcomes are equally predictable and tragic: more injuries, more deaths, more runaways, increased substance abuse, psychiatric hospitalizations and suicide attempts among women and children.[22]

To change things, we must see to it that those who staff our institutions are schooled in the causes and consequences of violence against women and children and trained to intervene effectively. What's more, we must see to it that *all* our community institutions change, for piecemeal change may be worse than no change at all. If police arrest offenders and judges release them without punishment, for example, the result is offenders who feel licensed by the court to carry on, and to scoff at the police as well. If social workers or journalists encourage women to take the dangerous step of running from batterers and no shelter is available, the result is homeless women who are doubly endangered. If judges issue restraining orders but police do not enforce them, the result is often another headline femicide: "Murdered Wife Had Protection Order."

Sometimes, with the best intentions, institutions work at cross purposes and do more harm than good. Social workers charged with child protection, for example, may routinely place abused children in foster care, heedless of the fact that their battered mother would protect herself and them if the batterer were held to account for his violence. On the other hand, some judges, determined to keep the nuclear family intact, pressure battered women into marital counseling, mediation, or child custody and visitation arrangements that are debilitating and profoundly dangerous to the women and their children. For their part, women who fear that they will lose their children or be bound into some continuing legal relationship with the offender, may not report child abuse or even seek help themselves.

To avoid these mistakes, and to plan an effective, coordinated community program, Schechter suggests that *every* institution establish "policies, standards, training programs and practices" to meet *one set of goals*:

1. to identify and respond sensitively to every victim in the family;

2. to protect and empower abused women so that they in turn may protect their children;

3. to make it safe for women and children to seek help;

4. to stop further harm by holding offenders, rather than their victims, accountable for maltreatment;

5. to ensure that every agency in the community adheres to these standards and works together to achieve them.[23]

To plan a coordinated community program members of *every* community agency, public and private, must *sit down together*. That includes agencies and institutions that may think they have no role to play in helping battered women: the housing authority, for example, the vocational school, the credit union. They must build in to their design specific ways to monitor one another's work, collaborate on reviewing and revising programs, hold one another accountable for ineffective policies and practices, provide mutual support, and work to overcome institutionalized sexism, racism, and homophobia; and they should hire a full-time coordinator to monitor and promote their continued collaboration. Every aspect of the coordinated community program must aim to protect victims and to hold offenders accountable.

The Criminal Justice System

In 1980, with the leadership of feminist organizers, the city of Duluth, Minnesota, undertook a Domestic Abuse Intervention Project, a system of coordinated criminal justice intervention in domestic abuse cases, a system involving police, prosecutors, civil and criminal court judges, and probation officers. The DAIP also runs batterers' reeducation groups and a center for supervised child visitation and parenting education. It works in close cooperation with battered women's shelters, with the Women's Coalition, which provides support groups and services and legal advocacy for battered women, and with the Women's Transitional Housing Program, which provides short- and long-term low- and no-rent housing and child care and facilitates job training. The goal of every segment of this coordinated effort is to make women and children safe and offenders accountable for their crimes. In twelve years of the Domestic Abuse Intervention Project, one in twenty men living in the Duluth metropolitan area (population 250,000) has been ordered by civil or criminal courts to attend the batterers' reeducation program, designed and conducted by profeminist women and men. This program doesn't seem to have decreased the number of violent men going through the system— deprived of one victim, many a batterer turns on the charm to recruit another, then is arrested again for assaulting his second, third, or fourth target—but the program has provided safety for thousands of women and children.[24] Eighty percent of women who have used the program report five years later that they are free of violence, and most no longer live with the man who assaulted them. Duluth also maintains, year after year, an exceptionally low rate of domestic homicide.[25] The Duluth model can be adapted to other communities.[26] Similarly, the San Francisco Family Violence Prevention Project, which provides advocacy for women and training for personnel at every level of the criminal justice system, is a model for other communities.[27]

To be effective, any criminal justice program must begin with a policy of arresting offenders and handing out serious consequences. Police must recognize assault as assault, a crime committed by a perpetrator against a victim. (They must get over the notion that a "domestic disturbance" is a "marital problem" of a "violent couple.") Given limited resources, police policy makers must reorder their arrest priorities, recognizing that domestic battery, the leading cause of injury to women, is far more serious, violent, dangerous, and costly to the victim and to the public than the petty thefts, car thefts, burglaries, and minor drug use offenses that typically engage the police. Police officers should be empowered and *required* to make warrantless arrests on probable cause in domestic assaults and to hold offenders overnight for arraignment; they should be shielded from civil liability for wrongful arrest in such cases. In sizable communities, police should computerize and review records of domestic calls so that they can easily identify repeat offenders. In responding to every domestic disturbance call, police should be required to give the woman (*not* in the man's presence) printed information about her rights and appropriate community services. Police should carry this information in the languages of all major ethnic groups in their community.

On their own initiative, prosecutors should prosecute men arrested for domestic assault. Although criminal justice personnel at all levels should consider the victim's wishes, it is their job, not hers, to arrest, prosecute, and punish the criminal. Salaried women's advocates (and translators if necessary) should be present in every prosecutor's office and every court to advise battered women of their rights and help them negotiate the system. Legal counsel should be available to all women, and it should be free for poor women. On their own, or in cooperation with a local battered women's program, prosecutors and courts should establish support and educational groups for victims of domestic assault, such as those now offered in the Quincy (Massachusetts) District Court.

Women should be able to obtain restraining orders quickly and easily, including at night and on weekends, and free of charge. Police should enforce protection orders by *seeking out* and arresting violators. Records of restraining orders should be computerized and centralized, especially in large cities, to avoid the all too common situation in which a judge, having no knowledge that the defendant is in violation of a valid restraining order, releases him to assault again and perhaps to kill. For similar reasons, civil court judges should routinely review the criminal court records of men who appear before them in any case in which battering is alleged, including proceedings for separation and divorce, child custody, and child support. Violation of a restraining order, which constitutes contempt of court, should be regarded as a very serious offense punishable by imprisonment. Any man who commits an assault in violation of a restraining order should be regarded as dangerous; the assault should be a nonbailable offense. A recent study indicates that between one-half and three-fourths of all murder-suicides are committed by battering men who fear the "infidelity" or departure of a wife or girlfriend.[28] The court should take at his word any man who threatens to harm or kill his present or former partner and/or himself; and prosecutors and judges should recognize that many attacks currently charged as "assault" are in fact failed murder attempts. Charging with assault or battery a man who has slashed, stabbed, shot, clubbed, run over with a car, or doused with gasoline and set fire to a woman—as happens again and again in our courts—is an invitation to him to try again. The court must also recognize that such a man presents a danger to the public at large.

Judges should have and exercise the power to remove batterers from their homes and order them to stay away so that women and children need not flee. In sentencing batterers, they should hand down some *combination* of sanctions and rehabilitation. Sanctions might include finding the offender guilty, ordering him to make restitution, limiting or terminating his visitation privileges, or sending him to jail. Rehabilitation should include substance abuse rehabilitation and programs, batterers' reeducation, and parenting education. In no case should judges regard rehabilitation as a *substitute* for sanctions. Judges should not be permitted to let a personal bias in favor of the nuclear family make them blind to the dangers women and children face; they should *never* require victims of abuse to enter mediation or counseling with their assailants.

When women apply for protection orders, judges should not issue "mutual protection" orders to both parties, thereby suggesting that the woman is as blameworthy and as dangerous as the violent man. And when a batterer persuades or forces a woman to let him in to her premises again, judges should not pronounce the restraining order "waived" or charge the woman as an "accessory" or "co-conspirator" in the violation of a protection order. (Such judicial action, founded on ignorance and hostility to women, is common and in some jurisdictions, mandatory.) Legal counsel should be provided to women seeking protection orders; and because many fearful women choose civil protection orders in preference to invoking the sanctions of criminal law, judges should try to determine with the woman and counsel whether the circumstances warrant additional criminal justice responses.

Because so many batterers assault again and again, attacking either the same woman or a series of women, legislators and judges should hand down heavier penalties for repeat offenders. Legislating significant jail time for repeat offenders, however, will bring sentencing judges up against the fact that there is nowhere in the United States enough jail space for perpetrators of domestic assault. The answer is not more jails and prisons in a country that already has too many, but a reordering of priorities in assigning jail time. State governors, legislators, judges, and state and local penal officials should recognize that assaultive men, particularly repeat offenders, are far more dangerous to individual victims and to the public at large than most nonviolent offenders who currently crowd our jails and prisons and who are good candidates for alternative punishments.

When judges are to decide custody of the children of a violent man, they must face the fact that joint custody can only be harmful to the mother and children. As Susan Schechter points out, "Forcing women to continually negotiate with their assailants puts them in a dangerous and inherently unequal position."[29] And children, trapped between parents in perpetual conflict, are bound both to suffer and to learn firsthand about the efficacy of physical violence.[30] In custody proceedings today, judges are to rule in "the best interest of the child." They must recognize and establish as a matter of policy that in custody cases involving battery the best interest of the child *is* a presumption against joint custody and against custody for the battering man. And when judges award custody to an abused woman they should grant her every possible assistance, ranging from child support payments to parenting education. If offending fathers are to have visitation rights, communities should establish centers where visits can take place safely under professional supervision and the mother need never encounter the battering father. (The Duluth Domestic Abuse Intervention Project provides a model.) In determining visitation arrangements, the safety of mothers and children must be the primary consideration.

The governors of every state should review the cases of women currently imprisoned for assaulting or killing a man.[31] They will find, in a great many cases, that the degree of homicide charged was greater than the facts of the homicide would support; that the homicide followed a long history of rape and assault about which the jury was permitted to hear nothing; that legitimate claims of self-defense were disallowed either by the court or by the woman's own attorney; that expert testimony about battering was wrongfully excluded; or that the sentence given was so long in comparison to the sentences assigned men who committed "spousal" homicides as to raise at least the suspicion of gender bias, not to mention cruel and unusual punishment. A fair-minded review will find hundreds of women now in state prisons who deserve immediate clemency if not reparations.

Instituting new policies is often the easiest part of the job of making change; getting officials, steeped in sexism, to carry them out is another matter. We've seen that police chiefs may have to bring disciplinary action against their officers to make them arrest batterers. Similarly, state governors may have to take action to compel criminal justice personnel to comply with state abuse prevention laws. In 1985, then-governor Michael Dukakis of Massachusetts took additional steps to bring police, prosecutors, court clerks, and judges into compliance after a task force found that they simply disregarded the 1978 abuse prevention statute. In 1991 the state legislature strengthened the law itself, and in 1992 Governor William Weld proposed that the legislature enact further reforms, particularly to the bail system.[32] The lesson to be learned from the Massachusetts experience is that every policy needs a built-in review procedure to hold accountable those who are charged with carrying it out and to review and amend procedures. Eight federally funded demonstration projects carried out in criminal justice and other community agencies in 1985 also found a need for "full-time domestic violence coordinators . . . to develop and monitor interagency coordination."[33]

Many advocates note that judges seem particularly resistant to change, and several state reports on women in the courts, federal and state reports on "domestic violence," and a National Institute of Justice study on civil protection orders all emphasized the need for judicial training.[34] Both civil and criminal judges should be *required* to attend profeminist in-service education and training programs on battering and child abuse, and so should police officers, prosecutors, and all other personnel in the criminal justice system who deal in any way with domestic assault cases. (In-service education should consist of more than a few token workshops.) Information on battery, sexual assault, and child abuse should be a regular and significant part of police training, law school education, and continuing education programs of bar associations, police, and judicial organizations.

If women are to use the legal remedies that now exist on the books, they must have legal counsel. Without lawyers, women are less likely to get orders of protection, and the orders they get are less likely to contain all the provisions they're entitled to, putting them and their children at a disadvantage in subsequent visitation, custody, and divorce proceedings. Nevertheless, most women today represent themselves in court, while their husbands, who often control the couple's money, are likely to appear with lawyers. A violent man facing charges for battery or violation of a restraining order is assigned a lawyer at public expense if he can't afford one, but the woman who complains against him is on her own. Noting these inequities in a report to the Ford Foundation on the current state of legal reform for battered women, law professor Elizabeth M. Schneider writes that despite an "explosion of legal reform activity around the country over the last 15 years, there are virtually no lawyers available to assist battered women to navigate the legal reform systems that have been established."[35] She cites the example of Connecticut, a state with a comprehensive system of statues against domestic abuse, but only one lawyer working full time on domestic assault cases.[36] Although women now have remedies for battery "on the books," Schneider concludes that "the lack of skilled legal representation effectively discriminates against battered women."[37]

In the absence of lawyers, lay advocates have long provided support and advice for battered women, run interference with the criminal justice system, instigated legal reforms, and monitored compliance—all this usually without formal training or pay. More federal and state money should be allocated to provide paralegal training programs for lay advocates, legal services for battered women, and paid lawyers and lay advocates for battered women's shelters or centers. (The Legal Center run by Women Against Abuse in Philadelphia is a model for other cities.) Law schools and bar associations should encourage and help in this work. Federal money should also support the two national centers that currently gather and disseminate information about legal matters affecting battered women and their children: the National Center on Women and Family Law in New York, and the National Clearinghouse for the Defense of Battered Women in Philadelphia, the latter devoted to the legal defense of women charged with crimes for defending themselves against battery or sexual assault.[38]

New Legislation and Policies

As we've seen, many of the women murdered each year by husbands or boyfriends are killed *after* they leave or as they are trying to leave—and as they are trying to get the police and courts to enforce a restraining order. The violent man engaged in separation assault often kills innocent bystanders as well as (or in lieu of) the woman who is his primary target, as Julio Gonzalez did when he set out to incinerate Lidia Feliciano. To save lives, then, stricter measures are required, as some states now recognize.

When Governor Weld proposed legislation in 1992 to prevent such homicides, Massachusetts men were murdering their wives and girlfriends at the rate of one every nine days.[39] Weld proposed to detain violent offenders before they killed. Often, in deciding whether to free a defendant on bail, courts are mandated to consider *only* whether the defendant is likely to show up for trial. Weld's proposal, which should be adopted in every state, requires judges also to consider whether a defendant poses a danger to any individual or to the community, and to jail dangerous defendants without bail.[40] As we've seen, many, many women are able to predict their own deaths precisely because their husbands or boyfriends pose such a clear and imminent danger, a danger consistently disregarded by the courts.

Every state should also enact an antistalking law, authorizing fines and imprisonment for "intentionally, maliciously and repeatedly following or harassing another person and threatening the other person with death or great bodily harm."[41] Such laws, already passed or pending in twenty states, give police the power to arrest and detain stalkers, and courts the power to sentence them to substantial terms behind bars for the act of stalking itself, *before* the deadlier crime of assault or murder. (Some civil libertarians mistakenly equate arrest for stalking with preventative detention, a violation of the stalker's civil rights. The mistake occurs because stalking was not previously thought of as a crime, undoubtedly because it so rarely happens to men. Rightly considered, stalking is a clear violation of the victim's civil rights for it may cause her to lose her freedom of movement, her freedom of association, her freedom of speech, her housing, her job, her health, and her peace of mind.)

Congress should act as quickly as possible to pass the comprehensive "Violence Against Women" Act sponsored in the Senate by Joseph Biden of Delaware and in the House of Representatives by Pat Schroeder of Colorado and Louise Slaughter and Charles Schumer of New York. This legislation would double federal funding for battered women's shelters and authorize $25 million in law enforcement grants for projects to combat violence against women. It would make restraining orders enforceable across state lines, provide federal penalties for stalking across state lines, and designate "crimes of violence motivated by the victim's gender" as violations of federal civil rights laws.[42] But legislators at every level must understand that new legislation will accomplish little or nothing until the criminal justice system is held accountable for law enforcement.

The Health Care System

Most battered women never call the police or go to court or flee to a women's shelter, but great numbers of battered women visit doctors and hospitals for treatment of injuries and other stress-related illnesses, their own and/or those of their children. In Massachusetts, for example, an estimated 190,000 women are assaulted every year, yet only 18,000 women seek help from existing programs and in 1991 only 44,000 received restraining orders from the courts.[43] Undoubtedly many more visit health care professionals, although most of them are not identified as battered women.

Clearly the greatest need among health care professionals is education. All colleges and universities that offer degrees in medicine, nursing, social work, psychology, and pastoral care must include education about male violence, battering, sexual assault, and child abuse in their standard curricula. All currently licensed health professionals, especially those in emergency care, obstetrics and gynecology, pediatrics, internal medicine, family practice, psychiatry, and substance abuse counseling should be required to undertake further education and training on battering and child abuse. All health care facilities should have clearly established protocols for identifying and treating domestic assault victims, and supervisors should be required to train their staffs to respond.

Mental health personnel, in hospitals, clinics, and private practice, must understand that battering is *not* primarily a mental health issue. Therapists may have a role to play in helping women survivors of violence who suffer from post-traumatic stress symptomology, but most battered women need material assistance and emotional support, not therapy, and they can find that empowering help within the battered women's movement in peer support groups, mutual service, and political action. Nevertheless, because many women victims of assault will consult them, mental health professionals must be well prepared to offer support to a battered woman, validate her experience and feelings, help her to make plans for her safety, and refer her to appropriate community resources. Before counseling couples, therapists must ascertain whether the man is violent; and, if so, the therapist should refer both parties to other *separate* and appropriate services and assist the woman in making temporary safety plans.

More often than not, woman abuse and child abuse occur in the same household. Women must be able to bring their abused children to health care facilities for treatment without fear that they will lose them to the authorities. To that end, every emergency facility should have a paid battered woman's advocate on staff or on call from a battered women's program in the community. In cases of suspected child abuse, the advocate can help evaluate what's going on in the household and help mother and child plan for their safety. A model program is Advocacy for Women and Kids in Emergencies (AWAKE) at Children's Hospital in Boston, the first program based in a pediatric hospital to intervene and advocate for battered women. AWAKE offers a range of supportive services, including telephone and in-person counseling, help in finding emergency shelter and housing and in going to court, referrals for legal and medical care, and support groups for battered women and for children who have witnessed abuse or suffered it. AWAKE also offers consultation and training to health care professionals on many aspects of identifying and treating domestic assault victims, and it helps other organizations to establish similar programs.[44]

Every emergency health care facility and the offices of gynecologists, obstetricians, pediatricians, family practitioners, and therapists should display and distribute information on battered women's rights and services in the local community. Doctors and nurses should learn about those services, by visiting them if possible, and be prepared to refer their patients accordingly. No physician or therapist should suggest that an abused woman enter marital counseling with her assailant. And no physician should seek to mask an abused woman's real pain and fears with pain killers or tranquilizers.

In June 1992 *The Journal of the American Medical Association* devoted the better part of an issue to violence against women. The AMA's Council on Scientific Affairs recommended that physicians routinely screen female patients to identify victims of violence; that they "validate" the seriousness of the patient's experience and its possible consequences; that they record the patient's history of victimization and refer patients to appropriate resources.

In addition, the Council recommended that training in interviewing techniques, risk assessment, safety planning, and procedures for linking medical services to other community resources be incorporated into undergraduate, graduate, and continuing medical education programs; that the AMA disseminate protocols for identifying and treating violence victims; and that the AMA launch "a campaign to alert the health care community to the widespread prevalence of violence against women."[45] The AMA, which certainly can not be accused of acting precipitously in this matter, should continue and expand its campaign.

Child Protection Agencies

These agencies, usually run by the state, are known in different localities by different names, such as child welfare, child protection, social services, or human resources. They investigate complaints of child neglect and abuse, offer services to families, and remove children in cases of serious risk. Since the abused child is likely to have an abused mother, child protection workers could be helpful to battered women. Unfortunately, they often take their task of helping "families" as a directive to keep the nuclear family intact. As a matter of policy, social service departments should acknowledge that the *family* they work to preserve may consist of *a woman and her children*, and that the best way to protect a child is to protect its mother. To that end, child protective workers should refer abused mothers to other helpful community services such as battered women's support groups, legal services, shelters, and housing authorities.

Too often social workers overlook woman abuse and label its victim a "neglectful mother." Too often they charge with "failure to protect" a woman who would protect her children if she had some help in getting away from her assailant. And too often they remove children from an abusive mother who would stop abusing her children if she could escape the man abusing her. Clearly, child protection workers should be educated about battering as well as child abuse during their professional training. Workers currently employed in child protection agencies should take in-service training about battering and marital rape, and every such agency should have a paid battered women's advocate on staff.

Child protection agencies should hold batterers and child abusers accountable for their offenses and refer them to batterers' programs. Laws and regulations should be redrawn if necessary to make boyfriends who are legally unrelated to the mother and child accountable for offenses against them.

Religion

Many members of the clergy believe in keeping the nuclear family together no matter what, and many still maintain that a wife's duty is to love and cherish her husband, even when he beats her nearly to death. But as one survivor of battery, now a member of the clergy herself, said: "I couldn't believe that's what God had in mind for my life."[46] Recent criminal trials and civil damage suits brought against priests and clergymen for child sexual abuse make clear that religious institutions are more likely to cover up abuse in their midst than to help the victims; but churches can not go on being accomplices to crime, not to mention sin. The clergy must educate themselves about battering and be alert to identify and help battered women and abused kids in their congregations. They should seek training or help from their local battered women's shelter or program. Alternatively, they may find help through their own religious organization; some religious groups now have specialists on "domestic violence" who can provide information to local clergy and congregations. The Center for the Prevention of Sexual and Domestic Violence, for example, has provided education and training on sexual abuse and domestic assault for clergy and lay leaders since 1977.[47]

When giving pastoral care to women, clergy—like all other counselors—should question them about violence, validate their experience, express concern for their safety, refer them to appropriate community resources, and *never* suggest they enter marital counseling with the assailant. They must put the safety and well-being of the woman first; and they must bear in mind that a woman and her children *are* a family. Clergy should participate in planning a coordinated community response to domestic assault, and they should take the lead in teaching that male violence against women and children is a moral wrong.

The Schools

Teachers, especially primary school teachers, will have abused children and the children of abused women among their students. High school teachers will work with victims and perpetrators of dating violence. All teachers can be instrumental in letting abused women, teenage girls, and children know about their rights and sources of help. Like other helping professionals, teachers should learn in college about male violence against women and children, and they should be required to learn through continuing education or in-service training about programs and resources in their own communities. In turn they should include information on battering and child abuse in their curricula, beginning in the primary grades. Teachers of young children should enlist the help of an experienced child advocate in presenting this information and handling the students' reactions. They must be particularly clear in delivering the message that the abuser is wrong and that the abuser's victims are blameless.

High school teachers should also include information on date battery and rape. They can work with local battered women's programs to develop such materials for the classroom. In Boston, for example, an improvisational theater troupe visits high schools to perform skits about male violence against women and kids; it is a joint project of Transition House, a women's shelter, and Emerge, a men's counseling center.[48] Some local schools and state departments of education have prepared materials on battering and child abuse for the classroom; teachers have only to make use of them. One example is a four-week course on "The Prevention of Family Violence" developed by a Louisville, Kentucky, high school and adopted in several other states.[49]

The Media

The press must clean up its act. Too often print and broadcast journalists, male and female, especially crime reporters, fall back on sexist cliches and ready-made scenarios instead of investigating and accurately reporting facts. They mask rape and battering in the language of "love." They quote police and lawyers as authoritative sources but rarely consult battered women's advocates, who might bring a different perspective to bear on the facts of the story. Sometimes they throw fairness and balance to the winds and sympathize with the offender, as most reporters did in covering the story of the poor, mistreated arsonist Julio Gonzalez. There are remarkably fair and valuable exceptions, of course—the *Boston Globe* coverage of the epidemic of male violence against women in Massachusetts is a good example—and such thoughtful journalism can go a long way toward setting the tone and providing accurate information for public discussion. But as long as routine coverage in both print and broadcast media presents rape and assault from the perspective of the offender, the press will be part of the problem women and children are up against.

The press also abets batterers by failing to report their "routine" crimes, just as it used to cover up for drunk drivers. But because violent men so often prey upon a number of women in sequence and because they are dangerous to the public at large, the public should know who they are. Newspapers should print the names of men who are subject to restraining orders, calling particular attention to men convicted of violating restraining orders. Many newspaper editors and publishers believe that such a policy intrudes upon the privacy of the men named, but we have seen that the crimes of these men and the danger they pose are not "private." (As readers, we can let our own newspapers know that we want this information.)

Reporters and editors in print and broadcast journalism must educate themselves about battering. Before they touch this beat they should have read *Battered Wives* by Del Martin, *Women and Male Violence* by Susan Schechter, *Rape in Marriage* by Diana E. H.

Russell, *Violence Against Wives* by R. Emerson Dobash and Russell P. Dobash, and *When Battered Women Kill* by Angela Browne. In addition, they should read *Virgin or Vamp: How the Press Covers Sex Crimes* by Columbia journalism professor Helen Benedict. Benedict gives the press low marks for its coverage of sex crimes, and much of her analysis applies equally to press coverage of domestic assault and femicide.

It is probably too much to expect of the entertainment media that artists and producers in the film, television, video, and music industries stop eroticizing male violence against women and depicting it with such obvious relish. But all of us as consumers can protest with our feet, our pens, and our pocketbooks; and we can organize others to boycott certain films, TV programs, recording "artists," magazines, and the products of companies that sponsor television programs glamorizing rape and battery or radio programs in which misogynistic records are played. And we must write our objections to the production companies and networks and sponsors; one complaint won't make a difference, but thousands might.

The Shelter Network

Federal and state funding for battered women's shelters and related services is pitifully short-lived and small. The federal government has initiated no programs for battered women since 1984; and Minnesota, which has one of the most progressive and best-funded abuse prevention programs in the country, spends less to help battered women than to kill mosquitos.[50] One result is that there are only about a thousand shelters for battered women in the United States. Everywhere, women in need are turned away. In Philadelphia, Women Against Abuse rejects 75 percent of the women who seek shelter. In New York City, Sanctuary for Families turns away one hundred battered women and their children every week. In Seattle, five hundred men are arrested for battering every month, but only thirty-nine shelter beds are available for battered women. In Massachusetts, women's shelters turn away 71 percent of the women in need of shelter and 80 percent of the children.[51] In all areas of the country, demand for temporary shelter, court advocacy, and peer support groups is rising, and budgets are being cut. Some shelters have had to discontinue support programs for children, while others have had to drop court advocates. Everywhere paid workers have cut their own salaries to make the money stretch farther; many carry on as volunteers. One Midwestern shelter laid off its custodian for lack of funds; later, when the shelter was criticized publicly for being dirty and unsanitary, she wrote to the local newspaper: "Until government and society commit themselves to ending violence in the home, there will always be battered women's shelters, they will always be full and there will always be dishes to wash and bathroom floors to mop. Token laws and band-aid funding are the real problem. If we're looking for solutions, why aren't we putting batterers in shelters and letting the women and children stay at home?"[52]

Shelters were never meant to become permanent establishments, but because community institutions do not act effectively to defend women, shelters are the single most effective way of saving lives. More shelters should be established, and all of them should be staffed primarily by women who are survivors of abuse, whether or not they have professional credentials. And because so many battered women cite the lack of affordable housing as the single greatest obstacle to getting free of an abusive man, shelters must have additional funds and the cooperation of municipal housing authorities to help women find transitional and long-term housing. Overburdened federal, state, and local governments will be hard pressed to find more money for shelters, but they must rearrange their priorities to provide it. Elizabeth Schneider points out that money spent on shelters is well spent, for "shelter work contributes to community education, abuse prevention, and institutional change as well as the welfare of children."[53]

Although shelters should be accountable for public funds they expend, they must be free to shelter any abused women and children in need. In 1992 an Iowa shelter became the subject of public controversy and an investigation by the state Division of Criminal Investigation after a former resident, who had risen through the ranks to become a staff member, was revealed to be a fugitive, sought for leaving Arkansas with her two children, of whom she had custody, in violation of custodial claims brought by her ex-husband. (Her children were returned to their father; she was arrested and taken to Arkansas to face prosecution.)[54] But as long as women must run from male violence, as long as some find safety only underground, it should neither surprise us nor discredit a shelter that among the thousands of women it aids there is the occasional fugitive from "justice."

Research

During a prolific academic career, sociologist Lee H. Bowker noted that scholarly journals welcomed his traditional articles but rejected his profeminist articles on woman abuse with a nastiness that would have sunk most young professors trying to build a career. Scholarship pretends to neutral, objective standards, but Bowker concluded "that there are many gatekeepers in the world of scholarship whose professionalism is insufficient to keep their antifeminist attitudes in check."[55] Reviewing the clinical literature on battering, sociologist and batterers' counselor James Ptacek noted that the sociologists, psychologists, and psychiatrists who write it accept "at face value" the victim-blaming excuses of the batterer.[56] One consequence of these transparent biases is that much of the research conducted by sociologists and psychologists, scholars and clinicians, during the last decade (often at the taxpayers' expense) has proved irrelevant or an impediment to the work of activists providing direct services to battered women and their children.[57]

Important and useful research is still to be done, particularly on the institutional and social supports for male violence, and on male violence itself. No study has ever been done, for example, of men who murder the women they say they love, although these men currently kill three out of four female murder victims. More important, no study has been done of the psychiatric criteria and legal standards that define as "normal" and "well adjusted" men whom ordinary uneducated women with no professional training whatsoever can plainly see are about to commit murder. What is it about psychiatry and the law that makes women's experience immaterial? What are the consequences for women, and what should we do about it?

Similarly, very little is known of the long-term effects on children who are subjected to abuse or witness it. Reports from women survivors on what helped them to escape and rebuild their lives, and what community institutions might have done to help, would be useful to service providers and policy makers. Given that we live in a country rapidly being consumed by violence, such studies could produce information helpful to everyone. And most helpful of all might be information to tell us how to break our peculiarly American habits of studying individual psyches and tabulating statistics. We must search for structural solutions to structural problems, find social answers to social questions, and think about things like safety and equality and justice as if we were in fact members of a *society*.

Public and private funds for research should go to studies and projects that address the felt needs of workers in the field. Any agency, foundation, or corporation funding "domestic violence" research should seek the guidance of nonacademics providing direct services to victims and offenders, particularly those who are themselves survivors of violence. They should also consult feminist theorists within the battered women's movement and profeminist men leading programs for offenders. No matter how much conservatives and misogynists might want to wish feminism away, it is eminently clear that the feminist analysis of male violence against women and children is the most accurate. What's more, it is the only analysis of male violence that offers hope of change.

Individual Action

Finally we come to the difficult question of what, if anything, individual women and men can do. Is the problem insurmountable? Hopeless? And if you are a nonviolent man or woman living with a nonviolent partner, is it even your problem?

As I've said, I believe that violence is everyone's problem, that we are all touched by it in some way, if only in the cost of an extra lock for the front door. How many kids are learning right now by example in their own homes that a man can get what he wants by slapping a woman or a child around? We could go over the economic costs again—the expense we all bear as taxpayers for the emergency services, police work, and court costs of undeterred male violence. We could consider how much our health insurance costs would diminish if men stopped hitting women. We could count casualties again—thousands of women dead, and almost every day more innocent bystanders killed as well. No one gets off free.

It's up to *everyone*, then, to recognize the principle that all women have a right to be free from bodily harm—and to act as if we believe it. That may mean overcoming a lifetime of training that tilts your opinions in the opposite direction. Whether you are a judge, a cop, a physician, a teacher, or an ordinary citizen talking over the latest shocking murder to hit the papers, it means holding the offender to account, even if you sympathize with him. It means biting your tongue before you blame the victim. It may mean educating yourself, reading some of the books I've mentioned, and becoming actively involved: volunteering at your local shelter or sending some money or becoming a big sister or brother to an abused kid.

And if a woman you know is being abused—or you suspect that she is—it means trying to talk to her, offering support, offering to help in whatever way you can *whenever* she feels ready to call on you, recognizing all the while that her life is more complicated than you can know, that she may not respond as you would like.

Many a would-be helper suggests to a battered woman that she "just leave," then turns away in frustration, anger, and disgust when she doesn't. (As if she hasn't thought of it herself.) Recognize instead that getting free is a *process*; offer your continuing support and you may become part of her process of saving herself. Two books that may be helpful to her and to you are *Getting Free* by Ginny NiCarthy and *When Love Goes Wrong: What To Do When You Can't Do Anything Right* by Ann Jones and Susan Schechter.

But before you can offer help to an abused woman, or seek it for yourself, you have to know what goes on in your own community. Is there a shelter in your town? Who pays for its operation, and how much? Does it have enough room, or does it often turn women in danger away? How long can a woman stay there, and will the shelter help her find a place of her own? What's the policy of your local police department? When the cops get a domestic disturbance call, what do they actually do? What's the record of the prosecutors and judges in your town when it comes to domestic assault cases? Do they follow through with prosecution and sentencing, or do they pin their failures on the women? Is there a batterers' counseling program in town, and how well does it seem to be working? Where can a battered woman find a support group? Is there any special housing that might be available for her? How about job training? What kind of legal aid can she get? What does a woman have to do to get a restraining order? If she gets one, how will it be enforced? Do you have an antistalking law in your state? Are there any special services for battered women at the local hospital? How do your senators and representatives plan to vote on the Violence Against Women bill? If you can't answer all these questions, then you know what your first task is. And if the answers you find leave you dissatisfied with the services in your community, then you have more work cut out for you and your friends. The most powerful and empowering thing you can do as an individual is to become involved in a social or institutional effort for *change*.

*   *   *

It's likely that many women reading this book will have been victims of violence. It seems to be more and more difficult to avoid it. In one survey of six thousand college students 42 percent of female students reported some kind of sexual assault; and college men who used violence on dates said they *chose purposefully* to do so to "intimidate," "frighten," or "force the other person to do something."[58] As these young men boast, violence against women does not happen by accident. And women who have been assaulted and raped are angry and afraid.

Most women, trained to stay safely at home to avoid the rapist in the streets, are appalled by the indisputable evidence that home is the most dangerous place for a woman to be. Experts on domestic assault dispassionately write lines like this: "The onset of systematic and severe violence against women is almost exclusively associated with entering a permanent relationship with a man. . . . Only in a prison or similar total institution would an individual be likely to encounter such persistent abuse, violence and terror."[59] Put that information together with the fact that *no* woman sets out to enter a permanent relationship *with a batterer*, and you see why women are uneasy—and why the lucky ones may prefer to believe that battering is something other women bring on themselves.

Women should listen to their own uneasiness—and get more information about male violence and control. Although no test is foolproof, there are early warning signs to watch for in the behavior of any potential partner. What is his attitude toward women? How does he treat his mother and his sister? How does he work with female colleagues or a female boss? (If he doesn't have any, that tells you something, too.) Does he make jokes about women in power? How does he treat your women friends? Does he understand that they are as important to you as he is? (Do you understand that yourself?) What is his attitude toward your autonomy? Does he respect the work you do and the way you do it? Or does he run it down, or meddle, or tell you how to do it better, or encourage you to give it up? Does he tell you he'll take

care of you? Does he want to spend the leisure time you have together on your interests, or his? How much time does he spend
listening to you talk about your interests, and vice versa? Does he
remember what you said? Is he possessive or jealous? Does he want
to spend every minute with you? Does he cross-examine you about
things you do when you're not with him? How does he feel about
your male friends? What happens when things don't go the way
he wants them to? Does he blow up in a traffic jam, fume about
his income tax, whine about your friends, or sulk about personal
slights?

Susan Schechter and I presented many more questions and lists
of control tactics in *When Love Goes Wrong*, a book of advice we
wrote not because we believe that a woman is responsible for the
violence done to her, but because it seemed to us increasingly unlikely that society would remove that responsibility from her. I
want to make it clear, though, that when I offer advice to a
woman, I don't hold her or myself to blame if the advice proves
ineffective. Male violence is *male* violence. But that said, the general principles women should keep in mind are these: stay away
from a man who disrespects *any* women, who wants or needs you
intensely and exclusively, and who has a knack for getting his own
way almost all the time. *Any* of the above should put you on
guard. And if, when you back off, he turns on the solid gold
charm, keep backing. Author Naomi Wolf gave good advice to
graduating seniors at Scripps College: "Never cook for or sleep
with anyone who routinely puts you down."[60] And, as a practical
matter, I would add: prepare yourself as best you can with education, training, and job skills to lead an independent life. Support yourself.

Women who have been assaulted or raped or sexually harassed
at home or at school or on the job or in the streets should report
the fact to officials and talk about it to other women. Spread the
assailant's name around. If officials take no action, spread that
around too. Anita Hill set us all an example. We must not keep
to ourselves the shameful secrets of men.

Women who have never been abused or battered and who believe that it couldn't happen to them should volunteer to help at a battered women's shelter. If their belief is wrong, as I think it is, they will learn something from working with battered women. If their belief is right, battered women will learn something from them.

It's important that men take action to end male violence as well. Violence against women is men's problem, just as racism is whites' problem, though it's women who pay the price of the one, people of color who pay the price of the other, and women of color who pay the price of both. Women can do much in our own behalf—almost everything already done to combat violence against women was done by women—but we can not *stop* violence against women by ourselves any more than people of color can stop racism by themselves. Men *choose* to use violence to get their way. They can just as well *choose* not to. Many men choose to be non-violent, and some take a stand with women against violence and emotional abuse. They must increase their numbers, raise their voices, and use whatever power they have for change. All men *can* change their behavior. Whether they *will* is another matter.

But there is no good reason that change must come slowly and painfully and only after the injury and death of thousands more. Things change when people stop being resigned to things as they are. Things change when people in large numbers get a hold of a principle and begin to act as if they believed it.

Notes

Introduction

1. Marilyn French, *The War Against Women* (New York: Summit, 1992), p. 187.

2. Femicide is on the rise worldwide. See *Femicide: The Politics of Woman Killing*, ed. Jill Radford and Diana E. H. Russell (New York: Twayne, 1992).

3. Susan Schechter, "Ending Violence Against Women and Children in Massachusetts' Families: Critical Steps for the Next Five Years," The Boston Foundation, unpublished report, p. 9.

4. Susan Schechter, *Women and Male Violence: The Visions and Struggles of the Battered Women's Movement* (Boston: South End Press, 1982).

5. Betty Friedan, *The Feminine Mystique* (New York: Norton, 1963); *Sisterhood Is Powerful: An Anthology of Writings from the Women's Liberation Movement*, ed. Robin Morgan (New York: Random House, 1970); *Voices from Women's Liberation*, ed. Leslie B. Tanner (New York: New American Library, 1970).

6. Schechter, *Women and Male Violence*, p. 20.

7. Ibid., p. 11.

8. Ibid., p. 124.

9. Evan Stark and Anne Flitcraft, "Women and Children at Risk: A Feminist Perspective on Child Abuse," *International Journal of Health Services* 18, no. 1 (1988); Linda McKibben et al., "Victimization of Mothers of Abused Children: A Controlled Study," *Pediatrics* 84 (September 1989): 3.

10. For a detailed history of this work see Schechter, *Women and Male Violence*.

11. David Adams, "Treatment Models of Men Who Batter: A Profeminist Analysis," in *Feminist Perspectives on Wife Abuse*, ed. Kersti Yllo and Michele Bograd (Newbury Park, Calif.: Sage, 1988), p. 191.

12. Christine de Pizan, *The Book of the City of Ladies*, trans. E. J. Richards (New York: Persea, 1982), p. 187; Mary Wollstonecraft, *A Vindication of the Rights of Woman* (1792; rpt. New York: Norton, 1988); Frances Power Cobbe, "Wife-Torture in England," *The Contemporary Review* 32 (April–July, 1878): 55–87; John Stuart Mill, *The Subjection of Women* (1869; rpt. Cambridge, Mass.: M.I.T. Press, 1970), see esp. part 2.

13. Patricia Nealon, "For abused, few places to turn," *Boston Globe*, June 2, 1992, p. 6.

14. Milt Freudenheim, "Employers Act to Stop Family Violence," *New York Times*, Aug. 23, 1988, p. 1.

15. Telephone interview with Anne Menard, Executive Director, Connecticut Coalition Against Domestic Violence, Dec. 31, 1992.

16. "Domestic Violence Is a Crime," report of the Family Violence Project, San Francisco Victim Witness Assistance Program, n.d.

17. French, *The War Against Women*; Susan Faludi, *Backlash: The Undeclared War Against American Women* (New York: Crown, 1991); Gloria Steinem, *Revolution from Within: A Book of Self-Esteem* (Boston: Little, Brown, 1992).

1. *Against the Law*

1. The Fourth Amendment "right of the people to be secure in their persons" has been interpreted as establishing a right not only to be free of intrusions on personal dignity and safety authorized by the state, but also to bodily integrity, recognized judicially, for example, in cases involving the rights of terminally ill patients to refuse medical treatment and of mentally ill people to refuse antipsychotic drug treatment. The right to personal integrity also inheres in Fourteenth Amendment guarantees of "life, liberty [and] property."

2. William Blackstone, *Commentaries on the Laws of England*, ed. Thomas M. Cooley, 4th ed. by James DeWitt Andrews (Chicago: Callahan, 1899), book I, pp. 134, 129, 134–38.

3. *Union Pacific Ry. v. Botsford*, 141 U.S. 250, 251 (1891).

4. Carol Smart, *Feminism and the Power of Law* (London: Routledge, 1989), p. 142.

5. Uncited case referred to in *Thurman v. City of Torrington*, 595 F. Supp. 1521, 1528 (1984).

6. Ibid. Emphasis mine. Note the court's reference to the thoroughly contemporary notion that some violence is *not* dangerous or damaging.

7. Elizabeth Pleck, *Domestic Tyranny: The Making of American Social Policy against Family Violence from Colonial Times to the Present* (New York: Oxford University Press, 1987), pp. 63–65.

8. Elizabeth Pleck, "Wife Beating in Nineteenth Century America," *Victimology* 4, no. 1 (1979): 60–74.

9. Cited in Sue E. Eisenberg and Patricia L. Micklow, "The Assaulted Wife: 'Catch 22' Revisited," 3 *Women's Rights Law Reporter* 138, 138–39 (1977).

10. Letter from Laurie Woods, Director, National Center on Women and Family Law, Dec. 15, 1992.

11. Schechter, *Women and Male Violence*, pp. 159–60. For a detailed summary of early efforts of the battered women's movement to effect change in the criminal justice system see Schechter, pp. 157–74.

12. Charles Thurman was convicted of attempted murder and, when the conviction was overturned on a technicality, allowed to plead guilty to first degree assault. Sentenced in 1987 to twenty years, to be suspended after fourteen, he was released in 1991. Ray Routhier, "Thurman to be freed April 12," *Hartford Courant*, March 15, 1991, pp. C1, C9.

13. *Thurman v. City of Torrington*, 595 F. Supp. 1521, 1523 (D. Conn. 1984).

14. P. G. Jaffe, D. A. Wolfe, and S. K. Wilson, *Children of Battered Women* (Newbury Park, Calif.: Sage, 1990), cited in *Family Violence Bulletin* 7, no. 1 (1991): 11.

15. U.S. Senate Committee on the Judiciary, "Violence Against Women: A Week in the Life of America," Majority Staff Report (Washington: Government Printing Office, October 1992), p. 33.

16. Smart, *Feminism and the Power of Law*, p. 67, citing M. J. Mossman, "Feminism and Legal Method: The Difference It Makes," 3 *Australian Journal of Law and Society* 30–52 (1986).

17. Carol Gilligan, *In a Different Voice* (Cambridge, Mass.: Harvard University Press, 1982).

18. John Stuart Mill, *The Subjection of Women* (1869; rpt. Cambridge, Mass.: M.I.T. Press, 1970), p. 59.

19. Patricia Nealon and Sean P. Murphy, "Thwarting the killers is complex, elusive goal," *Boston Globe*, June 2, 1992, pp. 1, 6.

20. *DeShaney v. Winnebago County Dep't of Social Servs.*, 489 U.S. 189 (1989).

21. Caitlin E. Borgmann, "Battered Women's Substantive Due Process Claims: Can Orders of Protection Deflect *DeShaney?*" 65 *New York University Law Review* 1280, 1320–22 (1990).

22. Elizabeth M. Schneider, "The Violence of Privacy," 23 *Connecticut Law Review* 973, 985 (1991).

23. Ibid., p. 985, in part quoting Martha Minow, "Words and the Door to the Land of Change: Law, Language, and Family Violence," 43 *Vanderbilt Law Review* 1665, 1671–72 (1990).

24. Catherine MacKinnon, "Feminism, Marxism, Method and the State: Toward Feminist Jurisprudence," *Signs* 8, no. 2 (1983): 644.

25. Amy Eppler, "Battered Women and the Equal Protection Clause: Will the Constitution Help Them When the Police Won't," 95 *Yale Law Journal* 788, 801 (1986).

26. *Montalvo v. Montalvo*, 55 Misc. 2d 699, 704, 286 N.Y.S.2d 605, 611 (Fam. Ct. 1968), cited in Maria L. Marcus, "Conjugal Violence: The Law of Force and the Force of Law," 59 *California Law Review* 1657, 1684 (1981).

27. Philip Bennet and Doris Sue Wong, "Judge regrets he didn't see Cartier's record," *Boston Globe*, June 2, 1992, pp. 1, 6.

28. Roberto Suro, "Husband Shoots 2 and Himself in Dallas Court," *New York Times*, Jan. 20, 1993, p. A18.

29. Michael deCourcy Hinds, "Once Orderly Sanctuaries of Justice, Courts Now Tremble With Violence," *New York Times*, Jan. 26, 1993, p. A14. See also Larry Olmstead, "When Passion Explodes Into a Deadly Rage," *New York Times*, May 18, 1993, pp. A1, B4.

30. Martha R. Mahoney, "Legal Images of Battered Women: Redefining the Issue of Separation," 90 *Michigan Law Review* 1, 43–49 (1991); letter from Laurie Woods, Director, National Center on Women and Family Law, Dec. 15, 1992.

31. Mahoney, "Legal Images," 44–45; the statistical estimate is reported by Lee H. Bowker, Michelle Arbitell, and J. Richard McFerron, "On the Relationship Between Wife Beating and Child Abuse," in *Feminist Perspectives on Wife Abuse*, ed. Kersti Yllo and Michele Bograd (Newbury Park, Calif.: Sage, 1988), p. 162.

32. Mahoney, "Legal Images," 45, citing Phyllis Chesler, *Mothers on Trial: The Battle for Children and Custody* (New York: McGraw-Hill, 1986), p. 81.

33. Mahoney, "Legal Images," 45, n. 202, citing Lenore Weitzman, *The Divorce Revolution: The Unexpected Social and Economic Consequences for Women and Children in America* (New York: Free Press, 1985), pp. 233–34. In Weitzman's study men won custody in 63 percent of "negotiated" cases and in 33 to 38 percent of cases fully contested in court.

34. *Sorichetti v. City of New York*, 95 Misc. 2d 451, 408 N.Y.S.2d 219 (1978), aff'd, 68 A.D.2d 1020, 417 N.Y.S.2d 202 (1st Dep't 1979).

35. Sheila Weller, *Marrying the Hangman: A True Story of Privilege, Marriage and Murder* (New York: Random House, 1992), pp. 239–43.

36. Sheila Weller, "Abused By the Courts," *Village Voice*, Dec. 1, 1992, pp. 32–33.

37. Letter from Laurie Woods, Director, National Center on Women and Family Law, December 1992.

38. For many other examples see Weller, *Village Voice*, Dec. 1, 1992, pp. 31–38.

39. *Morgan v. Foretich*, 846 F. 2d 941, 942–50 (4th Cir. 1988); Bob Trebilcock, "Hiding Hilary," *Glamour*, November 1988, p. 305.

40. Jane Sims Podesta and Paula Chin, "A Courageous Mother's First Taste of Freedom," *People*, Oct. 16, 1989, p. 78.

41. Steve Twomey and Elsa Walsh, "Morgan-Foretich Fight Ends—for Now," *Washington Post*, Dec. 1, 1990, p. A7.

42. Ibid.

43. The law does so much harm to women and children, over and above its failure to provide a remedy for such harms as child abuse, sexual abuse, and battering, that British sociologist and legal scholar Carol Smart coined the term "juridogenic" to describe the potential of the law and legal process to generate such injuries. See *Feminism and the Power of Law*, p. 12. See also Ann Jones, "When Battered Women Fight Back," *Barrister* 9, no. 4 (1982): 12–15, 48–51.

44. Ann Jones, *Women Who Kill* (New York: Holt, Rinehart & Winston, 1980), pp. 281–321.

45. Eileen McNamara, "Judge criticized after woman's death," *Boston Globe*, Sept. 21, 1986, p. 1.

46. Paul Langner, "Dunn given life term in wife's slaying," *Boston Globe*, May 20, 1987, pp. 1, 13. In July 1990 the Supreme Judicial Court of Massachusetts upheld the murder conviction. "SJC upholds conviction in slaying of battered wife," *Boston Globe*, July 4, 1990, p. 23.

47. Eileen McNamara, "Judge is viewed as erring on abuse law," *Boston Globe*, Oct. 24, 1986, p. 1; Mark Sommer, "Abused women battered again by judges," *Guardian*, Nov. 12, 1986, p. 3; Gail Goolkasian, "Judging Domestic Violence," 10 *Harvard Women's Law Journal* 277 (1987).

48. Sheila Weller, ". . . til death do us part," *Redbook*, Aug. 1989, p. 137.

49. U.S. Congress. Senate. Committee on the Judiciary, *The Violence Against Women Act of 1991*, 102d Cong., 1st sess., S. Rept. 102-197, p. 34, citing Supreme Court of Georgia, "Report on Gender and Justice in the Judicial System" (1991) at 235.

50. Transcript of "Frontline" documentary #619, "My Husband Is Going to Kill Me," WGBH Educational Foundation, Boston, 1988, p. 2. Subsequent details of the Guenther case are drawn from the transcript of

this television documentary which was originally broadcast on PBS on June 28, 1988.

51. "Man accused of murdering wife was free despite intimidation reports," AP dispatch, Columbus, Neb., n.d.

52. Ibid.

53. Maria K. Pastoor, "Police Training and the Effectiveness of Minnesota 'Domestic Abuse' Laws," 2 *Law And Inequality Journal* 557, 573 n. 82 (1984).

54. "L.I. Man Kills Estranged Wife; Commits Suicide," *New York Times*, Dec. 28, 1988, p. B2.

55. Eric Schmitt, "L.I. Man Fatally Shoots Wife, Then Himself," *New York Times*, Dec. 30, 1988, p. B1.

56. Dan Fagin and Phil Mintz, "Stabbing Survivor Shot to Death on LI; Ex-Spouse Sought," *Newsday*, Jan. 4, 1989, p. 7; Eric Schmitt, "Suffolk Woman Being Protected Is Shot to Death," *New York Times*, Jan. 5, 1989, p. B8.

57. Kinsey Wilson and Joshua Quittner, "Wife-Slay Suspect Found Dead," *Newsday*, Jan. 7, 1989, p. 5; "Man Found Dead in His Car Was Wanted in L.I. Killing," *New York Times*, Jan. 7, 1989, p. 30.

58. "Husband Slays Wife in LI Murder-Suicide," *Newsday*, Dec. 30, 1988, p. 25.

59. Weller, ". . . til death do us part," pp. 113–14, 137–38.

60. Jane O'Reilly, "Wife Beating: The Silent Crime," *Time*, Sept. 5, 1983, pp. 23–26; Caroline Knapp, "Open Season on Women," *Boston Phoenix*, Aug. 7–13, 1992, p. 21.

61. Weller, ". . . til death do us part," p. 114.

62. George James, "911 Operator Suspended Over Delay in Response to Call for Help," *New York Times*, June 24, 1988, p. B3.

63. Dick Polman, "In the shadow of violence," *Philadelphia Inquirer*, April 9, 1989, p. K1. Subsequent details of Lisa Bianco's story are drawn from this report.

64. Isabel Wilkerson, "Inmate on Leave Held in Death of His Ex-Wife," *New York Times*, March 12, 1989, p. 22.

65. Helen Kennedy, "Despite increased restraining orders, women not always protected," *Boston Herald*, April 6, 1992, p. 11.

66. Ibid.

67. John Laidler, "Unaware of threats, court freed Lawrence killer," *Boston Globe*, April 7, 1992, pp. 1, 8; Beverly Ford, "Estranged husband kills wife, 2 teens and self in Lawrence," *Boston Herald*, April 6, 1992, pp. 1, 11.

68. Eric Fehrnstrom, "Gov slams 'cockeyed' justice system," *Boston Herald*, April 7, 1992, p. 10.

69. Margery Eagan, "System lets batterers think they can get away with it," *Boston Herald*, June 2, 1992, p. 6.

70. Sharon Smith, quoted in "Frontline" documentary "My Husband Is Going to Kill Me," transcript, p. 26.

71. Frank Bruni, "Court-'protected' women fear for their lives," *New York Post*, Jan. 9, 1989, p. 18.

72. Michelle Gellen, reporting on "Women at Risk" on the NBC nightly news, Jan. 8, 1990.

73. Ibid.

74. Knapp, *Boston Phoenix*, Aug. 7–13, 1992, p. 1.

75. Bruni, *New York Post*, Jan. 9, 1989, p. 18.

76. Jan Hoffman, "By Her Husband's Hand," *Village Voice*, Aug. 13, 1985, p. 92.

77. Ibid.

2. *Rights and Wrongs*

1. *DeShaney v. Winnebago County Dep't of Social Servs.*, 489 U.S. 189, 193 (1989).

2. "Hitting Home," an episode of "48 Hours," CBS TV, June 18, 1988.

3. Robin Finn, "The Battering of Tracey Thurman: Why Didn't the Police Stop It?" *Northeast Magazine*, Aug. 25, 1985, pp. 14, 31–32; Amy Eppler, "Battered Women and the Equal Protection Clause: Will the Constitution Help Them When the Police Won't," 95 *Yale Law Journal* 788 (1986).

4. The conviction was later overturned on a technicality. At a second trial in 1987, Charles Thurman pleaded guilty to first degree assault and was sentenced to twenty years, to be suspended after fourteen, and five years probation. Ray Routhier, "Thurman to be freed April 12," *Hartford Courant*, March 15, 1991, pp. C1, C9.

5. The Fourteenth Amendment was proposed by resolution of Congress on June 13, 1866. It was adopted July 21, 1868.

6. 17 Stat. 13 (1871) [codified as 42 U.S.C. Section 1983 (1982)]. Section 1983 reads in part: "Every person, who, under color of any statute, ordinance, regulation, custom, or usage of any State or Territory or the District of Columbia, subjects, or causes to be subjected, any citizen of the United States or other person within the jurisdiction thereof to the deprivation of any rights, privileges, or immunities secured by the Constitution and laws, shall be liable to the party injured in an action at law, suit in equity, or other proper proceeding for redress."

7. *Monroe v. Pape*, 365 U.S. 167, 180 (1961), overruled in part in *Monell*

v. New York Department of Social Services, 436 U.S. 658 (1978). In *Monell* the Supreme Court expanded the holding in *Monroe* to include government entities as well as individuals in the definition of "persons" contained in 42 U.S.C. Section 1983, thereby making it possible for a citizen to bring an action charging discrimination against a government entity. *Monell*, 436 U.S. at 691, 694.

8. Eppler, "Battered Women," 806, n.74.

9. *Thurman v. City of Torrington*, 595 F. Supp. 1521, 1527 (D. Conn. 1984). Thurman's was not the first case of a woman denied police protection to reach the courts. Looking at earlier cases in which women's rights were denied, and hearing that language echoed in post-*Thurman* decisions denying women's rights, one could make an argument that the *Thurman* decision favorable to women was a judicial aberration. One earlier example is a suit brought in 1972 against police by survivors of the victim of a fatal attack. According to the complaint, Ruth Bunnell had called the San Jose (California) police more than twenty times in a single year to report that her husband was abusing her and her two daughters, but they arrested him only once. In September 1972 she called police and told them her husband was on his way to her house to kill her. Police told her to wait until he arrived. When police showed up later in response to a neighbor's call, she had already been stabbed to death. The California Court of Appeals upheld the trial court's dismissal, holding that police had not "induced decedent's reliance on a promise, express or implied, that they would provide her with protection." *Hartzler v. City of San Jose*, 46 Cal. App. 3d 6, 10, 120 Cal. Rptr. 5 (1975). See also Joan Zorza, "The Criminal Law of Misdemeanor Domestic Violence, 1970–1990," 83 *Journal of Criminal Law and Criminology* 44, 53–4 (1992).

10. The defendants appealed, and Thurman settled out of court for $1.9 million. The jury also awarded her son $300,000.

11. Howard Kurtz, "Battered by Husbands, Then by Laws," *Washington Post*, National Weekly Edition, May 16–22, 1988, p. 10.

12. *Bruno v. Codd*, 90 Misc. 2d at 1047, 1048, 396 N.Y.S.2d 974, 975–76 (Sup. Ct. 1977). Other early tort actions against police successful in state courts include *Baker v. New York*, 25 A.D.2d 770, 269 N.Y.S.2d 515 (1966); *Jones v. Herkimer*, 51 Misc. 2d 130, 272 N.Y.S.2d 925 (Sup. Ct. 1966); *Scott v. Hart*, No. C-76-2395 (N.D. Cal. filed Oct. 28, 1976); *Sorichetti v. City of New York*, 95 Misc. 2d 451, 408 N.Y.S.2d 219 (1978), *aff'd* 70 A.D.2d 573, 417 N.Y.S.2d 202 (1979); *Thomas v. City of Los Angeles*, Civ. No. 000572 (Cal. Super. Ct. filed Aug. 16, 1979, consent judgment entered Nov. 7, 1985); *Kubitcheck v. Winnett* (Or. Cir. Ct. Hood River County, filed Nov. 13, 1980); *Barnes v. Nassau County*, No. 12433 (N.Y. Sup. Ct. 1982); *Bonsignore v. City of New York*, 683 F.2d 635 (2d

Cir. N.Y. 1982); *Doe v. City of Belleville*, No. 81-5256 (S.D.Ill. consent judgment entered Sept. 9, 1983; *Nearing v. Weaver*, 295 Or. 702, 670 P.2d 137 (1983).

13. Laurie Woods, "Litigation On Behalf Of Battered Women," 5 *Women's Rights Law Reporter* 7 (1978).

14. Kurtz, *Washington Post*, May 16–22, 1988, p. 10.

15. Ibid.

16. Ibid.

17. *Balistreri v. Pacifica Police Dep't*, 855 F.2d 1421 (9th Cir. 1988). As amended Feb. 27, 1990 and May 11, 1990.

18. 341 U.S. 123, 162–163, cited in Steven H. Gifis, *Law Dictionary* (Woodbury, New York: Barron's, 1975), p. 66.

19. *Balistreri v. Pacifica Police Dep't* at 1427.

20. *Id*. at 1422.

21. *Id*. at 1426.

22. *Id*. at 1428.

23. The facts presented are those alleged by the plaintiff as cited in the opinion of the United States Court of Appeals, Tenth Circuit. See *Watson v. City of Kansas City*, 857 F.2d 690, 692–93 (10th Cir. 1988).

24. *Watson* at 696.

25. *Id*. at 697. Laura S. Harper notes: "Given the *Thurman* court's acceptance of the domestic assault/nondomestic assault classification as gender-based discrimination, *Thurman* was a seminal case with potentially monumental impact. To date, however, other district and circuit courts have applied stricter gender-neutral standards." "Battered Women Suing Police for Failure to Intervene: Viable Legal Avenues After *DeShaney v. Winnebago County Department of Social Services*," 75 *Cornell Law Review* 1393, 1404 (1990).

26. *Watson v. City of Kansas City*, 1989 U.S. Dist. LEXIS 2388, at *14 (D. Kan. 1989), *remanded by* 857 F.2d 690 (10th Cir. 1988).

27. *Id*. at *5.

28. *Hynson v. City of Chester, Legal Dep't*, 864 F.2d 1026, 1027 (3d Cir.), *vacating* 1988 U.S. Dist. LEXIS 3358 (E.D. Pa. 1988). The facts presented are cited in this opinion.

29. *Hynson*, 864 F.2d at 1030.

30. *Id*. at 1032.

31. *Id*. at 1031. Lauren L. McFarlane makes this point in a thorough discussion of these cases, "Notes: Domestic Violence Victims v. Municipalities: Who Pays When the Police Will Not Respond?" 41 *Case Western Reserve Law Review* 929, 947, n.104 (1991).

32. *Hynson*, 864 F.2d at 1031.

33. *Id*. The *Hynson* court follows the *Watson* court in citing *Personnel*

Administrator of Massachusetts v. Feeney, 442 U.S. 256 (1979), a case involving preferential treatment of veterans in employment, which held that a plaintiff bringing a gender-based discrimination claim must show that "a gender-based discriminatory purpose has shaped . . . the legislation" in question, or in other words that a law, rule, classification, or policy was adopted *on purpose* to discriminate against women. *Id*. at 275.

34. *Hynson*, 864 F.2d at 1032.

35. *Id*. at 1032. Note that the court, so eager to deny that police non-arrest policy affects *women*, refers to the plaintiff as "his or her," but it sees the "public official" as decidedly male.

36. *Id*. at 1027.

37. Benjamin Zipursky, *"DeShaney* and the Jurisprudence of Compassion," 65 *New York University Law Review* 1101, 1104–5 (1990).

38. *DeShaney v. Winnebago County Dep't of Social Servs.*, 489 U.S. 189, 193 (1989).

39. *Id*. at 194.

40. *Id*. at 192–93.

41. Zipursky, *"DeShaney,"* 1104.

42. *DeShaney*, 489 U.S. at 195–96.

43. *Id*. at 202–203. The majority opinion was joined by Justices Kennedy, O'Connor, Scalia, Stevens, and White. Dissenting, Justice Blackmun wrote that the Court's retreat into "sterile formalism" prevented it from recognizing both "the facts of the case" and "the legal norms that should apply." "The facts here involve not mere passivity," he wrote, "but active state intervention." *Id*. at 212.

44. *Id*. at 212. Emphasis mine. Justices Marshall and Blackmun concurred with Justice Brennan's dissenting opinion, and Justice Blackmun also wrote a dissenting opinion.

45. In a lengthy dissenting opinion, Judge Irving L. Goldberg argued: *"DeShaney* should play no role in McKee's case." *McKee v. City of Rockwall*, 877 F.2d 409, 417 (5th Cir. 1989) *cert. denied*, 493 U.S. 1023 (1990).

46. The allegations of the complaint are recounted and discussed by the appeals court in *McKee* at 409–11.

47. *McKee* at 409.

48. The affidavit is presented and discussed by the appeals court in *McKee* at 411.

49. *McKee* at 410. The court of appeals remanded McKee's claim against the City of Rockwall to the district court for further adjudication, but as Judge Goldberg observed in his dissenting opinion, "the majority's reasoning, that McKee made out no claim, virtually preordains judgment for the City of Rockwall on remand." *McKee* at 417, n. 2.

50. *Id*. at 417.

51. *Id.* at 412, 415. Dissenting, Judge Goldberg remarked: "A trial may demonstrate that a 'dislike' and a de facto policy are one and the same." *McKee* at 424.

52. *Id.* at 413.

53. *Id.*

54. The officers' affidavits are discussed in *McKee* at 411.

55. *Id.*

56. *Id.* at 420.

57. These allegations, brought by Gayla McKee in her complaint, are discussed in *McKee* at 410.

58. *Id.* at 414.

59. *Id.* at 410–11.

60. *Id.* at 412.

61. In *Bruno v. Codd*, the class action suit brought in 1976 to compel New York City police to enforce laws against assault, the state court noted: "Plaintiffs do not seek to abolish the traditional discretionary powers of the police; they merely seek to compel the police to exercise their discretion in each 'particular situation,' and not to automatically decline to make an arrest solely because the assaulter and his victim are married to each other." *Bruno v. Codd*, 90 Misc. 2d 1047, 1049, 396 N.Y.S. 2d 974, 976 (Sup. Ct. 1977).

62. *Watson v. City of Kansas City*, 857 F.2d 690, 695 (10th Cir. 1988).

63. *McKee* at 414. Emphasis mine.

64. *Id.* at 415.

65. *Id.* Dissenting Judge Goldberg disagreed with the majority's reasoning on this point and many others, but not with their decision favorable to the police. Following the *Hynson* court, he would have dismissed Gayla McKee's claims on grounds of police immunity.

66. Prior to *DeShaney*, at least two federal courts had dismissed battered women's due process claims on grounds that the state had no special relationship with the woman and no affirmative duty to protect her. In *Estate of Gilmore v. Buckley* 787 F.2d 714 (1st Cir.), *cert. denied* 479 U.S. 882 (1986), a battered woman with an order of protection was kidnapped and murdered by her ex-boyfriend. In *Turner v. City of North Charlestown* 675 F. Supp. 314 (D.S.C. 1987), a battered woman with an order of protection was repeatedly threatened and then shot in the head by her estranged husband. *DeShaney* makes this tendency to dismiss the due process claims of battered women the rule. The *McKee* court dragged *DeShaney* into equal protection claims as well.

67. *Balistreri v. Pacifica Police Dep't*, 855 F.2d 1421, 1423, 1426 (9th Cir. 1988). As amended February 27, 1990 and May 11, 1990.

68. *Balistreri v. Pacifica Police Dep't*, 855 F.2d 1421; 1988 U.S. App.

LEXIS 11594, **10, quoting *DeShaney v. Winnebago County Dep't of Social Servs.*, 109 S. Ct. 998, 1005–06 (1989).

69. *Balistreri v. Pacifica Police Dep't*, 855 F.2d 1421; 1988 U.S. App. LEXIS 11594, **11.

70. *Hynson v. City of Chester*, 731 F. Supp. 1236, 1239 (E.D. Pa. 1990), *remanded by* 864 F.2d 1026 (3d Cir. 1988).

71. The law distinguishes procedural due process rights from the substantive due process rights dealt with in *DeShaney*. Hence, a woman deprived by *DeShaney* of substantive due process claims might still enter a claim of violation of procedural due process rights.

72. *Hynson*, 731 F. Supp. at 1239.

73. See *Luster v. Price*, 1990 U.S. Dist. LEXIS 8444, at *1–2 (W.D. Mo. 1990). The facts presented are those alleged by the plaintiffs and recounted in the court's opinion.

74. *Id.* at *9–10.

75. *Id.* at *10. Emphasis mine.

76. See, for example, Caitlin E. Borgmann, "Battered Women's Substantive Due Process Claims: Can Orders of Protection Deflect *DeShaney?*" 65 *New York University Law Review* 1280 (1990). Some theorists suggest that state courts may provide a "more hospitable forum" for state constitutional and tort claims of battered women. Laura S. Harper, "Battered Women Suing Police for Failure to Intervene: Viable Legal Avenues After *DeShaney v. Winnebago County Department of Social Services*," 75 *Cornell Law Review* 1393 (1990). See also "Failure to Intervene" in *Women and the Law*, ed. Carol Lefcourt (Cranbury, N.J.: Clark, Boardman, Callaghan, 1992), section 9B.03.

77. *Dudosh v. City of Allentown* 665 F. Supp. 381, 385 (E.D. Pa. 1987), *vacated without op.*, 853 F.2d 917 (3d Cir. Pa. 1988) *cert. denied sub nom. Dudosh v. Warg*, 488 U.S. 942, *reh'g granted sub nom. Dudosh v. City of Allentown*, 722 F. Supp. 1233 (E.D. Pa. 1989). The facts presented are those alleged by the plaintiff and recounted in these opinions.

78. *Dudosh v. City of Allentown*, 722 F. Supp. 1233, 1235 (E.D. Pa. 1989).

79. *Losinski v. County of Trempealeau*, 946 F.2d 544, 547–48 (7th Cir. Wis. 1991), *reh'g denied*, 1992 U.S. App. LEXIS 195 (7th Cir. 1992) (en banc). The facts presented are those alleged by the plaintiffs and recounted in the court's opinion.

80. *Losinski*, 946 F.2d at 550.

81. *Brown v. City of Elba*, 754 F. Supp. 1551, 1555 (M.D. Ala. 1990). The facts presented are those alleged by the plaintiff and recounted in the court's opinion.

82. *Id.* at 1555–56.

83. *Id.* at 1555.

84. Borgmann, "Battered Women's Due Process Claims," 1314.

85. *Balistreri v. Pacifica Police Dep't*, 855 F.2d 1421; 1988 U.S. App. LEXIS 11594, **10. As amended Feb. 27, 1990 and May 11, 1990.

86. *Brown v. Grabowski*, 922 F.2d 1097 (3s Cir. N.J. 1990), *cert. denied sub nom. Borough of Roselle*, 111 S. Ct. 2827 (1991).

87. *Coffman v. Wilson Police Department*, 739 F. Supp. 257, 260 (E.D. Pa. 1990). The facts presented are those alleged by the plaintiff and recounted in the court's opinion.

88. *Id.* at 263.

89. *Id.* at 264.

90. *Id.* at 266.

91. *Id.* at 265–66 quoting *Archie v. City of Racine*, 847 F.2d 1211, 1226 (7th Cir. 1988), *cert. denied*, 489 U.S. 1065 (1989).

92. *Coffman*, 739 F. Supp. at 265–66.

93. *Siddle v. City of Cambridge, Ohio*, 761 F. Supp. 503, 510 (S.D. Ohio 1991).

94. *Id.* at 510–11.

95. *Id.* at 512.

96. Roberta M. Saielli makes this point in *"DeShaney v. Winnebago County Department of Social Services*: The Future of Section 1983 Actions for State Inaction," 21 *Loyola University of Chicago Law Journal* 191 (1989–90).

97. Daniel L. Schofield, "Domestic Violence, When Do Police Have a Constitutional Duty to Protect?" *FBI Law Enforcement Bulletin*, Jan. 1991, pp. 29–31.

98. U.S. Congress. Senate. Committee on the Judiciary. *The Violence Against Women Act of 1991*, 102nd Cong., 1st sess., S. Rept. 197 (1991), p. 52.

99. Joyce E. McConnell, "Beyond Metaphor: Battered Women, Involuntary Servitude and the Thirteenth Amendment," 4 *Yale Journal of Law and Feminism* 206 (1992).

100. Only five days after handing down *DeShaney*, the Supreme Court held that a city could be held liable under Section 1983 for injuries to individual citizens resulting directly from the city's failure to train its police force adequately. *City of Canton, Ohio v. Harris*, 489 U.S. 378 (1989).

101. Interview with Laurie Woods, Director, National Center on Women and Family Law, Dec. 22, 1992.

102. Telephone interview with Elizabeth Schneider, Professor of Law, Brooklyn Law School, Dec. 30, 1992.

103. "Calling it 'date rape' doesn't change a thing," *Boston Globe*, Dec. 10, 1989, p. A18.

104. Witness the public furor and the readiness of many reporters, ju-

rors, and members of the public to blame the victims who brought rape accusations against Mike Tyson, William Kennedy Smith, several St. John's College students, and several Glen Ridge (New Jersey) high school boys. Witness also the current popularity of fraternity gang rape as a kind of college intramural sport. See especially Peggy Reeves Sanday, *Fraternity Gang Rape: Sex, Brotherhood, and Privilege on Campus* (New York: New York University Press, 1990).

3. *What Is "Domestic Violence"?*

1. To see what "domestic violence" looks like, see Donna Ferrato, *Living with the Enemy* (New York: Aperture, 1991).

2. Susan Schechter, *Women and Male Violence: The Visions and Struggles of the Battered Women's Movement* (Boston: South End Press, 1982), p. 201.

3. Judith Lewis Herman, *Trauma and Recovery* (New York: Basic, 1992), p. 9.

4. Ibid., p. 69.

5. Telephone interview with Susan Schechter, Program Coordinator of AWAKE (Advocacy for Women and Kids in Emergencies), Children's Hospital, Boston, Mass., Jan. 22, 1993.

6. Gerald T. Hotaling and David B. Sugarman, "An Analysis of Risk Markers in Husband to Wife Violence: The Current State of Knowledge," *Violence and Victims* 1, no. 2 (1986): 101–124.

7. Lenore E. Walker, *The Battered Woman Syndrome* (New York: Springer, 1984), p. 59; Lee H. Bowker, Michelle Arbitell, and J. Richard McFerron, "On the Relationship Between Wife Beating and Child Abuse," in *Feminist Perspectives on Wife Abuse*, ed. Kersti Yllo and Michele Bograd (Newbury Park, Calif.: Sage, 1988), pp. 162–63.

8. Evan Stark and Anne Flitcraft, "Women and Children at Risk: A Feminist Perspective on Child Abuse," *International Journal of Health Services* 18, no. 1 (1988); Linda McKibben et al., "Victimization of Mothers of Abused Children: A Controlled Study," *Pediatrics* 84, no. 3 (1989).

9. Interview with Evelina Giobbe, founder of W.H.I.S.P.E.R., an organization of women used in prostitution and the sex industry, Oct. 3, 1987. See also Kathleen Barry, *Female Sexual Slavery* (New York: Prentice Hall, 1980), pp. 78–82.

10. Diana E. H. Russell, *Rape in Marriage* (New York: Macmillan, 1982), pp. 279–80.

11. Deborah Cameron and Elizabeth Frazer, *The Lust to Kill* (New York: New York University Press, 1987), pp. 17–34.

12. Sharon Lamb, "Acts Without Agents: An Analysis of Linguistic Avoidance in Journal Articles on Men Who Batter Women," *American Jour-*

nal of Orthopsychiatry 61, no. 2 (1991): 250–57. Lamb surveyed eleven journals from four academic disciplines. Among her findings: "At least half of the sentences about abuse refused to hold the man responsible for the violent acts he committed against the woman who was his wife, lover, or partner" (255). In *The War Against Women* (New York: Summit, 1992), Marilyn French observes: "So powerful and pervasive is the taboo against blaming men-as-a-class in our society that even social scientists who deplore male violence against women perpetuate a sense of male blamelessness for these acts" (p. 189).

13. Laura S. Harper, "Battered Women Suing Police for Failure to Intervene: Viable Legal Avenues After *DeShaney v. Winnebago County Department of Social Services*," 75 *Cornell Law Review* 1393, 1426, n.216 (1990).

14. Surgeon General Antonia C. Novello, quoted in "Physicians Begin a Program to Combat Family Violence," *New York Times*, Oct. 17, 1991, p. 15.

15. Sally Jacobs, "In Hub and beyond, HIV seen as latest whip for batterers," *Boston Globe*, Jan. 24, 1993, pp. 21, 24.

16. Marilyn French, *The War Against Women*, p. 187.

17. Herman, *Trauma*, p. 32.

18. Ibid., p. 28. For a complete list of the symptoms of post-traumatic stress disorder see Herman, p. 121.

19. Ibid., p. 119.

20. David Adams, "Treatment Models of Men Who Batter: A Profeminist Analysis," in Yllo and Bograd, eds., *Feminist Perspectives*, p. 191.

21. Ibid., p. 190.

22. Amnesty International, *Report on Torture* (New York: Farrar, Straus & Giroux, 1973), p. 173. See also A. D. Biderman, "Communist Attempts to Elicit False Confessions from Air Force Prisoners of War," *Bulletin of New York Academy of Medicine* 33 (1957): 616–25. The chart reproduced was adapted for use at a shelter in Northampton, Massachusetts. For lists of controlling techniques commonly used by batterers, see Ann Jones and Susan Schechter, *When Love Goes Wrong: What to Do When You Can't Do Anything Right* (New York: HarperCollins, 1992), pp. 17–22.

23. Adams, "Treatment Models," p. 194.

24. Ellen Pence, "How Society Gives Men Permission to Batter," *In Our Best Interest*, part 2, a videotape produced by the Women's Coalition, Duluth, Minn., n.d.

25. Lenore E. Walker, *The Battered Woman* (New York: Harper and Row, 1979), pp. 65–70. Walker was the first to identify a cycle of violence and to label its phases. Compare John Stoltenberg, *Refusing to Be a Man: Essays on Sex and Justice* (Portland, Oreg.: Breitenbush, 1989): "The appeal for 'forgiveness' . . . functions to trap and lock in any female who may have

been considering withdrawing her sustenance from him. The forgiveness asked—though it is always demanded, because even here pressure is applied—is a form of insistence that she remain in relation to him" (p. 23).

26. Russell, *Rape in Marriage*, p. 273; see also Lewis Okun, *Woman Abuse: Facts Replacing Myth* (Albany, N.Y.: State University of New York Press, 1986), pp. 113–39; and, for example, Ann Jones, *Everyday Death: The Case of Bernadette Powell* (New York: Holt, Rinehart and Winston, 1985), and Brian Vallée, *Life with Billy* (New York: Pocket Books, 1989).

27. Herman, *Trauma*, p. 75.

28. Interview with a survivor of battery who requested anonymity, in Minnesota, Sept. 2, 1987.

29. Interview with a survivor of battery who requested anonymity, in Hawaii, Nov. 28, 1987.

30. Linda Gordon, *Heroes of Their Own Lives: The Politics and History of Family Violence: Boston 1880–1960* (New York: Viking, 1988), pp. 286–87.

31. Gordon, *Heroes of Their Own Lives*, p. 287.

32. Interview in Indiana, May 5, 1979. Name withheld.

33. Carroll Smith-Rosenberg, *Disorderly Conduct: Visions of Gender in Victorian America* (New York: Knopf, 1985), pp. 90–93.

34. Gordon, *Heroes of Their Own Lives*, p. 255.

35. Robert Bly, *Iron John: A Book About Men* (Reading, Mass.: Addison-Wesley, 1990), p. 2.

36. Bly, *Iron John*, pp. 87, 8, 26.

37. Elizabeth Wilson, *What Is to Be Done About Violence Against Women?* (London: Penguin, 1983), p. 95.

38. Pence, "How Society Gives Men Permission to Batter," *In Our Best Interest*, part 2.

39. Pence, "Why Do I Feel So Crazy?" *In Our Best Interest*, part 2.

40. Susan Diesenhouse, "Women Driven to Kill Are Shown More Mercy," *New York Times*, Jan. 30, 1989, p. A10.

41. Charles Patrick Ewing, *Battered Women Who Kill: Psychological Self-Defense As Legal Justification* (Lexington, Mass.: D.C. Heath, 1987), p. 118.

42. Diesenhouse, *New York Times*, Jan. 30, 1989, p. A10. Interview with Kathleen (Kaplan) Brewster, March 28, 1993.

43. Angela Browne and Kirk R. Williams, "Exploring the Effect of Resource Availability and the Likelihood of Female-Perpetrated Homicides," 23 *Law and Society Review* 80 (1989). Browne and Williams report that between 1979 and 1984 the number of "male partners" killed by women decreased by more than 25 percent.

44. Holly Maguigan, "Battered Women and Self-Defense: Myths and

Misconceptions in Current Reform Proposals," 140 *University of Pennysyl-vania Law Review* 379, 397, n.67 (1991), citing statistics from the Department of Justice, Bureau of Justice Statistics. For discussion of "homicidal self-help" see Maria L. Marcus, "Conjugal Violence: The Law of Force and the Force of Law," 69 *California Law Review* 1657, 1658 (1981).

45. Faith McNulty, *The Burning Bed* (New York: Harcourt, Brace, Jovanovich, 1980); for cases of Francine Hughes and other battered women who killed their assailants see Ann Jones, *Women Who Kill* (New York: Holt, Rinehart & Winston, 1980), pp. 281–321; for other cases see Angela Browne, *When Battered Women Kill* (New York: Free Press, 1987); see also Joyce E. McConnell, "Beyond Metaphor: Battered Women, Involuntary Servitude and the Thirteenth Amendment," 4 *Yale Journal of Law and Feminism* 206 (1992); Cynthia K. Gillespie, *Justifiable Homicide: Battered Women, Self-Defense, and the Law* (Columbus: Ohio State University Press, 1989); Ewing, *Battered Women Who Kill*; and Vallée, *Life with Billy*.

46. Law professor Holly Maguigan exploded the popular myth that battered women typically kill "sleeping men." Reviewing 270 homicides, she found that 75 percent occurred during confrontations. Only 8 percent were "sleeping man" cases. In another 8 percent the woman acted during a lull in the man's violence against her; 4 percent were contract killings. (In 5 percent of the cases the circumstances could not be determined.) Maguigan, "Battered Women and Self-Defense," 396–97.

47. For discussion of this issue see Elizabeth M. Schneider, "Describing and Changing: Women's Self-Defense Work and the Problem of Expert Testimony on Battering," 9 *Women's Rights Law Reporter* 195 (1986); Lenore Walker, "A Response to Elizabeth M. Schneider's *Describing and Changing*," 9 *Women's Rights Law Reporter* 223 (1986). Expert testimony that a woman suffers from "battered woman's syndrome" is now used in child custody disputes to label her an unfit mother. Interview with Joan Zorza, National Center on Women and Family Law, Feb. 12, 1993.

48. Louise Bauschard and Mary Kimbrough, *Voices Set Free: Battered Women Speak from Prison* (St. Louis: Women's Self-Help Center, 1986), pp. ix–x; see also pp. 117–33.

49. Telephone interview with Leigh Dingerson, National Coalition to Abolish the Death Penalty, Feb. 12, 1991.

50. Isabel Wilkerson, "Clemency Granted to 25 Women Convicted for Assault or Murder," *New York Times*, Dec. 22, 1990, p. 1.

51. Janet Naylor, "Schaefer to free 8 battered women who fought back," *Washington Times*, Feb. 20, 1991, p. A1; Howard Schneider, "MD to Free Abused Women, Schaefer Commutes 8 Terms, Citing Violence," *Washington Post*, Feb. 20, 1991, p. A1.

52. Naylor, *Washington Times*, Feb. 20, 1991, p. A5.

53. William Blackstone, *Commentaries on the Laws of England*, ed. Thomas M. Cooley, 4th ed. by James DeWitt Andrews (Chicago: Callahan, 1899), book 4, pp. 93, 203–4.

54. "Fact File," *CA Reporter*, newsletter of the Correctional Association of New York, April 1991, p. 4.

55. Department of Justice, Bureau of Justice Statistics, telephone interview with statistician Stephanie Greenhouse, Nov. 30, 1992.

4. *The Language of Love*

1. *Brown v. Grabowski*, 922 F.2d 1097, 1117 (3d Cir. N.J. 1990), *Cert. denied sub nom. Borough of Roselle*, 111 S. Ct. 2827 (1991). The New Jersey Domestic Violence Act took effect in 1982. Deborah Evans was killed in February 1985.

2. Theodor H. Van de Velde, *Ideal Marriage: Its Physiology and Technique*, trans. Stella Browne (New York: Random House, 1930), pp. 158–59. Van de Velde quotes (without citation) from Ellis's "Love and Pain," vol. 3 of *Studies in Psychology*.

3. Alex Comfort, *The New Joy of Sex: The Gourmet Guide to Lovemaking for the Nineties* (New York: Pocket Books, 1991), pp. 98–99. Comfort's habitual use of pronouns without antecedents often leaves the meaning obscure; I represent the sense of these passages as best I can.

4. Robert Bly, *Iron John: A Book About Men* (New York: Vintage, 1992), p. 26.

5. George R. Bach and Peter Wyden, *The Intimate Enemy: How to Fight Fair in Love and Marriage* (New York: Avon, 1970).

6. Simone de Beauvoir, *The Second Sex* (New York: Vintage, 1989), pp. xxviii–xxx.

7. Bly, *Iron John*, p. 1.

8. Ibid., p. 175.

9. Bach and Wyden, *Intimate Enemy*, p. 27.

10. George Bach and Herb Goldberg, *Creative Aggression: The Art of Assertive Living* (1974; rpt. New York: Anchor, 1983), p. 272.

11. Ibid., p. 274.

12. In this context the smile, a sign of appeasement, has more to do with relative power than with gender as such.

13. Sigmund Freud, *Civilization and Its Discontents*, trans. James Strachey (1930; rpt. New York: Norton, 1961), p. 60.

14. Jean Baer, *How to Be an Assertive (Not Aggressive) Woman in Life, in Love, and on the Job: A Total Guide to Self-Assertiveness* (New York: New American Library, 1976).

15. Harriet Goldhor Lerner, *The Dance of Anger: A Woman's Guide to*

Changing the Patterns of Intimate Relationships (New York: Harper & Row, 1985), p. 2.

16. Carol Gilligan, *In a Different Voice: Psychological Theory and Women's Development* (Cambridge, Mass.: Harvard University Press, 1982), pp. 24–63.

17. Bach and Goldberg, *Creative Aggression*, p. 215.

18. Carol Tavris, *Anger: The Misunderstood Emotion* (New York: Simon and Schuster, 1982), p. 42.

19. Ibid., p. 121. Emphasis mine.

20. Lerner, *Dance of Anger*, p. 2.

21. Interview with a survivor of battery who requested anonymity, in California, March 15, 1989.

22. Bach and Wyden, *Intimate Enemy*, p. 116.

23. Ibid., p. 116. Emphasis mine. Note also the idea that a "tongue lashing may hurt more than physical violence," another common "justification" for assault, equating verbal and physical aggression, and conceptualizing physical assault as self-defense against women's "nagging" or "bitching." For discussion of this justification offered by batterers, see James Ptacek, "Why Do Men Batter Their Wives?" in Yllo and Bogard, eds., *Feminist Perspectives*, pp. 141–56.

24. Bach and Wyden, *Intimate Enemy*, pp. 116–17.

25. For an analysis of a paradigmatic "rough sex" murder case in which the woman was blamed for her own death, Robert Chambers's killing of Jennifer Levin, see Helen Benedict, *Virgin or Vamp: How the Press Covers Sex Crimes* (New York: Oxford University Press, 1992), pp. 147–88.

26. Comfort, *New Joy of Sex*, p. 99. Comfort adds the warning: "Don't ever put up with real violence—it will escalate, however much the aggressor apologizes." He does not explain the difference between "real" violence and violence that is not real.

27. Alison Carper, "The Danger Dance," *New York Newsday*, July 22, 1992, p. 5.

28. For a feminist analysis of pornography see especially Andrea Dworkin, *Pornography: Men Possessing Women* (New York: Perigee, 1981), and Catherine MacKinnon, "Part 3: Pornography," *Feminism Unmodified: Discourses on Life and Law* (Cambridge, Mass.: Harvard University Press, 1987), pp. 127–213.

29. Michael S. Kimmel, "Introduction: Guilty Pleasures—Pornography in Men's Lives," *Men Confront Pornography*, ed. Michael S. Kimmel (New York: Meridian, 1991), p. 1. Kimmel cites industry figures for 1984: 200 million issues of 800 hard- and soft-core magazines sold in the United States, generating over $750 million.

30. Kimmel, *Men Confront Pornography*, pp. 6, 8.

31. Diana E. H. Russell records reports from women whose partners forced them to "try" things they had seen in pornographic magazines or films. *Rape in Marriage* (New York: Macmillan, 1982), pp. 83–86.

32. Edward Donnerstein and Daniel Linz, "Mass Media, Sexual Violence, and Male Viewers: Current Theory and Research," in Kimmel, ed., *Men Confront Pornography*, p. 231.

33. Ibid., pp. 219–22.

34. Ann Jones, *Everyday Death: The Case of Bernadette Powell* (New York: Holt, Rinehart & Winston, 1985), pp. 158–59.

35. *People v. Powell*, 96 A.D.2d 610, 464 N.Y.S.2d 611 (1983).

36. Paula Chin and Civia Tamarkin, "The Door of Evil," *People*, August 12, 1991, pp. 35–36; *Estate of Sinthasomphone v. City of Milwaukee*, 785 F.Supp. 1343 (E.D. Wis. 1992).

37. "Tracy," music and lyrics by W. Antichrist, on *Rotting*, an album recorded by the heavy metal band Sarcofago, Kraze Records.

38. Niggas with Attitude, Priority Records, 1991.

39. "Mind of a Lunatic," The Geto Boys, Rap-A-Lot Records, 1990.

40. Interviews with Iris Fischer, Jennifer Fisher, and Margaret Rooks, South Hadley, Massachusetts, April 8 and May 11, 1992.

41. Dick Polman, "In the shadow of violence," *Philadelphia Inquirer*, April 1989, p. K1.

42. Victoria Benning and David L. Schutz, "Ex-boyfriend fatally shoots woman on Allston street, then kills self," *Boston Globe*, May 31, 1992, p. 28.

43. Ibid.

44. Peter Gelzinis, "Former victim tries to grapple with sense of relief and pain," *Boston Herald*, June 2, 1992, p. 7.

45. For analysis of bias in press coverage of sex crimes, see Benedict, *Virgin or Vamp*.

46. Batterers who accuse "their" women of infidelity are often projecting their own behavior. Jose Dolores Martinez of the Bronx, for example, shot and killed his wife, whom he believed to be unfaithful, and her niece, then killed his girlfriend, took another of his girlfriends hostage, and finally killed himself in her bed. Relatives said that Maria Altagracia Martinez, a faithful wife, never left her apartment without her jealous husband's permission. Cases like this occur frequently. Ray Sanchez and Bruce Stanley, "Suspect Kills Self," *New York Newsday*, July 4, 1992, p. 6.

47. Sheridan Lyons, "Man who killed wife gets 10-year maximum term," *Baltimore Sun*, June 24, 1989, p. 8A. Emphasis mine.

48. Ibid.

49. Maria Archangelo, "Man who strangled wife seeks early release from prison," *Baltimore Sun*, March 3, 1991, p. 6.

50. John Stoltenberg, *Refusing to Be a Man: Essays on Sex and Justice* (Portland, Oreg.: Breitenbush, 1989), p. 23. Emphasis mine.

51. Mary Murphy, "Why Robin Givens Has Rolled with the Punches—and Still Loves Tyson," *TV Guide* 37, no. 26 (July 1, 1989), 11.

52. "Accuser: Tyson laughed while he raped me," *Boston Herald*, Jan. 31, 1992, p. 1.

53. Michael Madden, "Strength rings in tiny voice," *Boston Globe*, Jan. 31, 1992, pp. 39–40; Beverly Ford, "Accuser described as intelligent, outgoing Providence student," *Boston Herald*, Jan. 31, 1992, p. 19.

54. E. R. Shipp, "Tyson Gets 6-Year Prison Term For Rape Conviction in Indiana," *New York Times*, March 27, 1992, p. 1. The sentence was ten years with four suspended. Judge Patricia J. Gifford denied Tyson's request to remain free pending an appellate decision.

55. Murphy, *TV Guide*, July 1, 1989, pp. 9, 11.

56. Michael Lev, "A Ballplayer's Life Turns on a Home Run," *New York Times*, July 20, 1989, p. B12.

57. AP Dispatch, "Officer Kills Lover in Suicide," *New York Times*, May 20, 1989, p. 31. Note the odd use of the singular possessive "lover's quarrel" in the police press release. It may be only a typographical error, but it is an accurate assessment of the one-sided nature of the "quarrel."

58. *New York Post*, May 20, 1989, p. 1.

59. Interview with a survivor of battery and stalking who requested anonymity, in New York, May 20, 1991.

60. For an example of the indictment of battered women as collaborators, see Susan Brownmiller, "Madly in Love," *Ms.*, April 1989, p. 64.

61. Gelzinis, *Boston Herald*, June 2, 1992, p. 7.

5. *Why Doesn't She Leave?*

1. "Hitting Home," an episode of "48 Hours," CBS TV, June 18, 1988.

2. Charles Thurman's conviction was overturned on a technicality. Retried in 1987, he pleaded guilty to first-degree assault and was sentenced to 20 years, to be suspended after 14, and 5 years probation. Under a 1990 Supreme Court ruling that grants more time off for good behavior to prisoners who were convicted twice, Thurman was released from prison eight months earlier than expected. Ray Routhier, "Thurman to be freed April 12," *Hartford Courant*, March 15, 1991, p. C1; Ray Routhier, "Thurman quietly escorted at night from prison to halfway house," *Hartford Courant*, April 13, 1991, p. C9; Ray Routhier, "Kentucky bars 'Buck' Thurman," *Hartford Courant*, April 19, 1991, p. B1.

3. Routhier, *Hartford Courant*, March 15, 1991, p. C1.

4. Telephone interview with Anne Menard, Executive Director, Connecticut Coalition Against Domestic Violence, Nov. 30, 1992.

5. "48 Hours," June 18, 1988.

6. Ibid.

7. Sam Roberts, "Indictment 62/87: A Battered Wife Turns to Violence," *New York Times*, April 9, 1987, p. B1; Sam Roberts, "A Victim's Peril: Lack of Money For a Divorce," *New York Times*, Oct. 1, 1987, p. B1.

8. Marilyn French, *The War Against Women* (New York: Summit, 1992), p. 188.

9. "The News at Six," WCBS TV, New York City, September 5, 1987.

10. Julie Johnson, "Queens Woman Acquitted in Killing of Husband," *New York Times*, Oct. 1, 1987, pp. B1, B4.

11. William Ryan, *Blaming the Victim*, rev. ed. (New York: Vintage, 1976), p. 15.

12. Ibid., p. 13.

13. Ibid., p. 16.

14. Ibid., pp. 8–9.

15. Ibid., p. 29.

16. John E. Snell, Richard J. Rosenwald, and Ames Robey, "The Wife-Beater's Wife: A Study of Family Interaction," *Archives of General Psychiatry* 11 (August 1964): 110–11.

17. Commenting on "The Wife-Beater's Wife," Judith Lewis Herman writes: "While this unabashed, open sexism is rarely found in psychiatric literature today, the same conceptual errors, with their implicit bias and contempt, still predominate." *Trauma and Recovery* (New York: Basic, 1992), p. 117.

18. Richard J. Gelles and Murray A. Straus, *Intimate Violence* (New York: Simon and Schuster, 1988), p. 89. Emphasis mine.

19. Susan Schechter, *Women and Male Violence: The Visions and Struggles of the Battered Women's Movement* (Boston: South End Press, 1982), pp. 192–95.

20. Leonard Buder, "A Police Study Challenges Belief Family Fights Are Riskiest Duty," *New York Times*, Feb. 11, 1979, p. 50; see also Ann Jones, *Women Who Kill* (New York: Holt, Rinehart & Winston, 1980), pp. 304–5.

21. Lawrence W. Sherman and Richard A. Berk, *The Minneapolis Domestic Violence Experiment* (Washington, D.C.: Police Foundation Reports 1, 1984), p. 2; see also Sherman, *Policing Domestic Violence: Experiments and Dilemmas* (New York: Free Press, 1992), pp. 30–32, and Joan Zorza, "The Criminal Law of Misdemeanor Domestic Violence, 1970–1990," 83 *Journal of Criminal Law and Criminology* 46, 51–52 (1992). Quoting a study

by Joel Garner and Elizabeth Clemmer, *Danger to Police in Domestic Disturbances—A New Look: Research in Brief* (Washington, D.C.: National Institute of Justice, 1986), Zorza reports: "The reality . . . is that domestic disturbance incidents, which account for thirty percent of police calls, account for only 5.7 percent of police deaths, making domestic disturbances one of the least dangerous of all police activities" (52).

22. U.S. Attorney General's Task Force on Family Violence, U.S. Department of Justice, *Final Report* (1984), p. 22.

23. Sherman and Berk, Police Foundation Reports 1, p. 2.

24. *Scott v. Hart*, No. C-76-2395 (N.D. Cal. filed Oct. 28, 1976).

25. *Bruno v. Codd*, 90 Misc. 2d 1047, 396 N.Y.S.2d 974 (Sup. Ct. 1977).

26. International Association of Chiefs of Police, "Wife-Beating," Training Key 245 (1976); "Investigation of Wife-Beating," Training Key 246 (1976).

27. Nancy Loving, *Responding to Spouse Abuse and Wife Beating: A Guide for Police* (Washington, D.C.: Police Executive Research Forum, 1980).

28. Sherman and Berk, Police Foundation Reports 1, p. 5.

29. Sherman, *Policing Domestic Violence*, p. 254. Although local law enforcement agencies in these cities reported that their pro-arrest practices, as part of a coordinated criminal justice system response, contributed to the decrease in domestic assault and homicide, Sherman attributes the falling rates of homicide to "chance fluctuation."

30. Ibid., p. 109.

31. Ibid., p. 115.

32. Zorza, "Criminal Law," 63–65.

33. Zorza, "Criminal Law," 64; *Brown v. Grabowski*, 922 F.2d 1097, 1116 (3d Cir. N.J. 1990), *Cert. denied sub nom. Borough of Roselle*, 111 S. Ct. 2827 (1991).

34. U.S. Attorney General's Task Force on Family Violence, *Final Report*, p. 23.

35. Zorza, "Criminal Law," 71.

36. "Immediate Arrest in Domestic Violence Situations: Mandate or Alternative," 14 *Capitol University Law Review* 243 (1985).

37. Zorza, "Criminal Law," 71.

38. Patricia Nealon and Sean P. Murphy, "Thwarting the killers is a complex, elusive goal," Boston *Globe*, June 2, 1992, p. 6.

39. Don Terry, "Woman in Divorce is Slain in Court," *New York Times*, May 6, 1992, p. A21.

40. Don Terry, "Killing of Woman Waiting for Justice Sounds Alert on Domestic Violence," *New York Times*, March 17, 1992, p. A14. Franklin was arrested at the scene and charged with first-degree murder.

41. Larry Olmstead, "When Passion Explodes Into a Deadly Rage," *New York Times*, May 18, 1993, pp. A1, B4.

42. Surgeon General Antonia C. Novello, address to an American Medical Association press conference on violence, New York City, Jan. 16, 1992.

43. Ibid.

44. "Domestic Violence Intervention Calls for More Than Treating Injuries," *JAMA: The Journal of the American Medical Association* 264, no. 8 (1990): 939.

45. "Violence Against Women: Relevance for Medical Practitioners," *JAMA: The Journal of the American Medical Association* 267, no. 23 (1992): 3186; Evan Stark, Anne Flitcraft, et al., *Wife Abuse in the Medical Setting: An Introduction for Health Personnel*, Domestic Violence Monograph Series, No. 7 (Washington, D.C.: Office of Domestic Violence, 1981), p. v.

46. "Wife Abuse: An Opportunity for Prevention," *Injury Prevention Network Newsletter* 5, no. 1 (1988): 3.

47. "Violence Against Women," *JAMA* 267 (1992): 3187.

48. Ibid.

49. Ibid., 3186–87.

50. Novello, address to AMA conference, January 16, 1992.

51. Stark, Flitcraft, et al., *Wife Abuse in the Medical Setting*, p. vii.

52. Patricia Nealon, "For abused, few places to turn," *Boston Globe*, June 2, 1992, p. 6.

53. "Domestic Violence Intervention," *JAMA* 264 (1990): 939.

54. Ibid., 940.

55. Ibid., 939.

56. Demie Kurz and Evan Stark, "Not-So-Benign Neglect: The Medical Response to Battering," in *Feminist Perspectives on Wife Abuse*, ed. Kersti Yllo and Michele Bograd (Newbury Park, Calif.: Sage, 1988), p. 253.

57. "Wife Abuse: An Opportunity for Prevention," *Injury Prevention*, 2–3.

58. "Campaign Alerts Physicians to Identify, Assist Victims of Domestic Violence," *JAMA: The Journal of the American Medical Association* 261, no. 7 (1989): 963.

59. Nealon, *Boston Globe*, June 2, 1992, p. 6.

60. "Campaign Alerts Physicians," *JAMA* 261 (1989): 963.

61. Surgeon General Antonia C. Novello, address to American Medical Association press conference on violence, Chicago, October 16, 1991.

62. Janice Perrone, "Doctors' attitudes affecting family violence problem," *American Medical News*, Feb. 3, 1992, p. 27. The study is the "Health Care and Family Violence Field Project," a Robert Wood Johnson Foundation study, the principal investigator Dr. Eli H. Newberger, Di-

rector of the Family Development Program at Boston's Children's Hospital.

63. Stark, Flitcraft, et al., "Wife Abuse in the Medical Setting," p. v.

64. "Domestic Violence Intervention," *JAMA* 264 (1990): 939.

65. Ibid., citing *American Journal of Orthopsychiatry* 56 (1986): 360–70.

66. Ellen Pence et al., *In Our Best Interest: A Process for Personal and Social Change* (Duluth: Minnesota Program Development, Inc., 1987), p. 61.

67. "Til Death Do Us Part," an episode of "48 Hours," CBS TV, Feb. 6, 1991.

68. Martha R. Mahoney, "Legal Images of Battered Women: Redefining the Issue of Separation," 90 *Michigan Law Review* 1, 65–66 (1991).

69. Arn Shackelford, "Decision shocks workers at women's shelter," *Grand Rapids Press*, May 12, 1989, p. A4.

70. Ellen Goodman, "Excuses, not penalties," *Boston Globe*, May 23, 1989, p. 15.

71. Tracy L. Sypert and Arn Shackelford, "Ratliff only recalls bits, pieces: lawyer," *Grand Rapids Press*, April 27, 1989, p. A1.

72. "Iron's friends decry verdict, but Ratliff's supporters satisfied," *Grand Rapids Press*, May 12, 1989, p. A1.

73. Tracy L. Sypert, "Ratliff's Defense: 'Diminished capacity,'" *Grand Rapids Press*, April 14, 1989, p. A2.

74. Tracy L. Sypert, "Ratliff judge bars details on 1st wife," *Grand Rapids Press*, May 2, 1989, pp. A1, A4.

75. Tracy L. Sypert, "Jurors felt Ratliff was 'provoked,'" *Grand Rapids Press*, May 12, 1989, p. A1.

76. Goodman, *Boston Globe*, May 23, 1989, p. 15.

77. Sypert, *Grand Rapids Press*, May 12, 1989, p. A1.

78. Ibid., p. A4.

79. Arn Shackelford, "New Ratliff trial unneeded, prosecutor says," *Grand Rapids Press*, Aug. 13, 1989, p. F1.

80. *Grand Rapids Press*, May 12, 1989, p. A4.

81. Elizabeth Pleck, *Domestic Tyranny: The Making of American Social Policy Against Family Violence from Colonial Times to the Present* (New York: Oxford University Press, 1987), p. 193.

82. Schechter, *Women and Male Violence*, p. 142.

83. Gerald T. Hotaling and David B. Sugarman, "An Analysis of Risk Markers in Husband to Wife Violence: The Current State of Knowledge," *Violence and Victims* 1, no. 2 (1986) 120.

84. Suzanne K. Steinmetz, "The Battered Husband Syndrome," *Victimology* 2, nos. 3/4 (1977): 499–509; Murray A. Straus, "Wife Beating: How Common and Why?" *Victimology* 2, nos. 3/4 (1977–78): 443–58;

Murray A. Straus, "Measuring Intrafamily Conflict and Violence: The Conflict Tactics (CT) Scales," *Journal of Marriage and the Family* 41 (1979): 75–88; Murray A. Straus, Richard J. Gelles, and Suzanne Steinmetz, *Behind Closed Doors: Violence in the American Family* (New York: Anchor/Doubleday, 1980), pp. 253–56.

85. R. Emerson Dobash and Russell P. Dobash, "Research as Social Action: The Struggle for Battered Women," in Yllo and Bograd, eds., *Feminist Perspectives*, p. 58; the most thoroughgoing critiques are Elizabeth Pleck, Joseph H. Pleck, Marilyn Grossman, and Pauline B. Bart, "The Battered Data Syndrome: A Comment on Steinmetz's Article," *Victimology* 2, nos. 3/4 (1977–78): 680–83; Schechter, *Women and Male Violence*, pp. 209–16; Mildred Pagelow, "The Battered Husband Syndrome: Social Problem or Much Ado about Nothing," in *Marital Violence*, ed. N. Johnson (Boston: Routledge & Kegan Paul, 1986), pp. 172–94; R. Emerson Dobash and Russell P. Dobash, *Women, Violence and Social Change* (London: Routledge, 1992), pp. 251–84.

86. Dobash and Dobash, *Women, Violence and Social Change*, p. 280.

87. Murray A. Straus and Richard R. Gelles, "Societal Change and Change in Family Violence from 1975 to 1985 as Revealed by Two National Surveys," *Journal of Marriage and the Family* 48 (1986): 465–79.

88. Tamar Lewin, "Battered Men Sounding Equal-Rights Battle Cry," *New York Times*, April 20, 1992, p. A12.

89. Dobash and Dobash, *Women, Violence and Social Change*, p. 274. For a full analysis of this "peculiar" family violence research, see pp. 251–84. In *The War Against Women* (New York: Summit, 1992), p. 189, Marilyn French cites this example drawn from Sharon Lamb's linguistic analysis of *Behind Closed Doors* by Straus, Gelles, and Steinmetz: "The authors describe a brutal scene of a husband beating his wife over the head with a cane and whipping her arms and legs with a hose, then ask, 'How could a couple inflict such a situation upon one another?' " See Sharon Lamb, "Acts Without Agents: An Analysis of Linguistic Avoidance in Journal Articles on Men Who Batter Women," *American Journal of Orthopsychiatry* 61, no. 2 (1991): 251.

90. Susan Schechter, "Building Bridges Between Activists, Professionals, and Researchers," in Yllo and Bograd, eds., *Feminist Perspectives on Wife Abuse*, p. 310.

91. Ibid.

92. Elliott Currie, *Confronting Crime: An American Challenge* (New York: Pantheon, 1985), p. 208.

93. David Bird, "Domestic Violence is Termed 'Insidious Criminal Problem,'" *New York Times*, Dec. 2, 1983, p. B3.

94. Currie, *Confronting Crime*, p. 208.

95. Lawrence W. Sherman, "The Influence of Criminology on Criminal Law: Evaluating Arrests for Misdemeanor Domestic Violence," 83 *Journal of Criminal Law and Criminology* 1, 16–17, 7–10 (1992).

96. Lawrence W. Sherman and Richard A. Berk, "The Specific Deterrent Effects of Arrest for Domestic Assault," *American Sociological Review* 49, no. 2 (1984): 261–72; for a summary see Sherman and Berk, Police Foundation Reports 1.

97. Sherman, "Influence of Criminology on Criminal Law," 21, 24.

98. Sherman, "Influence of Criminology on Criminal Law," 25–26. The cost estimate is drawn from Lisa G. Lerman, "The Decontextualization of Domestic Violence," 83 *Journal of Criminal Law and Criminology* 217, 218, n.6 (1992).

99. Sherman, "Influence of Criminology on Criminal Law," 25.

100. Franklyn W. Dunford, "The Measurement of Recidivism in Cases of Spouse Assault," 83 *Journal of Criminal Law and Criminology* 120, 135–36 (1992).

101. J. David Hirschel and Ira W. Hutchison III, "Female Spouse Abuse and the Police Response: The Charlotte, North Carolina Experiment," 83 *Journal of Criminal Law and Criminology* 73, 119 (1992).

102. Lawrence W. Sherman, Janell D. Schmidt, Dennis P. Rogan, Douglas A. Smith, Patrick R. Gartin, Ellen G. Cohn, Dean J. Collins, and Anthony R. Bacich, "The Variable Effects of Arrest on Criminal Careers: The Milwaukee Domestic Violence Experiment," 83 *Journal of Criminal Law and Criminology* 137, 168 (1992); Sherman, "Influence of Criminology on Criminal Law," 32.

103. Sherman et al., "Variable Effects of Arrest on Criminal Careers," 158–69; Sherman, "Influence of Criminology on Criminal Law," 32.

104. Cynthia Grant Bowman, "The Arrest Experiments: A Feminist Critique," 83 *Journal of Criminal Law and Criminology* 201 (1992); Lisa A. Frisch, "Research That Succeeds, Policies That Fail," 83 *Journal of Criminal Law and Criminology* 209 (1992); Lisa G. Lerman, "The Decontextualization of Domestic Violence," 83 *Journal of Criminal Law and Criminology* 217 (1992).

105. Sherman, "Influence of Criminology on Criminal Law," 43.

106. Sherman, *Policing Domestic Violence*, pp. 254–56, 130.

107. For the theory of "different folks" see Sherman, *Policing Domestic Violence*, pp. 154–87. One theoretical objection to mandatory arrest for domestic assault is that arrest will fall disproportionately on men of color. The Duluth Domestic Abuse Intervention Project reports that after arrest was mandated there, arrests of men of color markedly increased. Arrests of white men, however, increased far more dramatically, so that the proportion of men of color arrested actually fell to a level corresponding to

their proportion of the general male population. One may conclude that mandatory arrest, by overriding the discretionary racism of police, results in more equitable treatment for minority men, not less. For discussion see Caroline Forell, "Stopping the Violence: Mandatory Arrest and Police Tort Liability for Failure to Assist Battered Women," 6 *Berkeley Women's Law Journal* 215 (1990–91).

108. Sherman, *Policing Domestic Violence*, p. 258.

109. Sherman, "Influence of Criminology on Criminal Law,"1–5, et passim.

110. Sherman, "Influence of Criminology on Criminal Law," 37.

111. Bowman, "The Arrest Experiments," 204–205.

112. Sherman, *Policing Domestic Violence*, p. 251.

113. Sherman, "Influence of Criminology on Criminal Law," 37; Sherman, *Policing Domestic Violence*, pp. 252–60.

114. "Don't let abusers off the hook," editorial, *Milwaukee Journal*, Nov. 11, 1991, p. A22.

115. Bowman, "The Arrest Experiments," 203. See her essay for a thorough analysis of the male perspective in the arrest studies, 201–208.

116. Sherman, "Influence of Criminology on Criminal Law," 31–32.

117. Richard A. Berk, Alec Campbell, Ruth Klap, and Bruce Western, "A Bayesian Analysis of the Colorado Springs Spouse Abuse Experiment," 83 *Journal of Criminal Law and Criminology* 170, 173 (1992); Sherman, *Policing Domestic Violence*, p. 319.

118. Sherman, *Policing Domestic Violence*, pp. 319–24.

119. Bowman, "The Arrest Experiments," 205.

120. Sherman, *Policing Domestic Violence*, p. 213.

121. Ibid.

122. Schechter, "Building Bridges," in Yllo and Bograd, eds., *Feminist Perspectives*, p. 310; Judith Lewis Herman, *Trauma and Recovery* (New York: Basic, 1992), pp. 117–18.

123. Gelles and Straus, *Intimate Violence*, p. 138.

124. Pleck, *Domestic Tyranny*, p. 7.

125. "A Bill to Be Bashed," editorial, *Washington Star*, Oct. 13, 1980, p. A18. Note the cute headline which trivializes woman "bashing."

126. Schechter, *Women and Male Violence*, p. 146.

127. Dobash and Dobash, *Women, Violence and Social Change*, pp. 140–41. The bill carried an appropriation of $8.3 million for 1985 and 1986, and $8.5 million for 1987 and 1988.

128. Schechter, *Women and Male Violence*, p. 146.

129. "A Bill to Be Bashed," *Washington Star*, Oct. 13, 1980.

130. Roberts, *New York Times*, April 9, 1987, p. B1; Julie Johnson,

"Woman Describes How She Killed Her Husband," *New York Times*, Sept. 29, 1987, p. B3.

6. *A Woman to Blame*

1. Jimmy Breslin, "Below and Beyond the Call of Drugs," *Newsday*, Dec. 4, 1988, p. 2.

2. Pete Hamill, *New York Post*, Dec. 13, 1988, p. 2.

3. "A Tale of Abuse," *Newsweek*, Dec. 12, 1988, p. 56.

4. Testimony of Dr. Neil Spiegel, quoted in Erika Munk, "Private Lives, Public Fears," *Village Voice*, Nov. 15, 1988, p. 10.

5. Ronald Sullivan, "Witness Says Numerous Injuries to Nussbaum Were Nearly Fatal," *New York Times*, Nov. 5, 1988, p. 31.

6. Joyce Johnson, "What Lisa Knew," *Vanity Fair*, May 1988, p. 117.

7. *Newsweek*, Dec. 12, 1988, p. 56.

8. "Opening Up a Catalog of Abuse," *Newsday*, Dec. 2, 1988, pp. 5, 27.

9. Timothy Clifford, "Jurors Cringe at Videotape of Bruised, Battered Hedda," *Newsday*, Nov. 4, 1988, pp. 5, 22.

10. "Ex-Caseworker Tells of 'Filth,'" *Newsday*, Nov. 4, 1988, pp. 5, 22. The trancelike, zombielike, or detached state of consciousness which many observed in Nussbaum indicates severe, prolonged trauma and a coercive process very far advanced. See Judith Lewis Herman, *Trauma and Recovery* (New York: Basic, 1992), pp. 42–43.

11. Pete Hamill, *New York Post*, Dec. 13, 1988, p. 2.

12. William Glaberson, "Why Hedda Nussbaum Fascinates: Most Can Identify," *New York Times*, Dec. 9, 1988, p. B1.

13. Herman, *Trauma*, p. 84.

14. Herman, *Trauma*, p. 60. Herman also notes: "Though highly resilient people have the best chance of surviving relatively unscathed, no personal attribute of the victim is sufficient in itself to offer reliable protection" (pp. 59–60).

15. Herman, *Trauma*, p. 115. Herman also explains: "Most people have no knowledge or understanding of the psychological changes of captivity. Social judgment of chronically traumatized people therefore tends to be extremely harsh" (p. 115). Judgment also seems to depend upon how the victim sustained the trauma, a factor commonly related to gender. Public and press responded generously to the sometimes inappropriate behavior of candidate William Stockdale during the 1992 vice-presidential debate, sensing that allowances must be made for a man who was a longtime prisoner of war. Would allowances be made for a similar performance by a

woman if it were made known that she had been a longtime battered woman?

16. Sam Ehrlich, *Lisa, Hedda & Joel: The Steinberg Murder Case* (New York: St. Martin's, 1989), pp. 134–35; Timothy Clifford, "Nussbaum Got Break in Secret Deal," *Newsday*, Oct. 21, 1988, p. 4; Clifford, "Web of details clouded probe," and "Hedda to tell jury of events," *Newsday*, Oct. 27, 1988, pp. 5, 23.

17. Gail Collins, "Our values on trial, too," *Daily News*, Dec. 2, 1988, p. 33.

18. Judy Mann, "Steinberg's Excuse Works," *Washington Post*, Feb. 1, 1989, p. B3. Emphasis mine.

19. Douglas Martin, "Keeping Watch At a Funeral That Never Ends," *New York Times*, Dec. 17, 1988, p. 29.

20. Murray Kempton, "Judging Becomes Hard Job," *Newsday*, Jan. 19, 1989, p. 18.

21. Johnson, "What Lisa Knew," p. 184; talk show discussions included "Oprah Winfrey," "Metro Week in Review," "The Eleventh Hour," and "Nightline."

22. Susan Brownmiller, "Hedda Nussbaum, Hardly a Heroine . . ." *New York Times*, Feb. 2, 1989, p. A25. Brownmiller's novel is *Waverly Place* (New York: Grove, 1989).

23. Bob Herbert, "Abusive hands & helping hands," *Daily News*, Dec. 6, 1988, p. 4.

24. Mike Capuzzo, "A horror close to home," *Philadelphia Inquirer*, Feb. 19, 1989, pp. 1K, 8K.

25. See Paula Span, "Women Protest 'Hedda-Bashing,'" *Washington Post*, March 13, 1989, pp. B1, B4; Barbara Whitaker, "Feminists: Don't Blame the Victims," *Newsday*, March 25, 1989, p. 10.

26. Glaberson, *New York Times*, Dec. 9, 1988.

27. Carol Stocker, "The jury's out on Nussbaum," *Boston Globe*, Jan. 24, 1989, pp. 23–24.

28. Mike Santangelo and Stuart Marques, "Steinberg is guilty say alternate jurors," *Daily News*, Jan. 24, 1989, p. 3.

29. Jim Nolan and Karen Phillips, "Dismissed Juror: I Would Have Found Joel Guilty," *New York Post*, Jan. 24, 1989, p. 4.

30. John Kifner, "Steinberg Jury: Arguing, Laughter and a Verdict," *New York Times*, Feb. 1, 1989, p. B4.

31. Ronald Sullivan, "Steinberg Is Guilty of First-Degree Manslaughter," *New York Times*, Jan. 31, 1989, pp. 1, B5. In August 1991 the Appellate Division of the New York State Supreme Court upheld Steinberg's conviction, rejecting his contention that he had been denied a fair trial. "Steinberg Conviction Upheld," *New York Times*, Aug. 9, 1991, p. B3.

32. Kifner, *New York Times*, Feb. 1, 1989, p. B4.

33. Frank Bruni, Esther Pessin, Marilyn Matlick and Ann V. Bollinger, "Jury's Battle Over Hedda," *New York Post*, Jan. 31, 1989, pp. 4, 18.

34. Kifner, *New York Times*, Feb. 1, 1989, p. B4.

35. "On Trial," a BBC Television video documentary, filmed in New York City, February 1989.

36. Kifner, *New York Times*, Feb. 1, 1989, p. B4.

37. Timothy Clifford, "Steinberg Gets Top Term of 8⅓–25 Years in Prison, Ex-lawyer says, 'I'm the victim,'" *Newsday*, March 25, 1989, pp. 5, 11; Ronald Sullivan, "Steinberg Given Maximum Term of 8⅓ to 25 Years in Child's Death," *New York Times*, March 25, 1989, pp. 1, 32.

38. Stocker, *Boston Globe*, Jan. 24, 1989, pp. 23–24.

39. Ken Gross, reporting for *People*, quoted by Patricia Volk, "The Steinberg Trial: Scenes From A Tragedy," *New York Times Magazine*, Jan. 15, 1989, p. 25.

40. Beatrix Campbell, "The Trail of Terror," *The Guardian*, Jan. 2, 1989, p. 15.

41. Elaine Hilberman, "Overview: The 'Wife-Beater's Wife' Reconsidered," *American Journal of Psychiatry* 137, no. 11 (Nov. 1980), 1341–42.

42. Ibid.

43. Susan Schechter, *Ending Violence Against Women and Children in Massachusetts' Families: Critical Steps for the Next Five Years*, unpublished report (Boston Foundation, 1992), p. 3, citing studies reported in Lenore E. Walker, *The Battered Woman Syndrome* (New York: Springer, 1984); Evan Stark and Anne Flitcraft, "Women and Children at Risk: A Feminist Perspective on Child Abuse," *International Journal of Health Services* 18, no. 1 (1988); Linda McKibben et al., "Victimization of Mothers of Abused Children: A Controlled Study," *Pediatrics* 84 (September 1989); and a 1989 report of the Massachusetts Department of Social Services.

44. Coercing the victim to violate her own moral principles is the abuser's final step in bringing her under control; he often accomplishes this step by forcing her to witness or participate in abuse of her children. In *Trauma and Recovery*, Judith Lewis Herman describes this forced betrayal of "her basic human attachments" as the "most destructive of all coercive techniques." She writes: "This pattern of betrayal may begin with apparently small concessions but eventually progresses to the point where even the most outrageous physical or sexual abuse of the children is borne in silence. At this point, the demoralization of the battered woman is complete" (p. 83).

45. Judith Lewis Herman describes the powerless and severely traumatized battered woman in a passage in *Trauma and Recovery* that might have been written with Hedda Nussbaum in mind: "In most cases the vic-

tim has not given up. But she has learned that every action will be watched, that most actions will be thwarted, and that she will pay dearly for failure. . . . She will perceive any exercise of her own initiative as insubordination. Before undertaking any action, she will scan the environment, expecting retaliation. . . . To the chronically traumatized person, any action has potentially dire consequences. There is no room for mistakes" (p. 91).

46. The end result of the process I'm describing may suggest the concept of "learned helplessness" first applied to battered women by psychologist Lenore Walker. See Lenore Walker, *The Battered Woman* (New York: Harper and Row, 1979). Since Walker reported in 1979 the findings of her early studies of battered women, researchers and advocates have learned much more about the active strategies women use for coping, fighting back, and getting free. Even severely traumatized women, like Hedda Nussbaum, struggle, though their efforts may be counterproductive, misguided, or so dramatically constricted as to amount to inaction. (See Herman, *Trauma*, pp. 90–91.) In extreme cases, victims may lose the will to live. What makes one case worse than another is the severity of the trauma itself, and that depends directly upon the batterer's degree of violence and remorselessness, as Angela Browne found in studying battered women who killed extremely abusive men. See Angela Browne, *When Battered Women Kill* (New York: Free Press, 1987), pp. 181–86.

47. Ronald Sullivan, "Nussbaum Testifies to Not Hearing Noise," *New York Times*, Dec. 13, 1988, p. B3.

48. Ehrlich, *Lisa, Hedda & Joel*, p. 22; "A Love Betrayed, A Brief Life Lost," *People*, Feb. 13, 1989, p. 87.

49. Ehrlich, *Lisa, Hedda & Joel*, p. 22.

50. Interview with Naomi Weiss, Dec. 10, 1988.

51. Ibid.

52. Ehrlich, *Lisa, Hedda & Joel*, pp. 24–26.

53. *People*, Feb. 13, 1989, p. 87.

54. Herman, *Trauma*, p. 74.

55. Marianne Yen, "Sympathy for Nussbaum Has Limits," *Washington Post*, Dec. 9, 1988, p. A4.

56. *Webster's New International Dictionary*, 2d edition.

57. Suzanne Daley, "For Nussbaum, Journey To Understanding Is Slow," *New York Times*, Dec. 1, 1988, p. B9.

58. Ehrlich, *Lisa, Hedda & Joel*, p. 27.

59. *People*, Feb. 13, 1989, p. 88.

60. Ibid.

61. Ehrlich, *Lisa, Hedda & Joel*, p. 138. This information about Stein-

berg's history of violence was presented by Assistant District Attorney John McCusker at a closed bail hearing on June 8, 1988, and was excluded from the trial.

62. Ehrlich, *Lisa, Hedda & Joel*, p. 31. In press conferences, Adrian DiLuzio, one of Steinberg's defense attorneys, repeatedly cited Nussbaum's reference to "the best number of months . . . in my whole life" as evidence that Nussbaum loved being abused, a clear and probably deliberate distortion of her testimony that the "best times" were periods, sometimes lasting many months, when Steinberg did not physically abuse her.

63. In *Trauma and Recovery* Judith Lewis Herman describes the traumatic bonding that may occur between a battered woman and her abuser: "The repeated experience of terror and reprieve, especially within the isolated context of a love relationship, may result in a feeling of intense, almost worshipful dependence upon an all-powerful, godlike authority. The victim may live in terror of his wrath, but she may also view him as the source of strength, guidance, and life itself" (p. 92).

64. Dee L. R. Graham, Edna Rawlings, and Nelly Rimini, "Survivors of Terror: Battered Women, Hostages, and the Stockholm Syndrome," in Yllo and Bograd, eds., *Feminist Perspectives on Wife Abuse*, p. 221.

65. *People*, Feb. 13, 1989, p. 88.

66. Ibid., p. 87.

67. Many commentators misread symptoms produced by the *situation* as pre-existing qualities of Nussbaum's *character* and the "cause" of her victimization. Susan Brownmiller, for example, wrote that only an "extreme narcissist" could succumb to this "joint madness" with Steinberg, citing as evidence Nussbaum's intense preoccupation with self and self-improvement; but this program of renovating the self to suit the controller, undertaken at his insistence to please and pacify him, is a commonplace survival strategy, sometimes mistaken for "narcissism," yet clearly quite the opposite. See Brownmiller, *New York Times*, Feb. 2, 1989, p. A25.

68. Herman, *Trauma*, p. 57, citing B. L. Green, M. C. Grace, J. D. Lindy et al., "Risk Factors for PTSD and Other Diagnoses in a General Sample of Vietnam Veterans," *American Journal of Psychiatry* 174 (1990): 729–33.

69. *People*, Feb. 13, 1989, p. 89.

70. Maury Terry, "Joel Steinberg's Version," *Vanity Fair*, May 1988, p. 122. Nussbaum also told Bellevue doctors that Lisa had been sexually abused by friends with whom the child stayed on Long Island during the previous summer (while Nussbaum herself apparently underwent a "breakdown.") At Steinberg's trial, she testified about the incident of sexual abuse, which she believed, rightly or wrongly, to have occurred, and she

was widely criticized for her failure to report it earlier. In fact, she had reported it, albeit months after it supposedly took place, to the Bellevue doctors.

71. Ehrlich, *Lisa, Hedda & Joel*, p. 50.

72. *People*, Feb. 13, 1989, p. 90.

73. Ronald Sullivan, "Defense Tries to Show Nussbaum Liked Pain," *New York Times*, Dec. 9, 1988, p. B2.

74. *People*, Feb. 13, 1989, p. 90.

75. Sullivan, *New York Times*, Dec. 9, 1988, p. B2.

76. Graham et al., "Survivors," p. 222, citing Brooks McClure, "Hostage Survival," *Conflict* 1, nos. 1 and 2 (1978): 43.

77. Graham et al., "Survivors," p. 220, citing Martin Symonds, "Victim's Responses to Terror: Understanding and Treatment," in *Victims of Terrorism*, ed. Frank M. Ochberg and David A. Soskis (Boulder, Colo.: Westview Press, 1982); Elaine Hilberman, "Overview: The 'Wife-Beater's Wife' Revisited," *American Journal of Psychiatry* 137, no. 11 (1980): 1343, citing Martin Symonds, "Victims of Violence: Psychological Effects and After-effects," *American Journal of Psychoanalysis* 35 (1975): 19–26, and "The Rape Victim: Psychological Patterns of Response," *American Journal of Psychoanalysis* 36 (1976): 27–34.

78. Graham et al., "Survivors," p. 220.

79. *People*, Feb. 13, 1989, p. 90.

80. Ibid., emphasis mine.

81. Graham et al., "Survivors," p. 217.

82. Christine McGuire and Carla Norton, *Perfect Victim* (New York: Morrow, 1988), pp. 286–88.

83. Sullivan, *New York Times*, Dec. 9, 1988, p. B2.

84. Marianne Yen, "Former Lover Testifies To Control by Steinberg," *Washington Post*, Dec. 3, 1988, p. A3. Emphasis mine.

85. On the need for a new psychiatric diagnosis to distinguish the more complex syndrome that follows upon prolonged, repeated stress from simple post-traumatic stress disorder, see Herman, *Trauma* pp. 118–122.

86. Ehrlich, *Lisa, Hedda & Joel*, p. 56.

87. Ibid., pp. 56–57.

88. Patrick Clark and Stuart Marques, "Joel's 20 rules," *Daily News*, Dec. 2, 1988, p. 4; *People*, Feb. 13, 1989, p. 90.

89. Graham et al., "Survivors," p. 224.

90. Steven Erlanger, "Neighbors Say Abuse Was Reported," *New York Times*, Nov. 4, 1987, p. B4. Steinberg trained Nussbaum to be quiet by hitting her more if she "made noise."

91. Ibid.

92. Johnson, "What Lisa Knew," pp. 8, 181.

93. Ellis Henican et al., "Parents' Troubled Path," *Newsday*, Nov. 10, 1987, p. 3.

94. Erlanger, *New York Times*, Nov. 4, 1987, p. B2; Patrick Clark and Stuart Marques, "Neighbor tells of Hedda beatings," *Daily News*, Dec. 20, 1988, p. 7.

95. Ehrlich, *Lisa, Hedda & Joel*, p. 190.

96. Ibid., pp. 192–93.

97. Daphne Merkin, "The Couple Next Door," *7 Days*, Dec. 7, 1988, p. 8.

98. Johnson, "What Lisa Knew," p. 180.

99. Merkin, "The Couple Next Door," p. 8.

100. Johnson, "What Lisa Knew," p. 178. See also Joyce Johnson, *What Lisa Knew: The Truth and Lies of the Steinberg Case* (New York: Putnam, 1990).

101. Murray Kempton, "The Truth About Herself That Hedda Fails to See," *Newsday*, Dec. 18, 1988, p. 8.

102. Susan Brownmiller, "Madly in Love," *Ms.*, April 1989, p. 64.

103. "The Fascination of Abomination," editorial, *New York Times*, Feb. 1, 1989, p. A24.

104. Timothy Clifford, "Steinberg Gets Top Term of 8⅓–25 Years in Prison, Ex-lawyer says, 'I'm the victim,'" *Newsday*, March 25, 1989, pp. 5, 11. Nussbaum filed a civil suit against Steinberg, alleging in part that he subjected her to brainwashing and torture. Michele Launders and Nicole Smiegel, the birth mothers of Lisa and "Mitchell," also brought civil actions against Steinberg, Nussbaum, and various city officials. As of September 1993, the Nussbaum and Launders suits were still under litigation, the status of the Smiegel suit unknown.

105. Kenneth Keniston, "Wife Beating and the Rule of Thumb," *New York Times Book Review*, May 8, 1988, p. 12, reviewing Linda Gordon, *Heroes of Their Own Lives: The Politics and History of Family Violence: Boston 1880–1960*.

106. Interview with Naomi Weiss, Dec. 10, 1988.

107. Erlanger, *New York Times*, Nov. 4, 1987, p. B2.

7. *What Can We Do?*

1. Letter from Marilyn French, June 1992. Such men, incidentally, often abuse their wives most severely during pregnancy, fearful of their impending loss of power, jealous of the child who will compete for all that "wifely devotion" they've enjoyed. Such attacks, which may be seen as a kind of child abuse in utero, replicate within the individual family the

cultural/ historical competition between the privilege of the father and the rights of the child.

2. John J. O'Connor, "Downfall of the American Family," *New York Times*, March 24, 1992, p. C16.

3. Joan Zorza, "Woman Battering: A Major Cause of Homelessness," *Clearinghouse Review* 25, no. 4 (1991): 421–29.

4. Elisabeth Griffith, *In Her Own Right: The Life of Elizabeth Cady Stanton* (New York: Oxford University Press, 1984), p. 102.

5. Elizabeth Cady Stanton, *Eighty Years & More: Reminiscences, 1815–1897* (New York: Schocken, 1971), p. 225.

6. Griffith, *In Her Own Right*, p. 102.

7. Elizabeth Pleck, *Domestic Tyranny: The Making of American Social Policy Against Family Violence from Colonial Times to the Present* (New York: Oxford University Press, 1987), pp. 101–105.

8. Stanton, *Eighty Years & More*, p. 233.

9. For a full critique of the highly publicized Weitzman study which found divorced women and their children destined for "impoverishment" see Susan Faludi, *Backlash: The Undeclared War Against American Women* (New York: Crown, 1991), pp. 19–27.

10. Pleck, *Domestic Tyranny*, p. 102.

11. "Love Story Ends in Hate," *Newsday*, March 27, 1990, pp. 5, 28. Gonzalez was convicted in 1991 of all 176 charges against him, including 87 counts of felony murder and murder with depraved indifference, and imprisoned for 25 years to life (*Facts on File*, 1991).

12. Ibid.

13. Jimmy Breslin, "Too Great A Deed For a Weak Man," *Newsday*, March 27, 1990, p. 4.

14. Annette Fuentes, "Let's Get Lidia," *Village Voice*, April 10, 1990, p. 16.

15. Simone De Beauvoir, *The Second Sex*, trans. H. M. Parshley (New York: Vintage, 1989), p. 555.

16. John Stuart Mill, *The Subjection of Women* (1869; rpt. Cambridge, Mass.: M.I.T. Press, 1970), p. 3.

17. Ibid., p. 50.

18. Ibid., p. 19.

19. Representative Patricia Schroeder, commencement address at Mount Holyoke College, South Hadley, Massachusetts, May 24, 1992. Feminists around the world seek to have nations and international tribunals, such as the United Nations, declare gender violence a violation of human rights. See *Women, Violence And Human Rights*, Report of the Center for Women's Global Leadership (New Brunswick, N.J.: Douglass College, Rutgers University, 1992).

20. Interview with Sarah, New York City, Oct. 3, 1987.

21. R. Emerson Dobash and Russell P. Dobash, *Women, Violence and Social Change* (London: Routledge, 1992), pp. 73–76.

22. Susan Schechter, "Ending Violence Against Women and Children in Massachusetts' Families: Critical Steps for the Next Five Years," unpublished report (Boston Foundation, 1992), p. 19.

23. Ibid., p. 28.

24. Telephone interview with Michael Paymar, Training Coordinator of the Duluth Domestic Abuse Intervention Project, January 2, 1993. A follow-up study of 100 men who completed batterers' re-education under court order in the Duluth Domestic Abuse Intervention Project found 40 percent rearrested within a few years. Paymar estimates the actual rate of recidivism at closer to 60 percent.

25. Ibid.

26. Materials published by the program can be obtained by writing to Domestic Abuse Intervention Project, 206 West Fourth St., Duluth, MN 55806.

27. A prosecutor's manual, judicial training materials, and law enforcement curricula can be obtained by writing to the San Francisco Family Violence Prevention Fund, 1001 Potrero Avenue, Building 1, Suite 200, San Francisco, CA 94110, or calling 415-821-4553.

28. Anne H. Flitcraft, "Violence, Values, and Gender," *JAMA: The Journal of the American Medical Association* 267 (June 17, 1992): 3194, citing P. M. Marzuk, K. Tardiff, and C. S. Hirsch, "The Epidemiology of Murder-Suicide," *JAMA* 267 (1992): 3179–83. From the male perspective of the study, fear of "infidelity" and fear of "departure" are two different causative factors. From a female point of view "infidelity" *is* a departure.

29. Schechter, "Ending Violence Against Women," p. 63.

30. Reviewing studies of how children are affected by witnessing battery, Susan Schechter sums up: "Batterers place their children at risk in many ways. Marital violence is associated with low self-esteem in girls, aggression and behavior problems in boys and girls, reduced social competence, depression and anxiety." Ibid., p. 17. Another review of case studies found only one variable to be strongly associated with men's use of violence against female partners, and that was having witnessed parental violence in childhood. See Gerald T. Hotaling and David B. Sugarman, "An Analysis of Risk Markers in Husband to Wife Violence: The Current State of Knowledge," *Violence and Victims* 1, no. 2 (1986): 101–124.

31. A few women are imprisoned for long terms for killing a female intimate partner; their cases should also be reexamined for a history of battery.

32. Frank Phillips, "Legislative panel backs more power to deny bail," *Boston Globe*, June 6, 1992, pp. 15, 22; "Women lawmakers back bail-law change," *Daily Hampshire Gazette*, April 24, 1992, p. 7.

33. Elizabeth M. Schneider, "Legal Reform Efforts to Assist Battered Women: Past, Present and Future," unpublished report (Ford Foundation, July 1990), pp. 21–22, quoting Roehl, Harrell, and Kapsak, "Family Violence Intervention Demonstration Programs Evaluation," summary final report (Institute for Social Analysis, December 1988).

34. Ibid., p. 47.

35. Ibid., p. 51.

36. Ibid., p. 106

37. Elizabeth M. Schneider, "The Violence of Privacy," 23 *Connecticut Law Review* 973, 991 (1991).

38. For information, contact the National Center on Women and Family Law, 799 Broadway, Room 402, New York, NY 10003, and the National Clearinghouse for the Defense of Battered Women, 125 South 9th Street, Suite 302, Philadelphia, PA 19107.

39. Patricia Nealon and Sean P. Murphy, "Thwarting the killers is complex, elusive goal," *Boston Globe*, June 2, 1992, p. 1.

40. Frank Phillips, "Weld says quick move on crime bill could have prevented death," *Boston Globe*, June 2, 1992, p. 7. In April 1993 Massachusetts courts struck down the Weld proposal as an unconstitutional violation of the defendant's right to due process.

41. Antistalking legislation was first enacted in California in 1991 to protect movie stars, but many other states quickly recognized the value of such legislation in protecting the principal targets of stalkers, battered women. This language is drawn from legislation proposed in the Wisconsin State Legislature, 1992.

42. Schneider, "Legal Reform Efforts to Assist Battered Women," p. 23, quoting "Bill on Sex Crime Assessed in Senate," *New York Times*, June 21, 1990, p. A19.

43. Schechter, "Ending Violence Against Women," p. 9.

44. Information is available from AWAKE, Children's Hospital, 300 Longwood Avenue, Boston, MA 02115; phone 617-735-7979.

45. "Violence Against Women: Relevance for Medical Practitioners," *JAMA: The Journal of the American Medical Association* 267, no. 23 (June 17, 1992): 3189.

46. Interview with a woman who requested anonymity, in Massachusetts, March 17, 1992.

47. The Center, directed by Rev. Marie Fortune, also provides resources addressing religious issues that arise for victims of sexual and domestic

assault. For information: 1914 North 34th Street, Suite 105, Seattle, WA 98103; phone 206-634-1903.

48. Schneider, "Legal Reform Efforts to Assist Battered Women," p. 45.

49. Ibid., p. 66.

50. Ibid., p. 24.

51. All statistics are drawn from Schneider, "Legal Reform Efforts to Assist Battered Women," p. 61.

52. Tess Catalano, "Solve center's real problem," letter to the editor, *Iowa City Press Citizen*, Feb. 24, 1992, p. 5A.

53. Schneider, "Legal Reform Efforts to Assist Battered Women," p. 80.

54. Lyle Muller, "State asked to probe hidden children case," *Cedar Rapids Gazette*, Feb. 18, 1992, p. 1B.

55. Lee H. Bowker, "Publishing Feminist Research: A Personal Note by Lee Bowker," in *Feminist Perspectives on Wife Abuse*, ed. Kersti Yllo and Michele Bograd (Newbury Park, Calif.: Sage, 1988), pp. 170–73.

56. James Ptacek, "Why Do Men Batter Their Wives?" in Yllo and Bograd, eds., *Feminist Perspectives*, pp. 152–53. Ptacek notes that both clinical literature and the criminal justice system accept the most common excuse of the batterer (that he "lost control") and his most common justification (that he was "provoked" by the woman). Ptacek concludes: "Clinical and criminal justice responses to battering are revealed as ideological in the light of their collusion with batterers' rationalizations" (pp. 152, 155).

57. David Adams, Jann Jackson, and Mary Lauby, "Family Violence Research: Aid or Obstacle to the Battered Women's Movement?" *Response* 2, no. 3 (1988): 14–16.

58. "Violence Against Women: Relevance for Medical Practitioners," 3187.

59. Dobash and Dobash, *Women, Violence and Social Change*, p. 269.

60. Naomi Wolf, "A Woman's Place," *New York Times*, May 31, 1992, p. 19.

Index